OWD JOCKEYS AT WAR

The Dawley News 1915-16

Compiled by Toby Neal

**LANGRISH
CAIGER**
PUBLICATIONS

First published 2004 by Langrish Caiger Publications, PO Box 1916, Telford, Shropshire, TF7 5XZ. Email *langrishcaiger@aol.com*

The pages of the *Dawley News* are reproduced in this book approximately 15 per cent bigger than actual size. Some very faint or missing parts of the content have been reconstructed digitally.

Pictures and further details of the fallen soldiers mentioned in this book would be gratefully received by the publisher for potential use in any future edition.

Cover design by Pete Doherty.

ISBN: 0-9548530-0-8

INTRODUCTION

The *Dawley News* is a remarkable record of an ordinary English town at war. For nearly three years during World War One it was sent to the Dawley boys stuck in the trenches or in any of the other areas of service across the world.

It kept them up to date with news from home and was packed with snippets of gossip, soldiers' letters, and cartoons, with a bit of the Dawley dialect, the "Dawley twang", thrown in for good measure. The newsletter was started in autumn 1915 by the Brotherhood and Sisterhood of Dawley Baptist Church and sold at its meetings for an old penny "on condition it is sent, when read, to a Dawley soldier on foreign service".

Soon 300 or so copies were going out each week to Dawley's fighting men – the "owd jockeys" of the title – in all parts of the world, where they were eagerly read, even by soldiers with no connection with Shropshire.

Gathering and compiling material for the *Dawley News* magazine (which was in its early days called the *Weekly Report)* must have been a major task, and a recurrent theme in the pages is an appeal for the soldiers abroad to write, send cartoons and drawings, enter competitions, and so on.

As for the production team, a glimpse is given in the issue of April 18, 1916, which includes cartoons of those involved, showing that one of the artists was a woman and that the paper was run off on a Cyclostyle machine.

One figure who pops up in the pages now and again is Billy Lloyd, a local "character", from Station Road, Lawley Bank, who was very short (4ft 4ins) but nevertheless tried (unsuccessfully) to join up.

Sad news is not glossed over in the *Dawley News*, and many deaths are recorded. Although generally the magazine appeared weekly, there were some temporary breaks.

This compilation covers the period from the start of the magazine, in autumn 1915, to the end of 1916. A future volume will cover 1917 to the last date at which one of these newsletters survives (and if you know differently, let me know...), which was May 7, 1918. Altogether, this surviving collection comprises 64 issues. Most were of eight pages, but a few were just four pages.

All were handwritten – beautiful, error-free handwriting – and as this and its juxtaposition to the cartoons is so central to the "feel" of the *Dawley News*, it is reproduced here "as is" rather than being typed. The one exception is a magazine in which the writing has become very faded. This has been typewritten for clarity. Although I have tried to improve the quality of the originals, a few pages of some magazines are a little "fuzzy", and some others are slightly clipped, typically at the bottom edge.

This is not a complete set. Issues are missing. While 1916 and 1917 are well covered, only two survive in this collection from 1918. Were there more? How many? Perhaps, on reading this, somebody will come forward with some of the lost issues.

Those which do survive do so because of Mrs Mary Westbrook, the secretary of the church, and an unknown church member who had kept the copies for years.

"I was given them at our ter-jubilee in 1997. This person thought I would like to keep them in the archives for the church, which I have done. It's a shame really that they're not known about," said Mrs Westbrook, speaking in 2000.

The late Mrs Westbrook with some copies of the Dawley News in 2000.

Sadly, Mrs Westbrook died in May 2002. The original magazines were afterwards donated by her husband Clive, who himself died in June 2004, to Shropshire Archives.

Thanks to the Westbrooks, and that unknown church member who was such a good custodian of these magazines for so long, the Dawley News can now become better known, and modern generations can share in this part of Dawley's history.

Toby Neal

October 2004

THE TOWN OF DAWLEY

Dawley is a town in east Shropshire which, at the beginning of World War One, had about 7,700 inhabitants. Then, as now, it nestled in a landscape scarred by generations of mining which had left a legacy of barren pit mounds and mineshafts from the old workings. A few surviving pits of the East Shropshire coalfield continued to provide jobs for Dawley men when the war broke out in 1914, while many others earned their crust at various industrial enterprises in the area, such as the Horsehay Works.

Essentially there was one road through the town, and down Dawley High Street were all the usual shops and services that you could expect for a busy little community. There was a town park, a town hall, and a train station.

The most famous son of Dawley was Captain Matthew Webb who, a generation earlier, had been the first person to swim the English Channel. In 1909 a drinking fountain was erected in his memory at the head of the High Street (right), just a stone's throw from his birthplace.

So this was Dawley in 1914, a town which in many ways had more in common with the towns and villages of the Black Country than rural Shropshire. The men who went to war were mainly working class men, who spoke with a distinctive Dawley dialect and had a quiet pride in their special town.

They were typical of the thousands of men from across Britain who answered their country's call.

By 1915 hundreds of Dawley boys were serving their country in Britain and overseas, and Dawley Baptist Church struck on a way of keeping them in touch with news from their home town by producing a little magazine filled with gossip and goings-on. Whoever was the driving force behind the *Dawley News* must have had some idea of what the men would like, as the magazine included cartoons, letters, and gripes, and the religious content, such as it was, was not heavy handed.

It is clear that it rapidly became very popular with the men in the trenches, including with soldiers who had never heard of Dawley, and magazines were snapped up quickly on their arrival.

In their turn, the men sent their contributions to the mag from all parts of the world. In the early months, there appeared to be little or no censorship.

A central figure in the unfolding story of the *Dawley News* is the Rev Arthur Lester, who was the pastor at the time, and seems to have arrived in 1892. He was the Secretary of the Salop Baptist Association, and was chairman of the Dawley Military Tribunal, the proceedings of which feature regularly in the pages of the magazine. He continued as pastor after World War One and left in about 1919.

The old Dawley Baptist Church mentioned in these pages no longer stands.

It had been built in 1860, but was demolished in March and April 2000 to make way for a new church and community centre on virtually the same site.

As for the ordinary men and women recorded on the pages of the *Dawley News*, all are now dead. War memorial gates were erected at the entrance to Dawley park, and the plaques bearing the names of the fallen are kept indoors in what is now called Dawley House.

Dawley Baptist Church in the early 20th century.

Some examples of the 'Dawley Twang':
How bist owd jockey? – *How are you my old friend?*
Thee cosner do that – *You can't do that*
Dunna tek one, tek 'ontull – *Don't just take one, take a handful.*
Durst? – *Do you?*
Shut thee gob wut? – *Shut your mouth will you?*
Dawley Bonk – *Dawley Bank.*
Oss ay – *Horsehay.*

SHROPSHIRE ARMY UNITS

In Shropshire the coming of war meant a vast expansion of the county's military units. These were the King's Shropshire Light Infantry, the Shropshire Yeomanry, and the Shropshire Royal Horse Artillery.

They served all over the world. In Palestine, in the Balkans, in the Far East and, above all, in France and Belgium.

But not all Shropshire men served in Shropshire regiments. They served wherever they were told. And the converse was that Shropshire units were not comprised exclusively of Salopians.

However, some had more of a local flavour than others. In particular, the 4th Battalion of the King's Shropshire Light Infantry was a Territorial Army unit, made up of part-time soldiers, men who in civilian life were miners, shopworkers, farmers – you name it.

Of course, the men from Dawley served in all three services, and this is reflected in the pages of Dawley News. However, many will have served with the local Army regiment, the KSLI, of which there were only two regular battalions at the outbreak of war in 1914. This rapidly expanded to 10 battalions, of which eight saw action.

A wartime battalion would be between 700 and 1,000 men. The vast majority were peacetime civilians, many of whom would never have been abroad before. They paid a high price for their patriotism. In the KSLI, 4,710 men were killed, including 258 officers. Worst hit was the 7th Battalion, with 1,048 dead.

Here is a brief summary of who did what in 1915 and 1916, the period covered by this volume.

KSLI

First Battalion: Landed in France September 1914 with 27 officers and 969 other ranks. Commanding officer Colonel Luard was killed in action in 1915. Was engaged at Beaumont Hamel during the Battle of the Somme where it suffered heavy casualties.

Second Battalion: After returning from India in November 1914 it crossed to France December 1914. Fought in Second Battle of Ypres, before moving to Salonika in December 1915. It was a relatively quiet front and the main enemy was disease.

Fourth Battalion (Territorial Army): Spent early war years in the Far East, with some soldiers serving on the Andaman Islands and others in Hong Kong. The battalion was ordered in 1915 to put down a mutiny by some of the 5th Indian Light Infantry Battalion at Singapore. Many of the mutineers were executed.

Dawley soldiers of the 4th Battalion outside the Elephant and Castle pub in the town in a photo believed to have been taken in 1914 soon after war was declared. The sign in the background says 'C' Company – so no doubt they were members of that Company. In his 99th year, Cecil Bland of Dawley, who saw the photo being taken as a youngster (he is off camera, standing by a lamp) recalled: "The Territorials used to go to camp at Barry Dock every year and had only been there a couple of days when the war broke out. They were called back and given 48 hours leave, and were then sent to Hong Kong to relieve the garrison there.

"The soldier on the extreme left, standing, is Cliff Ball, who was a Corporal at the time. Later on he had a wholesale grocery shop in Dawley, with his brother Noah.

"Standing in the doorway (i.e. civilians, just left of centre of the doorway) are Joe Hall and his wife (they ran the Elephant and Castle), and the next one I recognise is Harry Poole, from Horsehay (the third soldier standing, from right). Next to him (holding baton and with cross-strap) is the Sergeant Major, and on the far right (with hand on hip) is Tommy Skelton, who was a Corporal at the time, but got to be a Sergeant Major. He lived at the Rough Ground, as they used to call it, at the back of the Royal Exchange, in a row there.

"Second from left of the four soldiers in the middle row is Alf 'Codge' Roberts. On the bottom row, on the extreme left (half kneeling, with moustache) is Tommy Jones of Old Park. Fourth from left is Alf 'Codge' Corbett, the gym instructor – if your name was Alf, you would get the nickname 'Codge'.

"Fifth from left is Tommy Price from Horsehay and the soldier crouching, far right, is Harry Skelton, Tommy Skelton's brother. The only

other person I know is Liz Gears of Horsehay, who is extreme right, with a hat." All the soldiers Mr Bland remembers survived the war.

Fifth Battalion: Went to France in May 1915. Heavily engaged in the Ypres sector in 1915 and the Battle of the Somme in 1916.

Sixth (Pals) Battalion: Moved to France July 1915, and first saw action in the Battle of Loos. Moved to the Ypres sector in January 1916, and in July to the Somme, taking trenches near Serre which were waist deep in British dead.

Seventh Battalion: Formed at Shrewsbury in September 1914 and moved to France a year later, going into action in October 1915 at Ploegsteert. Suffered heavily in the Battle of the Somme. After the Battle of Bazentin Ridge in July 1916 only six officers and about 135 other ranks survived, practically wiping out all those who had landed in France less than a year earlier. It attacked Serre in one of the last Somme battles on November 13. It was a dismal failure.

Eighth Battalion: Sent France September 1915, but soon transferred to Salonika, arriving in November.

Tenth Battalion: Formed March 1917 and so outside the scope of this volume.

The Shropshire Yeomanry: The 1/1st Shropshire Yeomanry was a cavalry unit but was dismounted in November 1915 and embarked for Egypt at Devonport in March 1916, arriving at Alexandria on March 20. With the age of the cavalry dead, it was destined to be turned into the 10th Battalion KSLI the following year.

Shropshire Royal Horse Artillery: Despite their status as Royal Horse Artillery (to support cavalry) since 1908, they actually served as field artillery (to support infantry) as A Battery, 293 Brigade, Royal Artillery. A second war-raised battery served as A Battery, 158 Brigade, RA. A Battery, 293 Brigade, served on the East Coast on Home Defence and on Salisbury Plain in 1915 and 1916 and did not go to France until January 1917.

Dawley in 1914

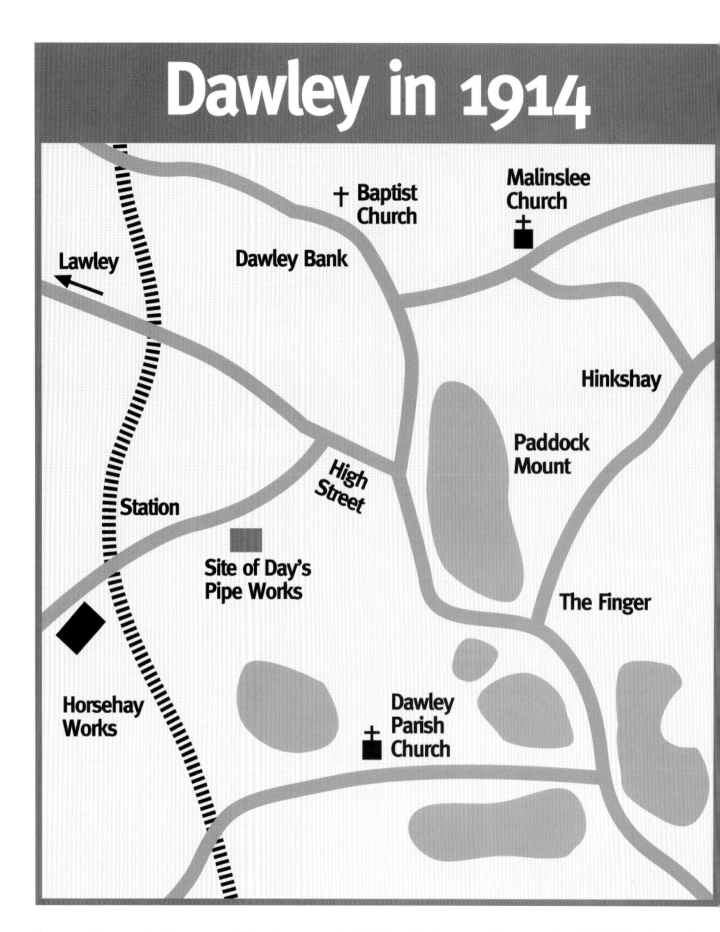

Lawley

Baptist Church

Malinslee Church

Dawley Bank

Hinkshay

Paddock Mount

High Street

Station

Site of Day's Pipe Works

The Finger

Horsehay Works

Dawley Parish Church

Some of the main features of Dawley area, including the barren pit mounds which dominated the landscape. The Anglican parish church and Dawley Baptist Church are about a mile and a quarter apart. Horsehay Works was one of the major employers in the area.

1915

"Well, to suffer is divine,

Pass the word along the line".

Weekly Report.
from the Brotherhood and Sisterhood.
Dawley Baptist Chapel.
Oct: 19th 1915.

A most interesting post-card has been received from Pte. J. Alford, who is a prisoner of war in Germany. Writing on Sept: 28th he says:— I am just writing to let you know I'm living, and glad to say I got wounded last Saturday, and taken prisoner with a good many more... We've been treated very well by the German hospital men, and have what we ask for." (His parents live at Heath Hill).

For several months we have been trying to find particulars of Pte. G. Kearsley (Bank Road) and have induced the search parties of the St. John's Ambulance Brigade to take the matter up. They now report to us (Oct: 14th) as follows:— "We are able to send you the detailed account of the fighting on Nov: 11th 1914, when Pte. Kearsley disappeared. The battalion (2nd West Riding) attacked the German trenches, and had to retire after heavy losses. Companies A and D suffered especially heavily, indeed D Company was in so hot a fire that those who survived had to surrender. Very thorough enquiry has been made in the Regiment of the men missing on this date, but very little information has been forthcoming. At this distance of time the one hope, and that I fear is a slight one, is for his name to come in on a Prisoner's list from Germany. If Pte. Kearsley's name so appears we will at once inform you."

Postcards have been received during the week from Pte. S. Small and Gunner Tart saying "Thank you!" for the communications they have received.

Pte. G. Jackson writes most weeks saying the letters and papers he receives so regularly are very welcome, and that he is alright, except that he has got a cold in the head!

The Diploma awarded by the French Republic to Corporal Tom Dunning for rescuing the French child from the burning house has been framed and sent to his home. It was on exhibition in the Sunday School on Sunday afternoon, and when the soldier comes home it will be shown at the Tuesday meeting. It is worded in French, part of which is as follows:—

République Française.

Actes de Courage et de Dévouement.

Au nom du Président de la République (En vertu du décret du etc)

The translation in English is:—

French Republic.

Acts of Courage and Devotion.

In the name of the President of the Republic (in pursuance of the decree of 16th Nov: 1901)

The Secretary of the Minister of State of the Department of the Interior has awarded a medal of honour and certificate of the 2nd Class to M. Dunning of the X.S.L.

This diploma has been entrusted to the care of his family and his fellow-countrymen as a souvenir of his honourable and courageous conduct.

The following is from Sergeant. S. Rowe who has been in the Dardanelles a long while and has had some terrible experiences. He has been wounded once before and then returned to the firing-line again. Now, for what reason we do not know, he is at Malta. "I am very weak, and it will be a long time before I am ready for the fray again. You should see me going for a drive in my hospital blues, you would laugh for I am nothing but bones. All the clothes I wear now are about two sizes too big for me. A lot of our fellows have been invalided home. I have not had any letters or papers for a month now — I suppose they have all gone where the good niggers go."

(This is a brave fellow who has had a lot of knocking about. Will several friends please write to him at once?)

Sergeant S. Rowe
1609. B. Co: 1st Lancashire Fusiliers.
86. Brigade. 29. Division.
St. Patrick's Hospital, Malta

Pte. W. H. Oliver of the 2nd K.S.L.I. writes from "Somewhere in Belgium." "It is very kind of you all to take up the work you are doing for us out here. All the boys are talking of the way they get papers and letters from the friends at Dawley, and they speak very well of them...... I have lost a lot of my pals - since we came home from India, and it is very hard to lose pals whom one has had for so long a time. B. Ball my best pal was killed last Whit-Monday, and I fear there will be a great many homes that will be bereaved while this terrible war is on."

Driver A. Round of the 459. Howitzer Battery, France, says:- "Thanks for the many letters and papers I have received. I am sorry I have not written before. We hope to be in England soon, we don't think the war will last a great deal longer. We wish you success and good luck with your good work, and hope to see you soon."

One of the men expected at the meeting this evening is Pte. S. Teece (Stone Row) 11381 - Grenadier Bomber, 5th K.S.L.I, who has been wounded in the heel at Hooge. His brother, unfortunately is missing entirely as the result of the same charge.

We are now printing special circulars giving the names of 100 Dawley soldiers who are on our weekly list, and with whom we are trying to communicate every week. We are also making an appeal to the general public to supply us with funds for the sending out of comforts, etc, to these men. To do all that ought to be done will require a considerable sum of money, and while our Tuesday meetings are able to provide part of the expenses, we must have considerable help from outside. We hope therefore all our friends will do their utmost to help us in our forward movement, and to secure new helpers.

We hoped to be able to get a Printer to produce copies of this Report cheaply, but an estimate, obtained from one of the cheapest local printers, is to the effect that 250 copies of this will cost £1.0 We do not yet sell 250 copies - for the present therefore we shall have to be content with it as it is - if you support it well, we hope presently to be able to print a monthly report of our work

Pte. Jack Williams (Old Park) writes on Oct: 9th :- "We are very pleased to get your letters as while we are in the trenches it is the only thing we get to cheer us up. Just at present we are in an old farm about 2 miles behind the firing-line, and we are getting plenty of shells. Fighting has dropped off a lot where we are just at present, there has not been much since we made that big charge where I got wounded. The Germans blew us out of the first line but it was only for a few hours, for as soon as it got dark we were ordered to get over the top and take the trench that we lost, and the best side had it – and it was the 1st Shropshires. This is a funny war, and when the shells are coming we are like a lot of rabbits. One man will shout to another "Get under, the gamekeeper is coming!" But we shall be very glad when it is all over, I have had about 10 months of it now, and I am just getting tired of it."

Corporal Tom Dunning writes from the V.A.D. Hospital, Wellingboro' on Oct! 14th thanking us for a copy of last week's "Report." He says it is most interesting to read the accounts of some of our brave comrades who are out at the front fighting for King and Country. He sees that last week, Pte. Thos. Powell said they were up to their knees in mud and water in the trenches, he has been up to his waist in water, but they did not mind so long as the Bosches are conquered. He is looking forward to coming home to speak at our meeting.

Pte. J. Bailey (King St) sends another long letter from Singapore thanking various friends, and saying that he hopes certain local soldiers who are reported wounded are progressing favourably. (These men who are at Singapore and Hong Kong have been rather neglected, we hope therefore our friends will write longer letters than usual to A. Corbett, N. Jones, J. Bailey, T. Powell, and others who appear not to hear too much news.

This 'Report' is sold weekly, price One Penny, and can only be procured at the Meeting. Friends wishing for copies must arrange to purchase them there, we cannot send them round. When the expenses are paid, the balance is spent in sending copies to soldiers, who are very interested in the doings of their companions.

Buy it regularly at the Meetings, and send it to a Soldier Friend at the Front, inside your next letter.

1916

"Away down communication trench,

Away down Whiz-bang Lane,

I've got a cosy little dugout,

Where the great Jack Johnsons rain.

Very close to the sniper's post,

Where the aerial torpedoes visit us most,

You can get some machine-gun toast,

Away down Whiz-bang Lane."

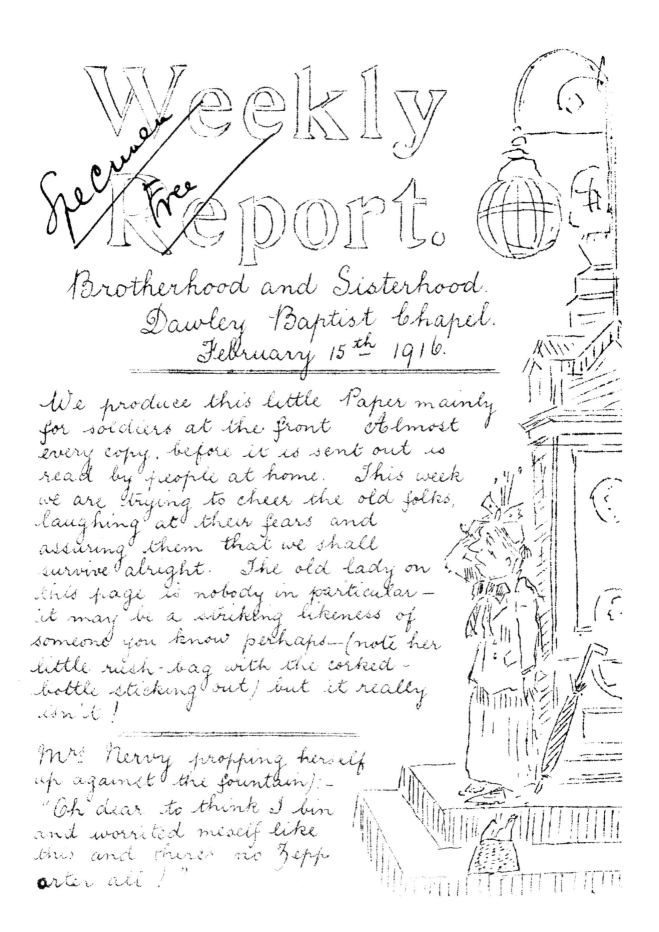

Weekly Report.
Specimen Free

Brotherhood and Sisterhood.
Dawley Baptist Chapel.
February 15th 1916.

We produce this little Paper mainly for soldiers at the front. Almost every copy, before it is sent out is read by people at home. This week we are trying to cheer the old folks, laughing at their fears and assuring them that we shall survive alright. The old lady on this page is nobody in particular — it may be a striking likeness of someone you know perhaps—(note her little rush-bag with the corked-bottle sticking out) but it really isn't!

Mrs Nervy propping herself up against the fountain):— "Oh dear to think I bin and worrited meself like this and there's no Zepp arter all!"

Alf wishes he could go to the Front!

Pte. A. E. Corbett writes from Hong Kong. "The Weekly Report is a treat for you can see in it letters from some of your old pals and then you know how they are going on I was very pleased to see that my old mate Ned Archer is going on alright in Serbia. also to hear of Jim Alford being safe. I am sorry he is in the hands of the Germans.

I am going to write a letter to him but I don't know whether they will let it go I shall have to be very careful what I put in it. We had a military funeral here last week! a sailor and a marine, the one was asleep in a signal cabin and fell through the window and broke his neck, the other died with heart trouble. It was a splendid funeral, all the Shropshires that could get went to show respect, they bought a wreath too. Our buglers blew the 'Last Post' and we fired the volley. It is awful cold and wet here now but of course it is not so bad as it is in the trenches, but all the same I wish I was at the front. We might stand a chance of going, for they are moving the German prisoners and the sooner they go the better."

DADDY'S GONE TO THE WAR

If a soldier's wife whose husband is out of the country does not receive an invitation for herself and her children of school age for our Tea-Party this next week, please let us know. The gathering will take place a few days ahead. We have received 10/- this week but we want more money yet.

More and More Men to be Called Up.

After midnight on March 1st there will be no more unmarried volunteers for the Army, for all who have not attested or been exempted by that date will be treated as members of the Army. On March 3rd the men of 19-29 are to be called up. That is, up to March 1st the door stands open and it is possible for any man to join as a volunteer. It is said that all the remaining groups and classes of single men are to be called up very shortly and that by the middle of April all single men who are fit and can be spared will be in training.

Dear Old England!

Pte. Len Roberts writes from Salonica :– "I have not found any place so dear to my heart as dear old England and it is very kind of the Brotherhood and Sisterhood to keep thinking of us. We are very busy day by day working and preparing against the enemy which I believe will be kept at bay. Thanks for the cigarettes it is good to have some out here it is almost the only comfort a fellow has when he begins to think about home and —— ! I trust I shall hear from some of you again soon."

Lights Out!

Dawley, in common with other towns in Shropshire now comes under the Restriction of Lighting Order which means blinds must be drawn over all our brilliantly-lighted shop-windows.

now that the enhancing diversion of studying shop windows is taken away the only diversion open to us is a study of the stars!

These dears are looking skywards from the High Street for Zomething they are never likely to see!

Where is it Hot in January?

Sergeant Eric Bailey writes:- "Please thank all for the parcel I received soon after I landed. It was very welcome after the absence of anything of the kind owing to the Postal arrangements. It seems queer to have such hot weather in January, but somehow it is not fully appreciated."

The Germans say they have got him!

In an official list from the German Government published in the English papers last Friday the name of Jim Alford of the 5th K.S.L.I. appears. This is the first official notification from the Germans.

OFFICIAL RECEIPT

This is to certify that we have got your Jim Alford.
Signed: Kaiser Bill.

We have been writing to him each week but no one has heard any word from him — his mother only received the one postcard. Please keep on writing — ask Mr Wooding for his address. No war-news in your letters, mind, and don't send any newspapers nor this Report (they will not get through) but just a cheerful letter telling him about his old "pals" here at home.

Fit for Anything!

Sergeant Percy Morgan writes from Salonica on Jan: 29th:- Just a few lines to let you know that I am still in the land of the living and fit for anything. All the Dawley boys are keeping very well. Thank you very much for the "Weekly Report" and the papers which you send out to us so regularly. Wishing you every success in your good work."

"It's a Treat to get it he says.

Pte. A. E. Thomas writes from France on Feb. 5th "Thank you for the papers and the "Weekly Report" it is a treat to get it and to know how the other boys are going on in other parts of the line, as it is seldom that we meet with anyone whom we know. We have been rather busy lately — "

M. P's Country Mansion – A Soldiers' Home.

Sir Charles Henry's house, Parkwood, near Wargrave, Berks, has been lent for a hospital for wounded soldiers, it appears. In the "Daily Sketch" last week there was a picture of some of the patients now there.

Slightly Wounded —— at Football !

Corporal Tom Dunning writes from Clifton Park, Blackpool. 'Lance-Corporal Ted Taylor and I are here, having a good time. We are on the staff of this hospital where, if we behave ourselves, we may stay till after the war. We got last week's "Report" and we sat up reading it till half past eleven.

Ted Taylor has got wounded playing football - a kick on his leg but we hope it will soon be better

THE BATTLE OF BLACKPOOL!

We are both very pleased to receive the "Report" which is most interesting. It is snowing very hard as I write this."

The Weather is Brightening!

Corporal R. G. Richards writes from France:- "It is indeed kind of you to be writing each week to soldiers from the Dawley district serving abroad..... Spring is approaching and things are getting much better. I read the "Weekly Report" each week and it is very interesting. A soldier leads a strenuous life abroad and he needs to be strong indeed to carry on for a few months in the firing line - one's nerves soon begin to suffer. Hence we greatly value your good work."

(Remember, we write to over 100 soldiers from the Dawley district each week.)

Pte. Joseph Shepherd of the R. A. M. C. writes from H M S "Letitia" in the Mediterranean. "I received the "Report" and thank you very much for it. Give my best wishes to the Brotherhood and I hope its good work will always have success."

On Furlough from the Front.

She :- "I'm not half proud of you, my boy, it must make the other girls sick with envy."

He :- "Oh, dry up!"

Recalled from the Front

A few local soldiers have been allowed to return home from the front for the purpose of working on munitions. A fair sample of this is that of an iron-turner — he was put through a test at the Base and then drafted home, after nine months at the front, to serve in a workshop.

The Boy Whose Bible was Bulletted.

Pte Percy Howells writes from Salonica:- "Many thanks for your 'Weekly Report.' I think it is a very good idea for it lets us know what our fellow comrades are doing in another theatre of war. We are having a good time, I can tell you, preparing for the Germans and what a shock they will get when they come. I have received letters and newspapers from friends of the Brotherhood but have been unable to answer them owing to there being no name or address so I hope you will tell them from me to put their name in so that I can write back to them. I was pleased to see that the boys in France were getting a few days' furlough. I don't think we shall get away from here until the war is over."

Pte. J. Tranter (Dawley Bank) writes from Victoria Barracks, Hong Kong. "I am glad to say I am very well. At present I am in the same company as P. Brown but they have changed it to A Company. I should like to have your 'Weekly Report' to read and I shall be glad when this dreadful war is over as I am tired of Hong Kong. The weather is very cold here at night - it has rained three days and never stopped yet.

READ YOUR BIBLE EVERY DAY, LADDIE!

I am keeping good company as I have got some good friends here. I read a chapter out of the Testament every night that Mr Lester gave me before I came out. The war does not look like being over yet - we may have to go but I hope not."

The Service last Sunday night was held in the Schoolroom, and it was crowded. It may be held there again next Sunday night at 6 o'clock but the service may be at 5.30 after next Sunday

To Our Lads in Salonica.

Some of us feel brave little Serbia deserves as much of our sympathy as Belgium. Have you seen any of the Serbian soldiers yet? Is this sketch anything like one?

If you are still at Salonica (which is of course quite close to Serbia) and go into the town we hope you will remember that it is the old Thessalonica of the Bible that St. Paul preached there and in the cathedral there is the pulpit which it is said he used. (Go and see it and send us a drawing of it for this paper.)

The Serbians have a fine lot of proverbs, here are some of them - (learn them) — "Where right is of no use wrong will not avail." "Better suffer injustice than commit it." "A victory is won not by shining arms, but by brave hearts." "Man gives all for honour, but honour at no price." "Trust not the smiles of the great nor a bright sky; both change in an instant." "He who is a hero has power enough; he who is no hero will never want any." "Better retire in honour than advance in disgrace." "Covetousness is the world's peace breaker" — a proverb which the Kaiser would do well to note.

The price of the "Weekly Report" is One Penny. The profits (if any) are used to send it out to Dawley soldiers abroad.

WEEKLY REPORT.

Tuesday.
Feb: 29th 1916.

Brotherhood and Sisterhood.
Dawley Baptist Chapel.

SOCIAL FOR SOLDIERS WIVES TO-NIGHT

We have produced a larger number of copies of this Report than usual this week in order to place a free copy in the hands of all the soldiers' wives who have to-day been our guests. We have been very pleased to meet the brave women whose husbands are abroad and we hope this affair is only the beginning of several pleasant and helpful gatherings. Some soldiers' wives are regularly with us every Tuesday, but others, owing to the care of their little children and from other causes have never before been in our Schoolroom. We hope to see these our sisters again. To cheer them to help them. They have made a very great sacrifice for us all in giving up their husbands to fight.

Two Bombardiers.

Bombardier R. Harley writes from France. Thank you for sending me the Weekly Report. If I do not answer often it is not because I am not interested. I can assure you it is always a pleasure to receive anything from Dawley. I was very pleased to see T. W. Archers letter in a recent number telling of his meeting with me on the battlefield. I was delighted to meet him as he has been out here since the beginning of the war the same as myself. I see in the Reports the names of lots of fellows that I know."

Bombardier T. Hardman gave a capital address at the meeting last Tuesday and we are grateful to him for it. His description of the horrors of war made everyone shudder

"We had —— big guns in action in that battle and the Germans had ——!"

but it was the sort of shudder which incites people to do more and more for the soldier at the front and the wife and children he has left at home. He told us of Loos and of the last battle of —— which was fought only 10 days before he came home and in which he took part. If only people would attend our meetings and hear thrilling speeches like Hardman's we should have no difficulty in keeping up interest

Sergeant S. Rowe writes from Malta:- "I should very much like to go to France for I have had enough of this end of the world. I was on the Gallipoli Peninsula twice and I don't want to meet the Turks a third time. It is very quiet now but I expect we shall be having a move in Egypt before long and then we shall see how Johnny Turk likes taking the offensive – he did not show up much on the Peninsula. I have a position in the Camp here now that I am better in health but in my time off I have had some nice tours round the island. There are some lovely sights

"THERE ARE SOME LOVELY SIGHTS I MUST SAY"

I must say

Such as the Dome at Musta which is supposed to be the second largest Dome in the world and the Chapel of Bones at Valleta — the inside of which is horribly decorated with human skulls, backbones, leg-bones, arm-bones and finger-bones."

<u>Note to Soldiers.</u> If you like this little paper sit down at once and write a letter for it describing your surroundings (less gruesome than the above please!) It will be inserted, then tell your home people to come to the Tuesday meeting and secure a copy.

The Doseley Railway Arch is being repaired and heavy scaffolding is placed under it — the workmen are taking out a perished brick here and there and making the whole thing good. We are now proposing to overhaul our Bridge — which carries letters, papers and parcels from Dawley to the fighting line. As might be expected after 18 months, some of our friends have got tired and ask to be replaced by others. The "traffic" therefore may have to go slowly for a week or two until repairs and re-organisation are complete. After that

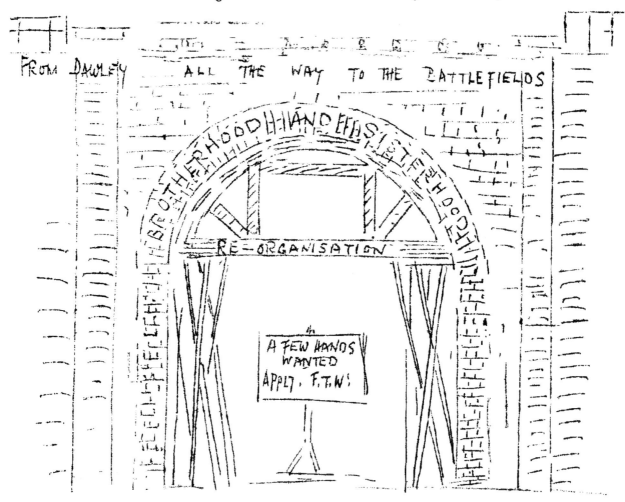

we shall be able to go ahead again — at a terrific rate, only equal to that of our local G.W.R. express between Lightmoor and Horsehay.
Note. A few new, clean hands to write letters wanted.

"The British Tommy is always Happy

Driver Harold Rowe writes from France. "So we are always happy, we never let anything dishearten us I think everything is going on very well all along the line, we keep going grand and winning victories and with patience we shall reach our goal. There has been some heavy bombardment going on the last few weeks and it is a treat to hear our friend Big Lizzie speak just at the back of our camp. When she does speak she nearly shakes you off your feet and lets the Germans know she is alive and kicking. I believe the gunner has been awarded the D. C. M. for his accuracy. I would sooner be out here than in training in England, for I know I am doing my bit."

From an Armoured-Aeroplane Mechanic.

Air-Mechanic G.S. Picken who is attached to the East Meditteranean Air-Squadron writes:- "I should be very pleased if you will convey to the members of the B and S my thanks for considering us in the way they do. It isn't as though they let us have one line and then forget us they seem to be busy all the time sending out one thing after another. I shall express every Dawley fellow's feeling in this. I shall be glad to visit the old place again, it isn't a large place I know still you miss it when you are away. I read a letter in one of the Reports from my cousin, Pte. George Phillips, I was jolly pleased to hear he was going on so well."

Away at the front, my boy, you may be interested to hear of the first meeting of the new Tribunal and of the Military Service Act. It took place in the Town Hall, the members sat round three sides of a long table on the platform. The hall was cold as usual the few people present crowding round the two fireplaces. The proceedings of the Tribunal are public and anyone may be present. A newspaper-reporter was there (though he put precious little in his newspaper!) so it is quite allowable to tell you one or two things.

Men who have attested and who consider themselves entitled to exemption state their case before this Tribunal, which is really a Committee of about twelve of their own townspeople. The Military Authority has a say, of course, through its representative but each case is carefully considered on its merits and the Tribunal has power to grant certificates either "Absolute Conditional or Temporary." There were about 20 appeals on Friday and none were given absolute exemption.

One or two conditional exemptions were granted – for instance a butcher's slaughterman, on condition that he remains a slaughterman. In the majority of cases temporary exemption was granted in order to give time to the applicants to make other arrangements. Among these were a hairdresser, a printer, a house-decorator, and workers who supply material for constructional work at a military camp. No one who was present would say these decisions were too hard. In the case of several young unmarried men the application for time was on the representations of the Military Authority refused.

Big works of the district appear able to secure exemption for all and sundry of their employees without reference to the local Tribunal at all which to some people appears rather puzzling.

Perhaps we will say more about this next week.

The Extinguisher

The Lighting Order puts out the lights of the Chapel one hour and a half after sunset — the lights which for many years have streamed across the hill and dale of many a mile of Shropshire landscape. If the Germans win they will put an extinguisher on Religion as Baptists understand it — the religion of tenderness, the religion of pity, the religion of sacrifice. That's why so many of our men have gone to the Front to fight. More are going!

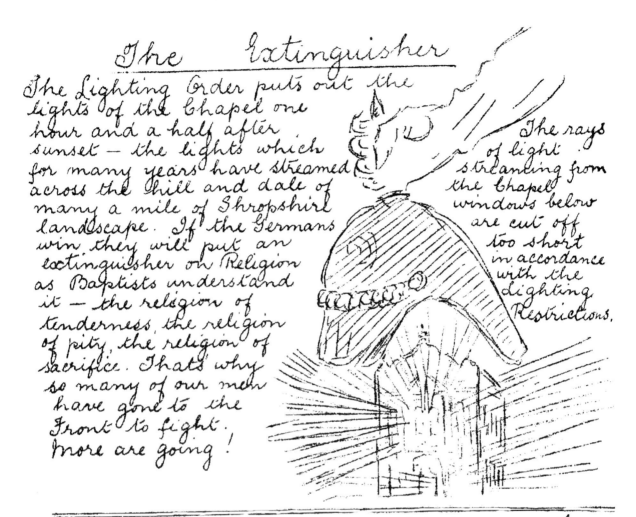

The rays of light streaming from the Chapel windows below are cut off too short in accordance with the Lighting Restrictions.

Pte. R. Deakin writes:- "I congratulate you on the way you are treating our boys. I am sure the parcels you send to us are most welcome and remind us of the fact that not only we but you at home are doing something to win the victory. Nearly every week I get one of the Reports and it helps to pass the time and I can see how my other friends abroad are welfaring."

Surprised to read of his Cousin.

Pte. J. Harley writes again from Salonica saying:- "I am greatly pleased with your Reports of which I have received several. I was surprised to read of my cousin Gunner Harley in one of them — I looked forward to meeting him in France but I did not do so as we had to come on here.

It's Bang, Bang all the While.

Pte. J. Hobson writes from France:- "Many thanks for all the papers which I am pleased to receive. I was glad to see in the Report that nearly all the Dawley lads have "toed the mark." I saw some of the boys here a week or two back — they tell me a good few have gone under but nothing else can be expected in war. Talk about Zepps, they are nothing out here for it is bang, bang all the while and the places are simply levelled to the ground."

We are

Before the Day's Pipe all their down, only a As you come Brandlee Horsehay across the site building used have not yet circular suppose that you one of the top of

levelling things!

war, you remember Works? Well, almost buildings are now taken few stacks remain. down the slope from you can now see the Hinder Hill, right where Day's main to stand. They touched the high chimney stack but I also is doomed. were the lads carried to this stack when it

was in building? If you wish to have one more glimpse of the glorious panorama of Dawley from the top of it you must make haste home or it will be down with a bang!

Price One Penny.

Profits (if any) devoted to sending this to our Soldiers at the front. It can only be purchased at the Tuesday meetings.

WEEKLY REPORT.

Tuesday. April 4th 1916.

Pte. H. Pugh writes from France. "I wrote home and told them all about the "Weekly Report" and now I get it every week. I think it's a jolly decent paper, and very interesting. The sketches are "great." You ask for some sketches from us but I'm no hand at that class of work. If I were I could send you some fine ruins. our present billet was once a fine place, now all the windows are out, there is a great

AWARDED

FOR

COURAGE
PATIENCE
CHEERFULNESS

FROM DAWLEY BAPTIST CHAPEL TO YOU.

shell-hole in the wall, half the roof is off and it looks as if it is only the plaster and the paper on the walls that keep the rest of the place together. We live in the cellar and as it's warm we don't mind, but we keep on smiling because it might be worse." "Later." "Alas, we have been moved into a dug-out on the other side of the village – it is very stuffy and we have got too much company in the way of rats and mice."

Price One Penny.

Issued at the Brotherhood and Sisterhood Meeting every Tuesday evening

The "Whisper"

A soldier writing from France last week, (quoting a remark on the front page of the "Weekly Report" of a few weeks ago) says:—
"I cannot say more but I will whisper something to you when I come home."

This is the sort of whisper which will be necessary to some of us! Many an old grandad who has been "hibernating" all the winter now sits outside his cottage in the warm spring sunshine. If a soldier happens to pass he wants a word or two with him — and a mere whisper is no manner of good to the old gent.

Tit - Bits.

A gauzeless miners' safety lamp, having an illuminant of one candle power, and so contrived as not to be extinguished by a knock or tilt to one side, has been shown to the Miners' Federation of Great Britain, and they have asked the Home Office to make special tests of it.

"Perhaps our Admiralty has a few little surprises in store for the enemy about which we do not talk," said Sir Robert Hadfield, the Sheffield steel manufacturer, at a company meeting.

The soap bubble which Sir James Dewar blew in a bottle at the Royal Institution on Feb. 17th has burst after an existence of thirty-seven days.

A small book will be sent to the soldier at the front whose postcard is first received correctly stating where in Dawley this is to be seen. (Answer to No. 1 next week)

W N E

IN THE

PUBLIC EYE.

NO 2.

"If the Germans came to Dawley."

They would "book" a Railway Station for a Dog-Kennel.

Gunner G. Tart of the R.F.A. writes:— "We have had a number of casualties lately — we have had our Captain and a gunner killed, also two other fellows last week.... We hear the Germans have achieved nothing at Verdun except that both they and the French have lost a lot of men. We are now out of action for a few days and we have been moved a long way behind the firing line in a country-village, something similar to Dawley" (Hold hard Gunner, "Dawley a village" with 7,700 people in it!) "I will try and send you a sketch for the "Report" in a short time."

We have received many Field Postcards during the week or which we thank the senders. One found us with the following address only "Weekly Report Brotherhood and Sisterhood, Dawley Baptist Chapel." What fame!

An Oakengates soldier, Driver A. E. Turner (Ambulance Section) writes to us.- 'I must write to you to thank you for sending the 'Weekly Report' to my old chum, Pte S. Small, whom I have known from a boy. We share the things you send out here and we are very grateful. We are much obliged for cigarettes for we are now in a place in France where we cannot get anything. I am sure I shall be pleased to come to your Tuesday evening meeting when we come home when this great conflict is at an end. My pal and I had a narrow escape the other day when riding on the Ambulance waggon, a large shell bursting over the top of us and pieces missing us by a few inches."

Bombardier R. Harley writes:- 'Thank you for the "W. R." which I keep on receiving - I can assure you your idea is a very good one as it keeps Dawley boys in touch with each other. I should like to meet one or two of the men whose letters you publish from time to time. I am glad to see Pte. W Ewings is following in his father's footsteps, he could not do better. I hope Dawley will still keep up its good record, which I think is excellent for a town of its size!

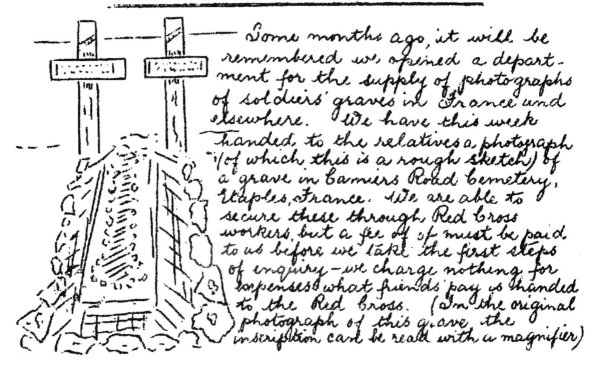

Some months ago, it will be remembered we opened a department for the supply of photographs of soldiers' graves in France and elsewhere. We have this week handed to the relatives a photograph (of which this is a rough sketch) of a grave in Camiers Road Cemetery, Etaples, France. We are able to secure these through Red Cross workers, but a fee of must be paid to us before we take the first steps of enquiry - we charge nothing for expenses, what friends pay is handed to the Red Cross. (In the original photograph of this grave, the inscription can be read with a magnifier)

Pte. E. Round (Meadow Road) who enlisted at the
outbreak of the war from Colwyn Bay into the Welsh
Fusiliers is a prisoner of war in the hands of the Germans,
who have sent him to an English Prisoners' Camp at
Hanover. Three loaves a week are being sent to him
to help to keep him alive! That's how the Germans
treat their prisoners. We are hoping to send out a
parcel of food for this man and his companions.
Who will help? Mark
contributions:- "Prisoners
of War in
Germany."

To Hanover

We have
received a copy
of the Sydney
"Daily Telegraph" sent
by Pte. A. E. Corbett
containing an excellent picture
of a detachment of Shropshire
Territorials marching through the
streets of the Australian city, to the
great interest of the spectators.

Mr. and Mrs. E. G. March are speaking and singing at
our meeting to-night. Mr. March has done practically
all the work in connection with the Soldiers' and Sailors'
Association (Allowances etc) in Wellington — for this
reason, if for no other, he deserves a warm welcome.

Next Tuesday Miss Dora Robinson and Miss Nora
Morgan of Wellington are coming to give us a
Musical Evening — which we anticipate with great
pleasure.

If Dawley soldiers at the front do not hear from us
regularly, please communicate with us.

In No Man's Land.

Lance-Corporal J. Davies writes from France:- "We are not a fighting corps, but a working corps - we try to make the other boys as safe and as comfortable as we can. I will try to tell you what happened on Friday night. We were going out into "No Man's Land" to put up barbed wire, but when we got there, the place was all crowded up and the boys were passing bags of bombs so we got the order to stand to with them for a counter-attack, then we thought we were in for a bit of fighting. When our officer said we must go out there to put up the wire again the Infantry said it was asking to be smashed up, but we did not grumble, we went out and worked at that wire till one o'clock in the morning. Nothing happened, I am glad to say, but when the star-lights go up one never knows what is going to happen. We could see the Germans moving about in front of us but they did not fire for if they did they knew they would draw our fire on them. But there in "No Man's Land" I must tell you it is a mass of shell-holes dotted about like spots on a piece of print-cloth, half-full of water and the ground is like clay. When we happen to slip into one of these holes in the dark we get up to our knees and it takes five to ten minutes to get out again, sometimes leaving one of our trench-boots in.... I wish you good luck in your work and with all the new hands that have been put to the plough."

We are deeply grateful to the Dawley Sewing Guild for the gift of 12 pairs of Socks and 4 Mufflers. During the week about 15 parcels have been despatched to needy soldiers in France and Salonica, containing shirts, socks, cigarettes, writing-paper, etc.

Off to France for the Third Time.

Pte. A. Holbrook writes from Pembroke Dock on April 1st "Thirty-two of us have now been liberated from special munition work here and they have put me back on my old job again – on the machine-gun and I shan't be long before I am out again for the third time. I can't 'grouse' much for I have had a good time at home and I am never likely to have such a winter as I had at the first on arriving from India. Thank you for the 'Report'."

"We are all doing our very best for you"

We used 105 Penny Stamps last Tuesday in sending copies of this little paper to soldiers to whom no one else would be sending and we have only received 6 stamps during the week. Please do not allow us to become bankrupt!
The amount of money placed in the box at the door on a Tuesday has been much too small of late. Next Tuesday therefore we shall take a collection from seat to seat for the Postage Fund at the special Musical Evening.

Many thousands of eggs have been collected by people in Dawley for the benefit of wounded soldiers in the hospitals.

The Bible Class in Hospital.

Your Lesson for April 9th

AENEAS.

Peter, one of the friends of Jesus was in a town called Lydda where he found a sick man, Aeneas, who had been in bed for 8 years. Peter said to him – "Aeneas, in the name of Jesus get up and make your bed!" Aeneas got up at once and found he was quite well. The miracle had such an impression on the people that many of them listened to Peter's preaching and became Christians.

It may be difficult to explain some of these old-time miracles but there is little doubt they took place, though the power to accomplish them may have died out with the first Apostles. Medical science to-day is able to perform miracles which would have astonished even Peter. The chief point is that Christ is to-day a Great Healer. Do you remember singing "Thy touch hath still its ancient power" "In Thy mercy heal us all." Ask to-day for a touch from the Great Physician.

"It makes a Soldier look "soft"!"

Pte Chas. Ayres writes from France. "I must say I am very glad when I am able to sit down to read the "Weekly Report." We are still fighting around the same old parts of France but really there is not much moving yet... I expect Dawley is very quiet now other men are being called up – never mind, you have got plenty of women, they will take our places and the work will go on just the same. I am sorry I can't tell you much but we are not allowed to in our Regiment. I should like to send you a good deal for your "Report" each week, but it does make a soldier look "soft" when he is not allowed to put as much in as he likes. I hope to be able to join you at one of your meetings soon."

(Never mind, old chap, if you can't tell us all you would like to, tell us what you can. Other soldiers please note this)

THE END

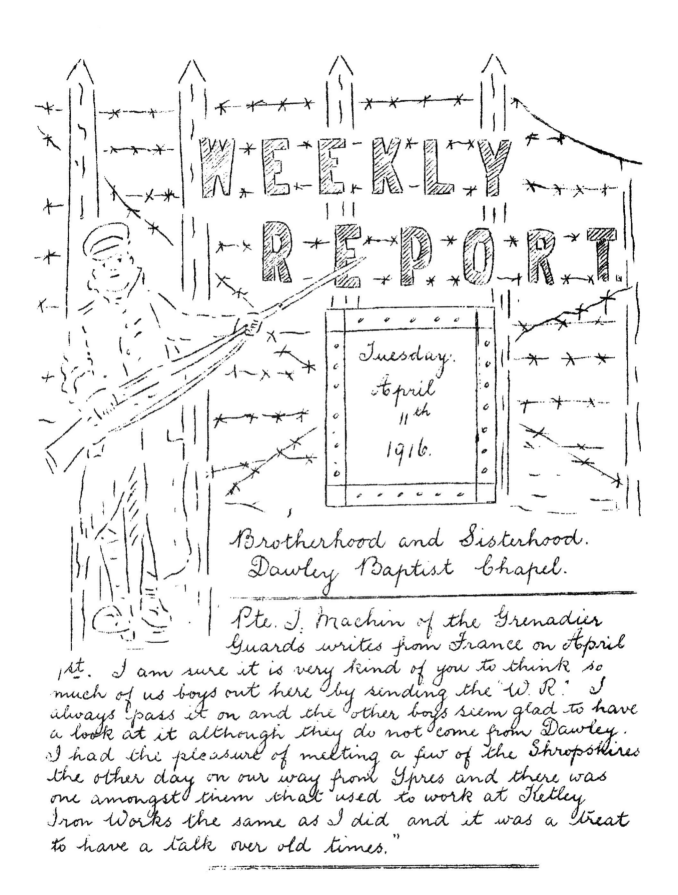

WEEKLY REPORT

Tuesday.
April
11th
1916.

Brotherhood and Sisterhood.
Dawley Baptist Chapel.

Pte. J. Machin of the Grenadier Guards writes from France on April 1st. "I am sure it is very kind of you to think so much of us boys out here by sending the 'W.R.' I always pass it on and the other boys seem glad to have a look at it although they do not come from Dawley. I had the pleasure of meeting a few of the Shropshires the other day on our way from Ypres and there was one amongst them that used to work at Ketley Iron Works the same as I did and it was a treat to have a talk over old times."

her (Scots Guards) writes from somewhere in April 2nd. "Since I wrote you last we have to the good old Shropshires at the place Battalion made such a gallant stand at ...ning of the war. I went up to the Shropshires' a few days ago and spent a short time with some the lads from the Dawley district – Pte. H. Bailey. A. Bailey from the Gid Park and Pte Willets from the Rock and Tom Hobson of Bank Road and I saw Pte. Frost – he is a rare boy. when I will come to say the spirit of our way the young soldier marvellous. Some of Shropshires were only for the Boer War is in them and they were going to a football

I hope to get leave soon your meeting.... I must lads is good and the takes to the life is simply the lads I met in the babies when I left home but the British pluck go off singing as if they match."

The Old Soldier is very Proud of the new Dawley Boys.

Travelling in France.

Driver Harold Rowe writes from France on April 3rd. "We have been moving about this last fortnight both by road and rail somewhere down —— France.... It is blazing hot here. I suppose you are still in darkness I noticed when we were travelling in the train at night towns were all lighted up and tramcars were running. After we left the train about 2 o'clock in the morning street lamps were lighted on our way till daybreak."

Latest Intelligence.

Randlay Brickworks are advertising in Dawley for girls to do light clay-work. Will the older men strike?

The Urban Council have recently summoned one of the citizens for keeping pigs too near the house — they say pigs ought not to be treated as members of the family.

Rev. E. Parry, on Saturday, in the presence of an admiring throng planted several young trees on his mount opposite Old Park School naming each tree after some celebrity commencing with the King!

One of the inhabitants has been pasturing his cows on the council's land at the Paddock for the past year or two and the councillors think, that with milk at 4d a quart this good dairyman ought to begin to pay something for the privilege.

"Every Bullet has its Billet."

Bombardier I. Hardman (who spoke at our meeting recently) writes a lengthy letter from France, in the course of which he says:— "Thank you for the parcel and Report. This is the liveliest place ever I was in, and I have been in a few. Things are looking brighter and I think the war will finish in July. We have them quite alright here. We have had a few casualties since I was with you, but we must not grumble. In the midst of life we are in death and we are out here. We always share our parcels — a pal of mine had a good one last Wednesday and we opened it together. Ten minutes after the parcel was all mine for he could not eat any more..... We buried him the same night..... I do not trouble — if I had to die in Belgium or France I shall have to die there. If there is a bullet or a piece of shrapnel made for a man he will get it. Thanking you again."

We deeply regret to announce to you the lo[ss]
Sergeant A. Eric. Bailey who died "somewhere"
March 29th or 30th. His burial-place is state[d]
cemetery at Ecoivres.

He enlisted at the outbreak of the war fr[om a sense]
of duty and his friends in the Army
all say that no soldier did his duty
better. He was above the average in
ability and universally popular.

As a lad he attended Lawley
School. While there he won a
County Council Scholarship
which secured him a place in the
Newport Grammar School. For a
year or two he was an elementary
school-teacher, first at Pool Hill
School, Dawley and later at
Malinslee. Presently he
went to Goldsmith's
Training College, connected
with the University College
of London, where he spent
two years, expecting at the
close to enter the teaching
profession.

Alas, that at the age
of 23 his life-work is done.

All at the Baptist
Chapel, where he was a
member and a Sunday
School teacher deeply
sympathise with his
parents, who live in
High Street. They have
two other sons now in
training.

"They
counted
not their
lives
dear unto
them."

'Platoon-
France" on
e the Military

keen sense

In   Honour
the   Memory of
ant. A. E. Bailey.

ve his life for his country
on the Battlefield.

"Be
thou
faithful
unto
death."

The sketch on the preceding page is adapted from a drawing by a professional artist, as anyone can see!

In the Public Eye. No. 3.

The Prize for No. 1. is awarded to Private J. W. Price, of the Cameron Highlanders whose postcard written on April 1st was received on April 5th. A book has been sent to him to-day. The answer was :- "The Key of Fire-Hose, etc. under glass in panel of the door of the Market Hall, High Street, Dawley."

A small book will be sent to the soldier at the front whose postcard is first received correctly stating where this is to be seen in Dawley.

(Answer to No 2 next week)

Correct answers were also received from Driver H. Rowe, Sergeant. J. Farr, Lance-Corporal A. E. Thomas and Private W. J. Harrison, but they were too late!

Sergeant S. Rowe is expected to arrive in Dawley from Malta, where he has been since the fighting in Gallipoli, this week.

Pte. E. Jackson is in hospital in Manchester and Pte. J. T. Simmons, slowly recovering from his "gassing" is at the R. C. Hospital, Esher, Surrey.

Lance-Corporal A. E. Thomas says he passes the "Weekly Report" round the boys of the Grenadiers, and they all like it.

Pte. T. Furber writes from France saying it is summer there now but they have a lot of water in the trenches, sometimes up to their knees.

Pte. Harry Corbett says he brought up the post to the trenches one night last week and he read every word of the "Report" before he went to sleep.

We gratefully acknowledge the receipt of the following for our Postage Fund. "Miss P. B." 12 stamps. and Mrs T. A. Jones. 24 stamps.

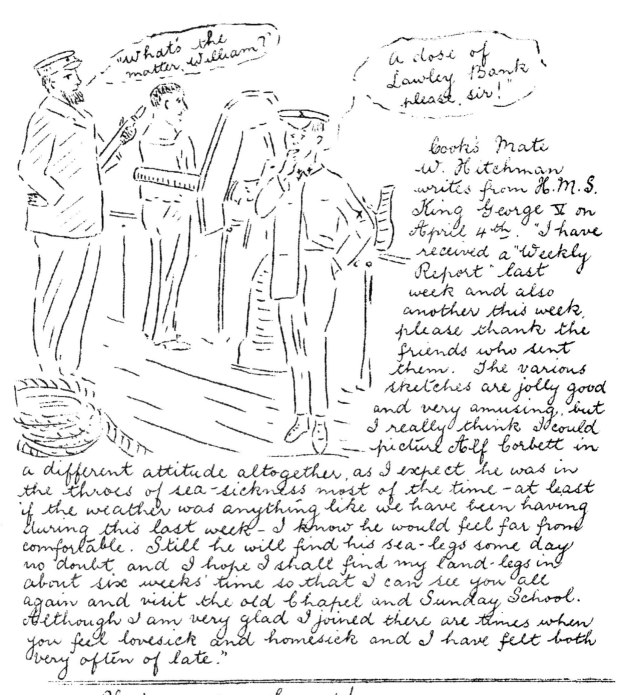

Cook's Mate W. Hitchman writes from H.M.S. King George V on April 4th. "I have received a "Weekly Report" last week and also another this week, please thank the friends who sent them. The various sketches are jolly good and very amusing, but I really think I could picture Alf Corbett in a different attitude altogether, as I expect he was in the throes of sea-sickness most of the time – at least if the weather was anything like we have been having during this last week – I know he would feel far from comfortable. Still he will find his sea-legs some day no doubt and I hope I shall find my land-legs in about six weeks' time so that I can see you all again and visit the old Chapel and Sunday School. Although I am very glad I joined there are times when you feel lovesick and homesick and I have felt both very often of late."

He's in Egypt!

Pte. M. Cadman – 38169 B Coy. 2nd Garrison Batt: R. W. Fusiliers writes from Egypt. – "Thank you for the "W. R" out here. It is not a bad country – only a bit hot. As I am in a Welsh Regiment I never see any Dawley boys but I am very pleased to hear about them and I hope we shall all meet again sometime in the old place when the war is over."

The Bible Class at the Front.

Your Lesson for April 16th

Peter and Cornelius.
(Acts 10. 1-23)

At Caesarea there lived a Roman officer named Cornelius who was a good-hearted chap and very kind to the poor. When he heard of the Christians he sent some of his servants to fetch the Apostle Peter from Joppa. But the woman of the house where Peter lodged did not want to interrupt him - she said Peter was praying on the flat house-top and must not be disturbed. The fact was Peter was a Jew and he had got the idea that the Gospel was only for Jews. But while he was at prayer he fell asleep and dreamed a dream which set him right. He saw that strangers and foreigners and good fellows like the Roman soldier Cornelius could be saved if only they wished. He therefore came down and went off with the soldier, who was afterwards converted and became a good soldier of Jesus Christ.

Lance-Corporal H. Dacre, 2nd South Staffords writes:-
"I liked that little sermon in the "Weekly Report" the other week, it is quite true if we ponder over it it makes things much easier, especially when we are in doubt. I think I. Machin who is mentioned in the Report is my cousin from down Dawley Green Lane if I am not mistaken, I am glad to know he is going on alright. Remember me to all friends at the meeting."

Price One Penny.

Sold only at the Tuesday meeting, from which we send out to about 150 soldiers a week.

Sold only at our
weekly meeting

For Tuesday,
April 18, 1916
Brotherhood and Sisterhood,
Dawley Baptist Chapel.

A Word of Cheer from "Neddock".
Pte Ned Archer writes from Salonica: "All the Dawley boys are well
and cheerful. We shall have quite a lot to tell you about our experiences if we
have the luck to get through. I cannot tell you how much I thank the B and S
for the good work they are doing. I wish my old friend Alf Corbett could come
here. We are all merry and bright just as we used to be at the Sunday School
at Lawley Bank. We realise the good you have done for us now we are away,
so your work in the Sunday School has not been in vain. P.S. Write soon.

Sunday Morning in Salonica
Sergeant J.G. Pitchford writes: "It is as hot as it can be here this Sunday
morning and we are waiting for Church Parade – we have it in the open
overlooking the docks. We strain our eyes looking across the water to dear old
England and we wonder how long it will be before we return. I can hear the
guns as I write, the sound seems to travel so far here across the mountains
and the blue sea. God has so far kept us safe from the dangers of this wicked
war."

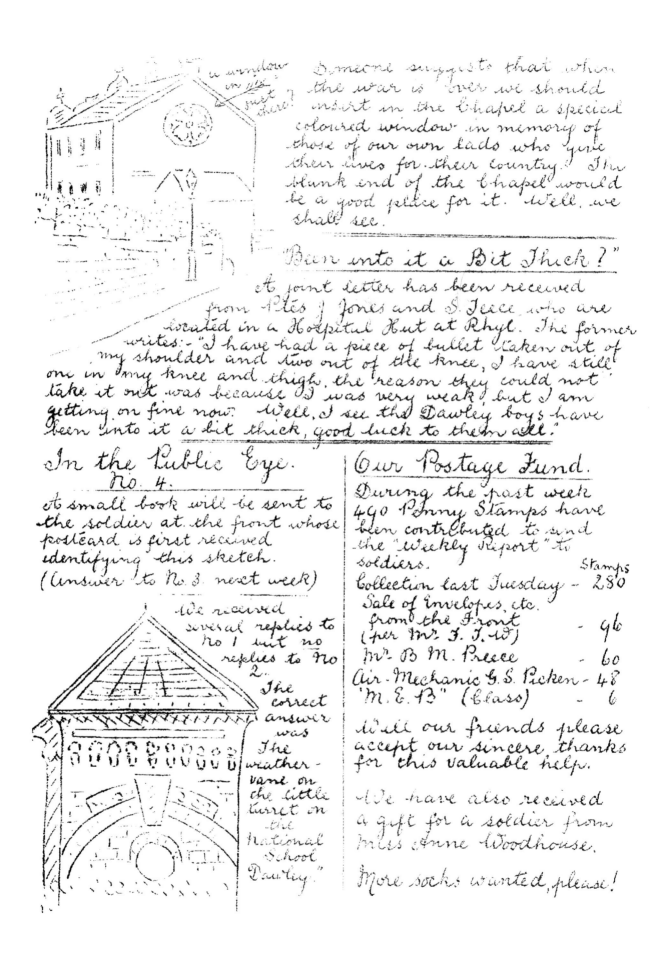

Someone suggests that when the war is over we should insert in the Chapel a special coloured window in memory of those of our own lads who gave their lives for their country! The blank end of the Chapel would be a good place for it. Well, we shall see.

"Been into it a Bit Thick?"

A joint letter has been received from Ptes J Jones and I Teece who are located in a Hospital Hut at Rhyl. The former writes:- "I have had a piece of bullet taken out of my shoulder and two out of the knee, I have still one in my knee and thigh, the reason they could not take it out was because I was very weak, but I am getting on fine now. Well, I see the Dawley boys have been into it a bit thick, good luck to them all."

In the Public Eye.
No. 4.

A small book will be sent to the soldier at the front whose postcard is first received identifying this sketch.
(Answer to No. 3 next week)

We received several replies to No 1 but no replies to No 2. The correct answer was "The weather-vane on the little turret on the National School Dawley"

Our Postage Fund.

During the past week 490 Penny Stamps have been contributed to and the "Weekly Report" to soldiers.

	Stamps
Collection last Tuesday	280
Sale of Envelopes, etc. from the Front (per Mr. J. J. W)	96
Mr B M. Preece	60
Air-Mechanic G. S. Picken	48
"M. E. B" (Class)	6

Will our friends please accept our sincere thanks for this valuable help.

We have also received a gift for a soldier from Miss Anne Woodhouse.

More socks wanted, please!

"O Risen Christ! O Easter Flower!
How dear Thy Grace has grown!
From East to West, with loving power,
Make all the world Thine Own."

"Thou art spending this Easter far away from the old spot my lad! but I have brought you my Easter Blessing out here"

"Lo, I am with you alway even unto the end of the world."

"I am He that liveth and was dead, and behold I am alive for evermore."

With our sincere Easter Greetings to you.

An Old Soldier's Prayer.

"O God, if in the day of battle I forget Thee, do not Thou forget me."

Who is this Anonymous Artist? A Sketch drawn at the Front

A Quiet Day in the Trenches

The sender of the above writes from Somewhere in France.
"Being as we appreciate seeing your sketches at the front I and my chum
being artists of no mean order and everything so quiet, we've drawn a bit of
the fiercest part of the firing-line, also it's a veritable rat-warren. But being
short of cheese we couldn't hie one out as we are no good as artists unless we
have the objects in front of us. That also accounts for the absence of Germans.
I and a small patrol were out in 'No Man's Land' the other night and we
caught one of those wicked Huns, but he pleaded so hard – you know the old
game 'Loving Wife and seventeen children' – all of us being married it
touched our manly breasts. He said he had had nothing to eat for 2 or 3 days
– result, we gave him our Iron Rations though they were a bit ancient and
then we conducted him back to his lines. He has promised to write us regular.
We are expecting the Non-Combatant Corps up any time so we've the barbed
wire for repairing s-h-h. Tell them not to get alarmed, there are only 90-100
Machine Guns in front of us and they only fire half that number at once.
There is a Firework Display to-night and we are going to see it. Don't forget
to send the Weekly Report every week as we look forward to it. Yours – One
from Dawley.

P.S. if you appreciate our sketch we will send you some more later on also our names."

(Yes, my boy, names please, we don't reproduce anonymous sketches or letters – yours are both very good – you need not hesitate to tell us who you are, it will add considerably to the interest of your future communications.")

Some of our friends have kindly made enquiries as to the production of the "W. R." There are several people on the staff and we beg to give a few portraits, which we hope will be easily recognised! After the frank disclosure of the works" no more inquisitive questions please.

Thank You !

We express our thanks to Miss Dora Robinson and Miss Nora Morgan for the excellent little entertainment they gave at last Tuesday. The collection amounted to £1·3·4 which has been devoted to the Postage Stamp Fund.

We hope to be able during the summer to arrange to send out to all Dawley married soldiers who have not been home lately a small specially taken photograph of their wives and children We hope to persuade one of our good friends to take charge of this but if other amateur photographers care to help we shall be very grateful Every soldier on foreign service note this.

About Ourselves.

One of the literary editors thinking out next week's number.

One of the artists on "If the Germans came to Dawley"

at express speed.

Working the Cyclostyle machine

"One Penny please"

One of the newsagents selling it at the Tuesday meeting.

The Belle of which French Village?

Pte. G. V. Lovatt sends a sketch (of which this is a rough reproduction) which he calls "The Belle of the Village" but he does not say what village! He writes:— "I am very comfortable at present, there are three of us in a snug little cellar – we have been in it for a month now and we have made it like a palace. We each have a real bed which is better than the hard floor. We have also erected a stove which springs into activity every night, either for making cocoa, or when we are in luck, frying eggs. I like your idea of putting into sketches various bits of Dawley because it brings before us again visions of the dear old place"... I have not met a Dawley chap out here for a long time, I can't make out where they have all gone to."

Death of Sir Charles Henry's Son Confirmed

In the daily papers last Friday morning the following note appeared:— "Lieutenant Cyril Charles Henry, 2nd Worcestershire Regiment, who is reported killed in to-day's casualty lists, was the only son of Sir Charles S. Henry, Bart., M.P, and Lady Henry.

He was born 22 years ago, and educated at Harrow. At the outbreak of the war he was a second lieutenant in the 4th Hussars. He was reported "wounded and missing" in the action at Loos on Sept 26th and it is now learnt that he was killed by machine-gun fire on the night of that date." There is no one, either at the front or at home but regrets to hear this.

Pte. J. W. Price of the Cameron Highlanders called to see us a day or two ago. He brought the contents of the parcel he received a few days before he left France to his home at Woodhouse Lane, Horsehay

The Events of the Week.

The weather has been very rough, cold and wet, which to people susceptible to influenza has been an outstanding feature of the week

Wednesday is to be kept as Red Cross Flag Day in Dawley when it is hoped a good sum will be realised.

The project of a Toy Factory for Dawley appears to be "off" for the present, Messrs Johnson Bros. of Harborne having purchased the Wesleyan School Hall in Wellington for the purpose.

Last week it was decided to arrange a Church Parade for the Red Cross and local Nursing Association Funds

The Dawley Military Tribunal has not met for three weeks, but there is a special meeting on Wednesday when it is understood a large number of cases have to be dealt with.

The workmen are still engaged in repairs to Doseley Railway Bridge — it having been necessary to almost rebuild the structure on the side towards Doseley Church.

Easter Monday of years ago.

Will it happen again next Easter?

Air Mechanic G. S. Picken writes from London on the 16th saying he was sorry he was unable to come to our meeting when home on leave. He expected to leave for foreign service again before this but he is kept back with four others to act as instructors to fellows just joining the air-service. He incloses 4/- in stamps for the Postage Fund and we thank him very much.

"If the Germans came to Dawley"

They would not be allowed to use the Bandstand in the Park on Easter Monday.

Pte C Ayres (King's Liverpool Regiment) writes from France "I only know one man in my regiment and that is L/Corp Jorgrove he lives near Bayston Hill. I dropped across him in the last draft. I was glad to see my little bit of news in the "Report" this week – I always hand it round to my chums when I get it. I am sorry to say I am not much of a hand in drawing but I will do my best to send a sketch soon if I can possibly do it, I am

willing to try but if it is not very good you might finish it off for me. No one knows what they can do until they try. I will see that a few coppers come to the meeting every Tuesday towards sending the "Report" every week because I would not like them to be stopped.

Pte J Furber writes from France on April 8th "Thank you for the Weekly Post and for your welcome parcel – we shall indeed have something to thank you for when the war is over. We are having some very nice weather here now I hope it is the same in England.

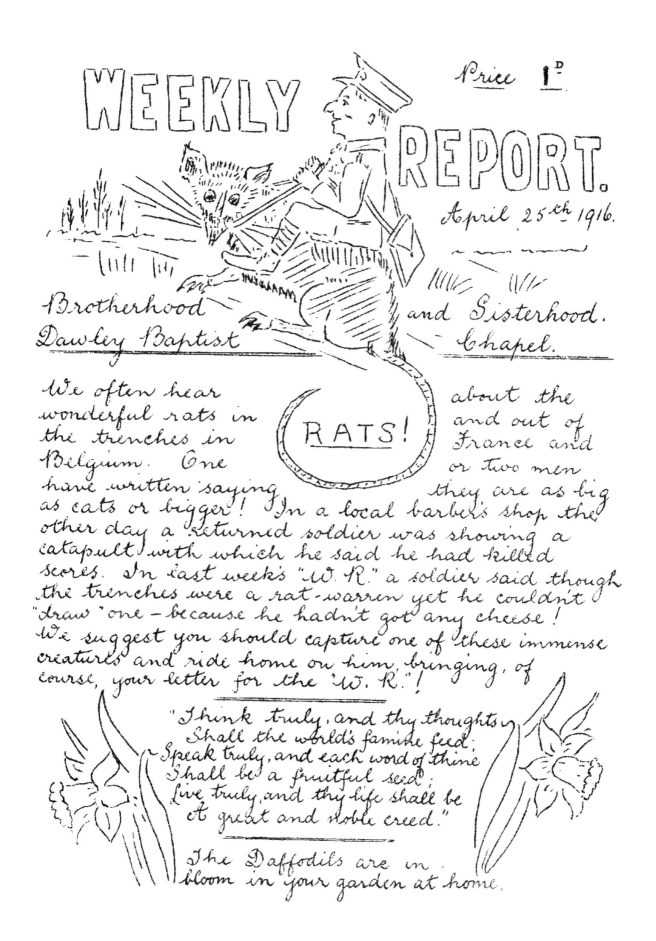

WEEKLY REPORT.

Price 1^D

April 25th 1916.

Brotherhood and Sisterhood.
Dawley Baptist Chapel.

We often hear wonderful rats in the trenches in Belgium. One have written saying **RATS!** about the and out of France and or two men they are as big as cats or bigger! In a local barber's shop the other day a returned soldier was showing a catapult with which he said he had killed scores. In last week's "W. R." a soldier said though the trenches were a rat-warren yet he couldn't "draw" one — because he hadn't got any cheese! We suggest you should capture one of these immense creatures and ride home on him, bringing, of course, your letter for the "W. R."!

"Think truly, and thy thoughts
Shall the world's famine feed;
Speak truly, and each word of thine
Shall be a fruitful seed;
Live truly, and thy life shall be
A great and noble creed."

The Daffodils are in bloom in your garden at home.

Some Dawley Doings.

The weather during the Easter holidays was cold and wintry, with some rain. A few visitors were over, but not nearly so many as in the old days.

Mr. J. Weaver of High Street last week resigned the chairmanship of the Madeley Board of Guardians – a position he has held for 20 years.

The two new coal-pits in the meadows under the mounds which lie between Days' old works and the Horsehay Pottery appear to be doing a flourishing business. One man has commenced to sink a coal-pit in his garden at Lawley Bank.

The Red Cross Flag Day in Dawley last Wednesday brought in £12-13-6. The organisers were Mrs J. Simpson, Miss Phillips and Miss Muriel Jones. The following took part in the collection:- Mrs Fletcher, Misses Bayley, Morris, Parvin, J. Passey, M. Wilkes, K. Growcott, R. Lane, Phillips, O. Hudson, M. Tranter, G. Bowen, D. and G. Wooding, M. and B. Smith, W. Rhodes, D. and E. Ruscoe, M. and C. Briscoe, A. and M. Woodhouse, G. Lester, D. Smith, K. Machin, M. Ketley, E. Callear, E. and B. Merrington.

One of the most interesting cases before the Dawley Military Tribunal last week was that of a man who had been called up before his appeal case had been finally settled.

He asked exemption on domestic grounds which the Tribunal hesitated for a time to grant. In the meanwhile his time was up and he joined. When the appeal form followed him and he had the opportunity to state his case again he told the military officer at the camp on the East Coast where he is now located that since he was in khaki he had no wish to return to Dawley.

"No, thank you sir, no more Dawley for me just yet!"

Fresh appeal for attested man

One Good Turn Deserves Another!

(The Xmas parcels sent out to our soldiers at Hong Kong were enclosed in one package addressed to Private A. E. Corbett, who was away towards Australia at the time, the presents are therefore only now being acknowledged.)

I'm real glad to do a bit for Dawley lads for they treated me well at Wellington.

SYDNEY →

Pte. et. E. Corbett writes from Hong Kong on March 16th. "The fountain-pen is the best present I have ever received since I left home, you can write when you go on guard without troubling to take a pen and ink with you. We have only just got back from Australia where we took the German prisoners. Tom Tranter has gone now with another batch, he was not with us. We had a nice time there – one would not know there was a war on, only they have got a lot of Australian soldiers home wounded. We had a fine time of it – one gentleman was a soldier who had been over to England and he was once billeted at Davies' at Wellington – when he knew we came from Dawley he took us for a ride in his motor all round Sydney..... At the different ports we stopped at the women made such a fuss of us, a lot of them had come from different parts of England. We met with one man from Dawley in Australia who had been out there 20 years – I forget his name, but I will get it off George Roberts – he knows it."

Lance-Corporal W. H. Oliver writes from Salonica :- "It is very good of you all to send out letters to me ever since I came from India – first to Belgium, then to France and now to Greece – I have never been short of hearing how Dawley people are going on. It is six years since I left Dawley for soldiering and on my return from India I had only three days at home but I hope to return some day."

Our Horses are well cared for

Sergeant J. Farr writes from France "I often read the Report over four or five times. I cannot tell you much news you probably know more about the war than we do. I don't suppose in the history of man horses have been so well-cared for as they are out here. We are not in a fighting unit "(Sergeant Farr is attached to the Canadian Veterinary section) "but we are workin just as hard. I have been at the front and here and I know the difference (if any) between the two."

(Yes, my boy, treat those Canadian horses well, but you should have seen how some of the creatures treated us when we were getting them into condition at Horsehay and Old Park!)

"The Guns Draw the Rain" - What about Dawley Rain?

Pte. G. Round writes:- "We are having bad weather here it is raining day and night - the guns draw the rain. How I wish the war were over but it cannot last much longer. I am glad to see by the "Weekly Report" that the Dawley boys are doing their bit. Candlin, Butler and J. Bailey are in the same regiment so I often see them but they are the only men from Dawley district I have dropped on."

War Economies.

Notice to our Readers.

Owing to a very considerable increase in price as well as restriction upon importation of paper and paper-pulp and at the same time an increasing demand on the part of soldiers for the "W.R" it has become necessary for us to follow the lead of other great newspapers. Instead of raising our price, however we shall in future use a cheaper paper. We are paying 25/- this week for paper — what a demand we make on the shipping trade!

To the gentleman who on Wednesday evening last gave Mr. Lester a 10/- Treasury note "for the support of your interesting soldiers' paper — thanks are given

<u>Do not forget</u> the <u>Old</u> Soldier please!

We have received a letter from an old Dawley soldier now stationed as a member of the National Reserve on guard at Brunner-Mond Works in a neighbouring county. He asks why we forget old soldiers — who have seen service in previous wars and who would be out at the front now if only the doctor would pass them. If some of the old Shropshire boys were not on guard at explosive and other works we should all know it, he says. (We are putting this soldier on our list for the "Weekly Report", etc)

"If it were not for us old soldiers in England you would know it"

Gunner Tart writes from France :- "We are now in a village for a rest — we can hear the big guns a good many miles away. I give the "W.R" to another fellow — Jones of St. Georges. We had a very nice concert in the village schools last night — a school about a quarter the size of Langley School. I wish I was having a walk just now up to Dawley Bank."

We have this week sent our first parcel to our Dawley man who is a prisoner of war at Hanover, Germany. It contained butter, cheese, cooked bacon and café au lait

Nearly 200 soldiers, out of this country will have this "Weekly Report" posted to them and it is safe to say practically all, at some time or other have attended our School Sermons. Some were our scholars right up to the time of their enlistment at the outbreak of the war. Since we have been sending out the "W.R" we have received letters from many men saying they too, once upon a time were scholars in our school.

Well now, we shall not forget you next Sunday. On the back page of our circular we have put the following: "In connection with our Tuesday meeting we are sending out to nearly 200 soldiers every week. We shall send them copies of the Anniversary Hymns left in the seats on Sunday evening. If you care to sign your name, please do so."

When the services are over we expect quite 200 copies of the circular to be left in the seats – many of them will no doubt be signed by people who attend the services. We shall send out these copies to you. You will see that the Hymns chosen are appropriate for you, as well as for us who are fighting other battles at home. The booklet ought therefore to be of great interest, especially as it was actually used by someone or other on Sunday night, perhaps by the person whose name is written on the back cover.

Remember also my lad, that not only on this Sunday but every Sunday we pray for you.

The title of our booklet is "Fight for the Right."

Pte. H. Corbett writes from France:- "Thank you for your parcel, the clothing came in very handy as we don't get a change very often. It will be a blessing when this terrible war is over and we can all come back again to the old place."

Pte. A. Lloyd says:- "After having a warm time with the Germans we are being moved for a rest. It is nice to be a little further back from the cannons. I hoped to be home for a bit but they have stopped all our passes and we shall have to be content."

Pte. J. Machin of the Grenadiers writes from a Rest Hut in France (he sends this picture of it) "There is no mistake as to the "W.R." cheering us up. I have now been transferred to Headquarters as Cycle Orderly and it is a far better job than being with the company. We do not have to go into the trenches except it is with a message to our officers. I think I am lucky to get such a job as I have only been out here six months, but during that time I have seen quite enough fighting to last me for a long while. "I hope to see you before long."

"In the Public Eye" (No. 3) The lettering "Calais" is to be found on the right-hand top curve of the portrait medallion on the Captain Webb Fountain in High Street.

We gratefully acknowledge the following amounts for our Postage Fund. "C.H." 60 stamps; Sergeant Sidney Rowe 60 stamps. (In making this gift Sergeant Rowe says he knows from his own experience in Gallipoli and elsewhere nothing better could be devised than this weekly letter posted to soldiers.

For our Soldiers' Comforts Fund we have received 17/6 from the Dawley Sewing Guild for which many thanks.

Pte. P. Brown writes from "Somewhere East." "It is very good of you to keep sending, we are in such a position I never know what address to give but your letters follow me. A word from home acts as a tonic. I have just completed my twelve months, what with dodging bombs and shells I am quite an old soldier now. Where I am at present it is just as hot as it was cold on the Peninsula so you see we get the extremes. My belief is the war will be over in a few weeks – but you can never tell for certain. I wish success to your paper – the good old "Weekly Report" I can honestly say it is quite a treat to me to read it."

"When You Boys Come Home."

Will you walk the High Street in a very 'Frenchified' fashion?

"Bow-wow"

Corporal J. Bullock writes from Hong Kong. "Your valuable Xmas presents came as a great surprise to me when I returned from Australia. We had a glorious time, free train and tram rides and we saw all the principal places in Sydney..... All we want now is another change – a chance to go to the front."

We invite all soldiers to write to us.

Weekly Report.

Tuesday,
May 2nd,
1916.

Brotherhood and Sisterhood.
Dawley Baptist Chapel.

"If the Germans came to Dawley"

and dared to bring one of "them Zeppelins"
we certainly should have something to say!

Pte. Crocker (who patriotically gave up his business in front of the Market Hall, to enlist) is now a Regimental Barber and he says "is enjoying himself immensely."

Easter at the Front.

Pte Percy Jones writes:- "Most of the fellows here are interested in the "Report" particularly a Londoner friend of mine. I see by the, "W. R" one of the Guards met some of the Shropshires - I met them too and am staying within sight of the place mentioned. And dear old Fritz is throwing his souvenirs and iron rations in this direction pretty freely. As a matter of fact I shouldn't wonder if the work we are doing hasn't tickled Fritz up a bit and this is how he expresses himself. As to the dear conscientious objectors I wonder if they will object to struggling to Heaven in the ordinary way or whether they will want to be driven there (if they know the way) in a motor car. Yesterday being Easter Sunday I and a friend went for a gentle stroll along the "beautiful" country lanes, past a burning house and through a village where fields appeared to be jumping up — not rejoicing as at Dawley in the spring-tide, the motive power not being the sunshine but something equivalent to T.N.T. "

Easter at the Sea-Side.

Lance-Corporal Joe Davies writes from France:- "We have had a rough two months but the sea-breeze is now doing us good although it has been mostly rain and wind. It is Easter Sunday and it looks more like England on a Sunday morning with so many Church Parades going on. I feel a bit out of sorts to-day because I am Corporal of the Guard and cannot get on to the sands only the sands our tents are pitched on, but I cannot complain. The town itself is like one of our large cities in England."

Please do not think that the sketch on the back page is our idea of what "mining" at the front really is. In some cases neither pick nor shovel are used (to say nothing of tubs and rails and a lofty fairway. Old disused bayonets are often used for excavations, the earth is collected by hands, put into sandbags and so silently conveyed to the rear.

We had our Anzac Day.

You have probably read in the papers of the fine reception the Australians and New Zealanders (who did so splendidly in Anzac a year ago) received in the streets of London. The same evening. one of our own men, Sergeant Sidney Rowe of Old Park, of the Lancashire Fusiliers gave us an account of the famous landing.

Everyone has heard of the deliberate running aground of the transport "River Clyde," close in to Sedd-el-Bahr. Among the Munsters who leaped from her, ran along barges to the shore in face of Turkish fire was Pte. J. K. Hyde who is still on sick leave here at Lawley Bank. Sergeant Rowe's regiment landed at Cape Helles from small boats, towed for a certain distance from the transport and then rowed.

He described how, as soon as the men rose in the boat to land many were picked off by Turks hidden in the cliffs – man after man as he leapt over the side of the boat was unable to get much further. Sergeant Rowe says he and others owe their lives to the precaution of getting out of the other side of the boat and waiting patiently there under cover for a few minutes till a diversion could be made. He says it is impossible to describe the difficulties of the charge up steep clay-cliffs. They had to clear the Turks off the cliffs and then sweep down through valleys of bushwood to other ridges, that rose in steps higher and higher against the sky.

The wonder of the landing on Gallipoli has been one of the military miracles of the war and we are glad two at least of our own men took part in it.

Pte. W. J. Harrison says:— "I am very pleased indeed with the "Weekly Reports"— they get more and more interesting every week! We all think something has happened if they do not arrive at the proper time. I am very sorry to hear of Sergeant Bailey being killed, I knew him quite well and I sympathise very much with his family."

"When You Boys Come Home!"

A B & S Meeting

"Did you send me the W.R.?"

Pte. C. Butler writes from France:—"We have come up again to the firing-line after a six weeks' rest and I can tell you it don't go down very well but we all came back with a good heart to have another smack at them. I think the Huns know when we are here, for they tell me as soon as we shifted they started coming over but I am pleased to say they found someone at home. If they keep coming over we will see what we can do in the way of thinning them out."

Sergeant C. P. Ball writes from Hong Kong:— "No doubt you will think I have forgotten my many friends at Lawley Bank but I can assure you such is not the case. Although we have not been in the trenches fighting the enemy or had the opportunity of winning the V.C or D.C.M we have been busy doing our duty at this far outpost of the British Empire. Thank you very much for the fountain-pen and the cigarettes you sent me — the pen is proving very useful. We have sent another escort with some more German prisoners to Australia to-day— not being one of the escort myself I am sorry I cannot give you an account of the voyage. Please thank the helpers at the B and S for what they are doing for the men at Hong Kong and may God's richest blessing rest upon their good work."

Nothing Doing in this Line of Business.

"What we should like to see" ➤➤

"What we never see" ➤➤

"They won't show the top button of their caps nor the spike of their helmets above the parapet."

Pte. George Jones writes from France:- "They won't they won't show anything. The shelling in our part of the line is getting more violent but we can snap our fingers at the Germans now. The awful wastage of their shells makes us smile at their anger. A few days ago one of our airmen kept going over the German lines and drawing their fire, we counted hundreds of shells fired at him but he came out smiling. I can tell you the "W. R" greatly lightens our task for it shows that you do not forget us at home."

To many soldiers abroad who receive this we are sending a copy of our Anniversary Booklet which was used at the Chapel last Sunday. We are sorry we cannot send you the tunes of the hymns as well but the words in most cases are very applicable to you.

What we would send you, if we could.

JAM

PLUM CAKE

LOVE-LETTER

WEEKLY REPORT.

TOF-FEE

B.D.V.

Pte H. Pugh writes from France:- "Thanks for the "Report" I received on Sunday. I was basking in the sun watching the Germans shelling an aeroplane when it came, so I let to and read it all through. The Hun had some shells up on Saturday and at night they gave us the benefit of their over-supply - they always let us know when it's Sunday, they start early and finish late."

A Soldier's Sermon from the Front.

A soldier writing to us on the regretted death in action of Sergeant A. Eric Bailey, says:- "I was exceedingly sorry to see from the "Report" that Eric was put out. I see no reason why we should not thank God that through Christ He has shown us that life is certain, though death is uncertain. We may be sure that Eric still possesses his individuality and also his life, for that is indestructible.

God grant that all we soldiers may know the truth of the passage- "He that dwelleth in the secret place of the Most High shall abide under the shadow of the Almighty ..... He shall not fear for the arrow that flieth by night nor for the pestilence that walketh at noonday. A thousand shall fall at thy side and ten thousand at thy right hand but it shall not come nigh thee."

"A Gunner from Dawley" writes anonymously, sending us a drawing indicating the sort of work on which he is engaged. But we must have your name, please — we cannot deal with letters which bear no name.

Driver Bodkin writes:- "I have received your "W.R." for several weeks — my wife and parents are well known to

THE DRIVER DRAWS HIMSELF.

"Driver F. J. Bodkin 1st Canadian Heavy Battery taking Ammunition to the Guns somewhere in Belgium."

We regret we have not room for the whole of the ammunition waggon.

This is a copy of part of the soldier's own sketch.

you but, you do not know me and it is very kind of you to send to me. I am not a very good artist but I have done my very best. Thanking you again."

Pte. T. Furber says:- "All the boys in my platoon wait for the "W. R." every week now. We have just had a new draft from England and there are a few Dawley boys among them and it is a great pleasure to meet them" (Will Pte. Furber kindly send us their names?)

Bombardier T. Hardman writes from France on Easter Sunday:- "In the last "Report" I found names of several Dawley men who are in this Division and they must be very near me, but the funny thing is I have never come across a Shropshire man out here yet. There are 22,000 men in our Division so it is perhaps not surprising, but your precious "Report" tells us about lots of them week after week and we are very grateful to you for it."

The Sunshine has made us a lot more lively in Dawley.

We are pleased to say our Sunday School Anniversary was again a success and the collections amounted to £51-9-8.

The preacher was Rev. Walter Wynn, the minister of a large church at Chesham in Bucks and he is also the editor of "The Young Man and Woman" – a monthly magazine (3d) which should be read by all of you.

This week, Rev. Frank A. Smith leaves Doseley Church for a living at West Bromwich. What Church people have thought of his work may be imagined when it is said that £75 has been handed to him as a good-bye gift.

A short but effective speech was made last Tuesday by Pte. J. W. Price of the Cameron Highlanders who, in no half-hearted fashion spoke of the value of the "W. R."

The answer to no 4.-"In the Public Eye" is the top of the tower of the Wesleyan Chapel, High Street, Dawley.

Acknowledgments.

We are grateful to the following for kind donations for our Postage Fund:- "J. M. H" 240 stamps; Pte. J. H. Price, 18 stamps, also to a lady friend for the sum of 4/6 towards the support of this little weekly paper.

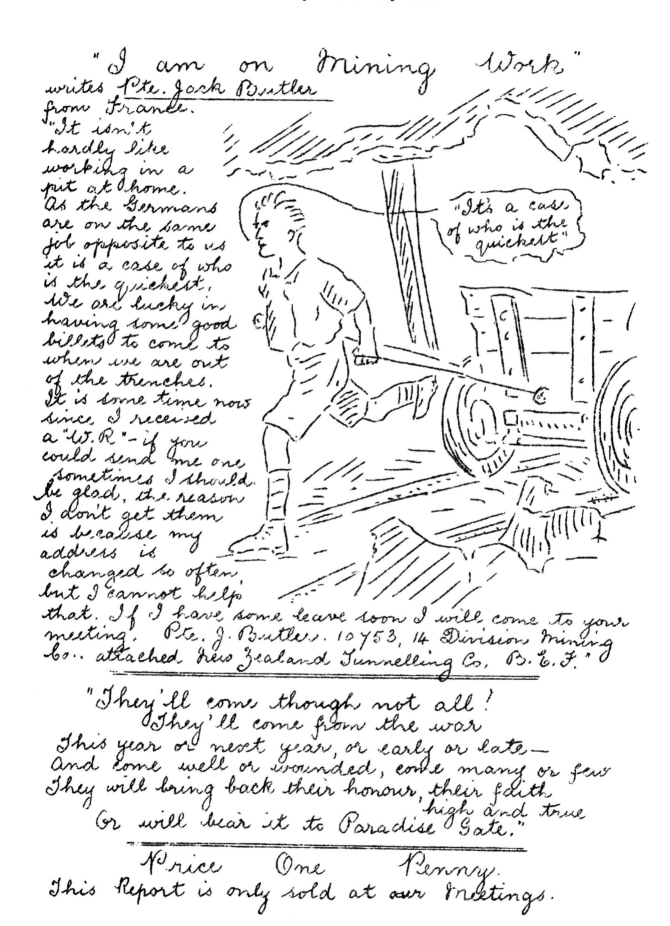

"I am on Mining Work"

writes Pte. Jack Butler from France.

"It isn't hardly like working in a pit at home. As the Germans are on the same job opposite to us it is a case of who is the quickest. We are lucky in having some good billets to come to when we are out of the trenches. It is some time now since I received a "W.R."– if you could send me one sometimes I should be glad, the reason I don't get them is because my address is changed so often, but I cannot help that. If I have some leave soon I will come to your meeting. Pte. J. Butler. 10753, 14 Division Mining Co., attached New Zealand Tunnelling Co., B.E.F."

"It's a case of who is the quickest"

"They'll come though not all !
They'll come from the war
This year or next year, or early or late—
And come well or wounded, come many or few
They will bring back their honour, their faith high and true
Or will bear it to Paradise Gate."

Price One Penny.
This Report is only sold at our Meetings.

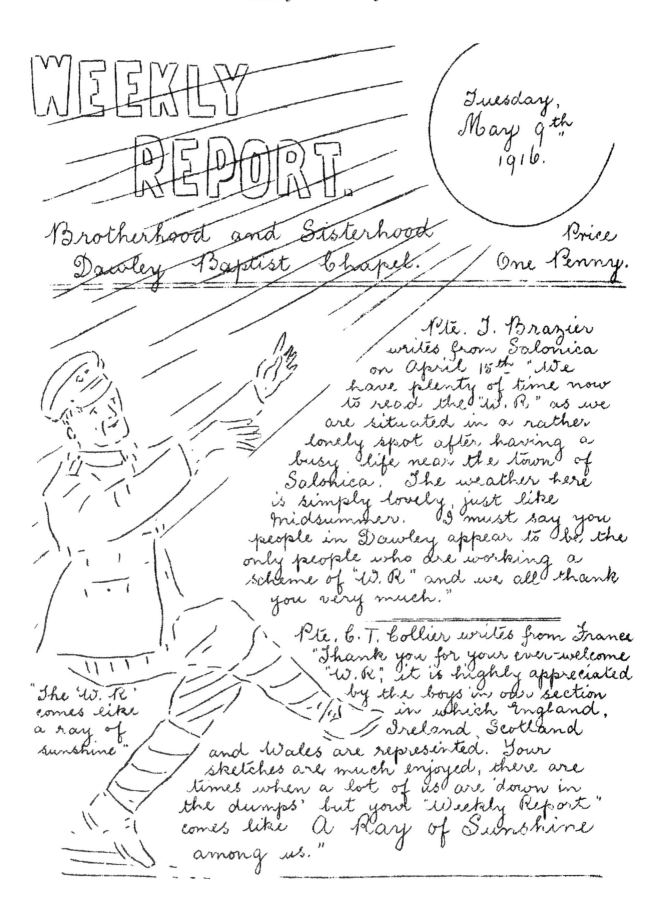

WEEKLY REPORT.

Tuesday,
May 9th
1916.

Brotherhood and Sisterhood
Dawley Baptist Chapel.

Price
One Penny.

Pte. J. Brazier writes from Salonica on April 15th "We have plenty of time now to read the "W. R." as we are situated in a rather lonely spot after having a busy life near the town of Salonica. The weather here is simply lovely, just like midsummer. I must say you people in Dawley appear to be the only people who are working a scheme of "W. R." and we all thank you very much."

Pte. C. T. Collier writes from France "Thank you for your ever-welcome "W. R." it is highly appreciated by the boys in our section in which England, Ireland, Scotland and Wales are represented. Your sketches are much enjoyed, there are times when a lot of us are 'down in the dumps' but your "Weekly Report" comes like A Ray of Sunshine among us."

"The 'W. R.' comes like a ray of sunshine"

A woman at the Nabb was fined £1 last week for having made a fire in her garden "which might have served as a signal, guide or landmark to the enemy." This is the way we deal with our garden fires one hour and a half after sunset. (This does not often happen, as the rain lately has made it impossible to light a garden fire.

"No fear of Zepps now farder!"

me-ow!

A Lawley Man has a Narrow Escape.

Lance-Corporal Deere says:- "I am very poorly at present. I have had the misfortune to see a comrade killed by a German shell and the Corporal and I were knocked down by a fall of sandbags. But we escaped death which our comrade did not. He was a Sergeant and a D.C.M. I feel thankful that I have been spared and I have thanked God for His wonderful mercy to me."

A Happy-Go-Lucky Lot.

Driver A. E. Turner writes from France:- "The weather is rotten out here now and we are up to our necks in mud, but we are a happy-go-lucky lot. Please send the "Weekly Report" each week. Pte Sam Small and I are expecting leave and then we will come to your meeting. The other day my pal had a large parcel come out here and it was more like a Sunday School Treat than anything else."

An Airman's Charmed Life.

Pte. G. V. Lovatt writes:- "It is May-day and so beautiful. A blue sky and a sun which threatens to turn one brown. It seems a shame to have a war on in such weather - it ought to be postponed!   As to my sketch, I cannot name the village which possesses the fair maiden because it is against the rules of the Censor.   At the moment of writing one of our airmen is having a hot time by the sound of the machine-guns which are at him.   The other day one of our aeroplanes went over the German lines no less than eleven times - the Germans got tired of firing at him - they stopped at his seventh journey.   He deserved something for his pluck.

SEE, THE CONQUERING HEROES COME! BLOW THE FIFES AND BEAT THE DRUM.

When You Boys Come Home

The Town Band and the Friendly Societies will march you down the High Street!!

Corporal J. Smith. R.M.R.E. writes from France:- "I am sorry the "W. R" has been delayed - it is six weeks since I left the Base to which it was addressed.   I saw Pte. J. Archer (Scots Guards) out here the other day but did not get a chance to speak to him and I also met Pte C. Butler - no doubt he will be with you by the time you receive this.   I will endeavour to send you a sketch at an early date.   No doubt some of you will remember me, for at one time I was a delegate on the Sunday School Union Committee.

A Tale of the Trenches.

Pte. T. W. Archer of the Scots Guards, who was in the trenches a few days before, gave us a capital speech last Tuesday. He is an old soldier, having served through the Boer War. He has been corresponding regularly with us while in France and he received a warm welcome from the people who crowded round him to shake hands. A few weeks ago we pictured him in the "W.R." looking after the younger Dawley boys. That sketch appears to have "suited him to a T" for he endeavours to play that part to his younger comrades. His speech on this point was most interesting, indicating how a young soldier faces the situation for the first time when he finds himself face to face with the Germans. He told an amusing story of a new lad who mistook the dug-out for a canteen, asking to be served with tea, sugar, etc. The old soldier entered into the joke, selling the boy a pennyworth of tea, sugar and a third of a candle, then finished up by laughing at the lad and telling him when he wanted his money he would come for it. We are grateful to Pte. Archer for his speech – we hope many other soldiers will similarly favour us.

Pte. A. Morton of the 14th Division Mining Section attached to the New Zealand Tunnelling Corps writes from France:–
"When we receive anything from the Homeland it gives us good spirit and we go about our work a lot cheerfuller. I received your small parcel to-day and especially the smokes are well received."

You must mind what you write to us!

Pte. Sam Davies writes as follows:- "There is one letter in the "W.R" I do not like - the one without a name. He says he went out into "No Man's Land" and dropped on a Hun and after hearing his tale went to the trouble to take him to his own lines. You can take it from me that is not the truth and if men cannot tell the truth to you they should not write for the "W.R" at all. What he says he did he is not allowed to do, and what is more I would not give much for the life of the man who ever did go close up to the German lines."

A much "Sketched" Subject.

The famous Dr. John Clifford of London preaches at the Chapel next Sunday and I wish you could be here to hear him. He has always been a fighter as these sketches, which years ago were drawn by a popular caricaturist and sent throughout the world, suggest. Only he fights with his mouth. Since the outbreak of the war he has done a great deal of good in stirring people up to do their duty. At a great meeting in the City of London a few months ago he was on the front line with Kitchener, Asquith and the Archbishop of Canterbury and it will be a great day for Dawley when he comes here.

On the war path.

Dr. Clifford, all his life has been a man of peace, but he believes we were forced into this war and there was no escape. He says it is not only a war between Britain and Germany but between the forces of freedom and those of slavery — it is a war for the most precious things that control the development of humanity. At the same time, he says, we have got to see that this is the very last war.

— Preaching some new crusade.

In the Baptist Pulpit at Dawley Bank.

HENRY HOWELLS.

We deeply regret to announce that Private Henry Howells of the 7th. K.S.L.I. was killed in action on April 25th in France at a place not stated. He was formerly a miner working at the Stafford Pits, and was 34 years of age. He enlisted on Nov: 18th. 1914 and had been in France about five months. His wife and 5 children live at 29. Old Park. Immediately Mrs Howells received the intimation from the War Office she came to Mr Leeter, who did what he could to help her by filling up her papers, etc. But how little anyone can do for a bereaved woman at such a time – how much one would like to do!

We are informed by the friends of Private William Tart of the Finger that the War Office on Friday last reported he was "missing". We hope further particulars will be forthcoming soon. If any soldier who reads this is able to give any information please communicate with us at once.

Lead, Kindly Light.

Lead, Kindly Light.
the bells are softly telling,
Till night be gone;
In many a heart the
silent song is welling –
Lead Thou me on;
Oh bells! That sing the
hymns my mother sung –
Oh bells! That sing the
hymns my mother sung –
Lead Thou me on!

Life's cup I lift, with
braver lips to drain it,
For that ye sing;
My cross I kiss, nor may
I dare disdain it,
Whate'er it bring;
Oh bells! Ye voice, the
voice of one passed on!
Oh bells! Till night be
gone – Till night be gone.

I hear the grasses o'er
a dead face growing
Beyond your song;
From out the years, my
mother's sweet eyes showing –
And night is gone:
Oh bells! That sing
above the rain and cold!
Oh bells! That sing ajar,
the gates of gold!

Lead, Kindly Light, the
bells are softly pealing –
Lead Thou me on;
A child again against
her heart I beat kneeling –
Till night be gone;
Oh bells! That sing the
gracious story on –
Oh bells! Till night be
gone – Till night be gone!

Pte. J. Brickley writes from France:– "It is quite a treat to get the "Report" – it keeps one in touch with home and it is so well put together."

At the beginning of the winter, it will be remembered, we started a £25 Soldiers' Comforts Fund. We received in money £22-18-7 and at the moment the treasurers Miss Breeze and Miss Walker have about £2-13-6 in hand. (Many friends have given us materials in lieu of money and these have been acknowledged). It is now proposed to produce a balance sheet and wind up this account. Auditors will be appointed to-night and all subscribers will receive a copy of the accounts when complete. We are still open to receive subscriptions but it is thought well during the summer to have one fund only - the ordinary B and S Fund. (Treasurer: Mr Lavender)

— — WALTER DAVIES. — —

Yesterday afternoon there was placed in the Square at Wellington just outside Davies' (outfitters) Shop a 77 m.m German gun captured at Loos by the 7th Division on Sept: 25th 1915. While one of our artists was sketching it Private Herbert Buckley of Old Park came up saying he had to return to the front on Tuesday or he would have come to our meeting to tell us about the taking of those trenches by the Germans a week or two back, in which he took part.

Postage Fund.

We remind our friends that our new system of posting the "W. R" to soldiers direct from our meeting each Tuesday evening is quite successful. We shall need about 10/- a week to continue this. During the week we have received 2/- for which we are grateful.

Lance Corporal A. E. Thomas writes from a Chelsea Hospital :- "I have landed in England, I have been wounded in my left eye. I am thankful to have got off with just that! I am looking forward to a short furlough now, when I will come to your meeting."

Pte. G. Growcott writes from France. "I hope you are still having as good a time at the Brotherhood as you did when I used to attend it. If you could send me a Mouth Organ I should be very pleased and that would make us quite happy. My address is :- Pte. G. Growcott, 8451, 96 Machine Gun Company, B.E.F."

"It's a long way to"

"We're a bit old for the job, matey, but we've got 'em to help 'em out"

Many older married men in Dawley are now preparing to "join up."

Pte P. Jonks writing from France says:- "I will try to send you a sketch next time I write. The weather out here is lovely now – we are not doing so bad but enjoying ourselves as much as possible under the circumstances."

We send out this Report each week to at least 130 soldiers. If any soldier who receives this copy does not receive it regularly will he kindly communicate with us? This paper is only sold at our Tuesday meeting.

Weekly Report.

Tuesday.
May 23rd
1916.

Brotherhood and Sisterhood
Dawley Baptist Chapel.

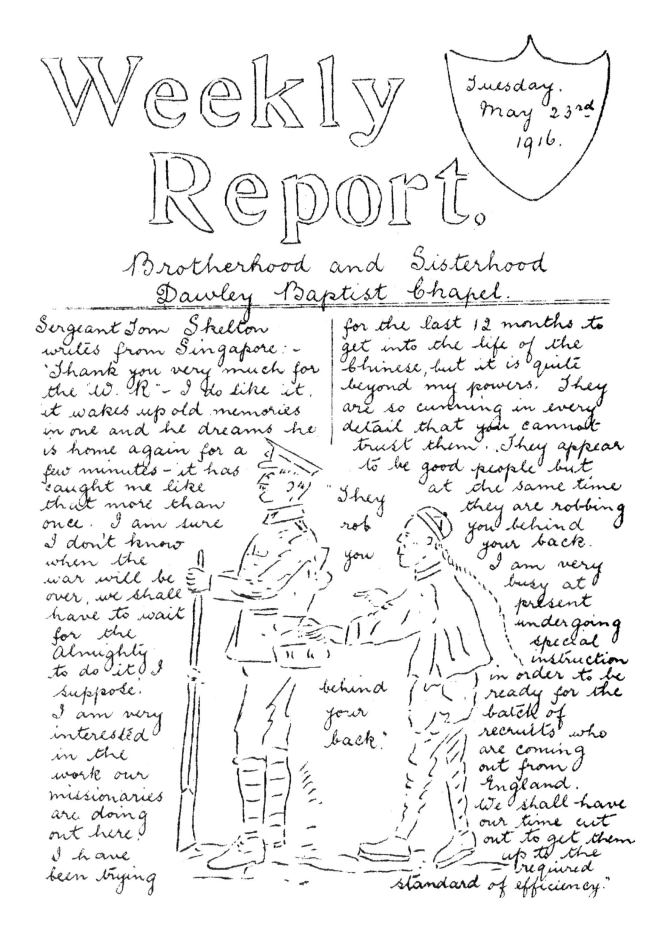

Sergeant Tom Skelton writes from Singapore:- 'Thank you very much for the W. R - I do like it, it wakes up old memories in one and he dreams he is home again for a few minutes - it has caught me like that more than once. I am sure I don't know when the war will be over, we shall have to wait for the Almighty to do it I suppose. I am very interested in the work our missionaries are doing out here. I have been trying for the last 12 months to get into the life of the Chinese, but it is quite beyond my powers. They are so cunning in every detail that you cannot trust them. They appear to be good people but at the same time they are robbing you behind your back.

"They rob you behind your back."

I am very busy at present undergoing special instruction in order to be ready for the batch of recruits who are coming out from England. We shall have our time cut out to get them up to the required standard of efficiency."

Pte. George Jackson writes from Salonica "I have been removed from the Convalescent Camp. I have been before a Board and I was marked for the Hospital Ship. We had to go to the 21st Hospital Ship to get in, but when we got there they only wanted three men to make the boat up. The first man I saw at the 21st Hospital was Pte. W. H. Parton of the R.A.M.C. from Dawley Bank. I was proud to meet him and I am writing this in his ward. We are sorry to read of the death of Mrs. J. H. Ball of Church Road for she was a good friend to me and other Dawley boys out here."

Pte. W. H. Parton writes from Salonica:- "It is really inspiring to feel that you at Dawley Bank are wanting to do something for the soldiers and that you do it — I hope you will get plenty of support. Your Weekly Report is one of the best papers I have ever read and we look forward to their coming.... Please excuse writing as I am using my knee for a writing desk in my little bell-tent."

Pte. J. Holmes of the Balkan Expeditionary Force says:- "I am writing this in my little dug-out with my comrades. We are talking about English cigarettes, we cannot get any out here worth smoking, if you care to send us a few they would be very much appreciated. We are very thankful for the 'W.R.' which comes every week to us who are living here in the mountains in Greece." (Cigarettes are being sent this week)

At our meeting last Wednesday we had with us Corporal A.E. Thomas of the Grenadiers who expressed on behalf of himself and other soldiers appreciation of our work. He has, unfortunately, lost one eye in a recent engagement.
Pte. J. W. Price, who has been often present at our meetings lately, has been sent to a military hospital for special treatment.

my ma wishes me to say—

There was a Meeting of the Dawley Tribunal on Friday when about 30 appeals were heard, chiefly of married men. The general idea of Dawley people appears to be that the Tribunal is too lenient and that any slacker who cares to stand up and say "his ma wishes him to remain at home" can secure exemption, but it is not so. The Tribunal has never given absolute exemption to anyone yet, at most — in the case of butchers, bakers and men connected with food-supply it only gives a conditional six months. Where single men, without any responsibility have appealed for exemption, they have always been refused. In cases of married men recently dealt with, a short time has been allowed in order to get their affairs in order, sometimes one month, in other cases two months. This is only fair as many married men, although they attested long ago, did not anticipate until quite recently, being called up. The members of the Tribunal have a thankless job. If they exempt men they are blamed, if they do not exempt men they are blamed. There is not a man on the Tribunal therefore but who would gladly give up his job to some-one else!

We send out this little paper to nearly 200 soldiers every week. We invite soldiers who appreciate it to write to us occasionally. When you come home give us a call at our Tuesday meeting.

Rather Strong!

"That night we killed 1,000,000 Germans!"

"When You Boys Come Home." You'll cure Grandad's rheumatics!

The manner in which the authorities are now enforcing the Military Service Act is well illustrated by the following incidents. For a night or two last week a party of gipsies encamped on the rough ground opposite Brandlee chapel. They were visited by the local police-sergeant and the men of military age were required to explain their registration-place or attestation. The next day they left but the local military authority made out an order calling them to the Army, and which is now following them through the agency of the police.

At Wellington Police Court on Saturday a young farm labourer was charged with failing to register and report himself under the Military Service Act. The policeman stated he saw the man at work in a field. When he accosted him he said "I have no time to bother with you, I have something else to do." The man was fined £2 and detained in custody to await a military escort.

We may have compulsion now but our great armies have been raised on the voluntary principle — thanks to the willingness of you brave boys

Daylight Saving.

1st Gentleman:- "This 'ere new Act is a bit of 'orl right, it allows us to get a drink an hour earlier!"

2nd Gentleman:- "But what about the other end, Bill?"

1st Gentleman:- "Bother the other end, what do we know about that."

Most people put on their clocks one hour on Saturday night or early Sunday morning A few "wanna going to bother about the clock" but it is anticipated their clocks will therefore bother them.

"I don't know how often I have had this bit of dialogue with some French R.C.O. almost in the same words," says a British soldier in France:-

"Frenchy: 'Vous vous êtes engagé, sergent?'
"I. 'Oui, caporel'
"F. 'Volontaire?'
"I. 'Nous sommes tous volontaires - jusqu'à présent.'
"F. 'Toute cette grande armée - deux millions et demi?'
"I. 'Oui - tous.'
"F: 'C'est beau, ça'"

"If the Germans Came to Dawley!"

"You would have to pay a Mark. For courting in the Park!"

An Open Letter to the Kaiser. By "Polybe" (M. Joseph Reinach) in the Paris Figaro. "You have a battle Fleet. Why do you not use it to break through the British blockade? The blockade is only maintained by the British Fleet, and if it were destroyed in fair fight the empire of the seas would be no longer closed to German merchant ships, which would be able to obtain

all the foodstuffs, raw materials, reinforcements, and munitions they liked from North and South America, and bring them to Germany. The United States have not two sets of rules, one for the Allies and the other for the Central Powers. They will place no hindrance in the way of your commerce, so that nothing is more simple — we say it with an entire impartiality of judgment — nothing is more honourable. Order out your Fleet to go and look for the British Fleet. Do you want its exact address? Sink and scatter the British Fleet and the seas are yours."

The programme at our meeting to-night is being arranged and carried out by members of the Oakengates Brotherhood and Sisterhood. The Y.M.C.A. Flag Day in Oakengates (worked mainly by the Brotherhood) brought in between £50 and £60.

He returns after 9 months

We are hoping to see at our meeting to-night two Belgian soldiers, who have just arrived in Lawley Bank from certain trenches in Flanders held by the Belgian Army. The one is Alphonso Mortier with his companion whose only English is "Yes" and "No". They are both in khaki and would be taken for British soldiers. On his previous visit Alphonso was dressed in poor make-shift Belgian military clothes but now he is as smart as you are.

Pte. A. Kelsey writes from Salonica - The "W.R." I received by this mail greatly surprised me I well, one of the letters did. It was one from Holbrook - I thought he was killed at Ypres last May. You can picture how glad I was to know he was alive and, according to his letter ready to come out again and make up for the good time he has had at home. We are not having any fighting but plenty of hard work. P.S. Excuse the stained paper - I dropped it in rifle oil." (And it smells like it, too!)

To the Skylark behind your Trenches.

Thou little voice! Thou happy sprite.
How didst thou gain the air and light -
That sing'st so merrily?
How could such little wings
Give thee thy freedom from these dense
And fetid tombs - these burrows whence
We peer like frightened things?
In the free sky
Thou sail'st while here we crawl and creep
And fight and sleep
And die.

How canst thou sing
while nature lies
Bleeding and torn beneath thine eyes,
And the foul breath
Of rank decay hangs like a shroud
Over the fields that shell hath ploughed?
How canst thou sing, so gay and glad,
While all the heavens are filled with death
And all the World is Mad?

"You can picture how glad I was.

Pte. J. Machin of the Grenadier Guards says:- "I had the pleasure of meeting an old friend yesterday - J. Yapp of our 3rd Battalion. It is the first time I have seen him since he left Chelsea Barracks 8 months ago so you may guess we had something to tell one another".

Pte. W. J. Harrison writes from France:- "There are a few new Dawley boys sent to us out here - Harold Hollis, Bert Archer and Howard Brothwood and a few others, I cannot think of their names now. I am glad to hear your sermons were a success - I should have been glad to be there."

"Ladies and Gentlemen, I have now great pleasure in taking the Chair!"

Pte. Noah Jones writes from the Straits Settlements:- "I am sure we shall not know how to thank you when we return to Dawley. We shall have a good Tuesday meeting that night, I suppose some of us will have to take the chair!" (Very good, Noah, but preparing a speech in Singapore is one thing delivering it in Lawley Bank is another. We'll wait and see!)

Cyclist A. Barker of the Salonica Forces says:- "I read in the "W.R" of your offer to send books to us, I beg to say I shall be able to scrape through a few. Prior to my enlistment I used to live at 14, Wellington Road and I was a member of the Horsehay Primitive Methodist Chapel. I was employed at Coalmoor Pipe Works. The other night we had a taste of Macedonian rain and wind — it broke our tent ropes and swept our tent away leaving us without any covering but our blankets." (Some books have been sent this week to this soldier)

Pte. H. R. Pugh of the Royal Welsh Regt. writes from France:- "I often see a lot of K.S.L.I's but though I scan every face I haven't seen any Dawley boys - they occupied the right on the line of our lot. A week to day the Germans started shelling us at breakfast-time but they finished in time for dinner. We had just got over our dinner safely when we heard the scream of another shell - we almost stopped breathing but we escaped. Our dug-out is cut out of the chalk about six feet below the surface. There is one thing about life in the trenches - there is plenty of fun to be got out of things. For instance you are sitting quietly when all at once you hear the whistle of a Shell, then you jump up and waiting a second, bolt for the nearest cover, the moment the Shell has burst and the pieces cease falling you come out and start laughing, not that there is really anything to laugh at."

"The German shelling was finished in time for dinner."

Pte. John Bishop writes from Salonica district acknowledging the receipt of a very belated parcel. "I hope the B and S will keep up their good work till we come home again. I used to hear my mother say "Home sweet home, there's no place like home" and I shall say that if I can get there once more. We are all looking forward to the time when we can get back."

Price One Penny.
Only sold to Dawley people who attend our Tuesday meetings. If any Dawley soldier on foreign service does not receive this regularly, please let us know.

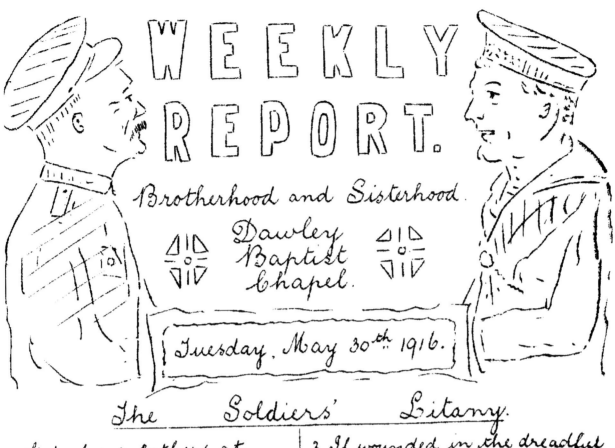

WEEKLY REPORT.

Brotherhood and Sisterhood.

Dawley Baptist Chapel.

Tuesday, May 30th 1916.

The Soldiers' Litany.

1. God of our fathers at whose call
We now before Thy footstool fall.
Whose grace has made our Empire strong
Through love of right and hate of wrong;
We pray Thee in Thy pity shield
Our soldiers on the battlefield.

2. Asleep beneath thy ample dome
With many a tender dream of home,
Or charging through the dust and glare
With bullets hurtling thro' the air.
We pray Thee in Thy pity shield
Our soldiers on the battlefield.

3. If wounded in the dreadful fray
Be Thou their comfort and their stay.
If dying may they in their pain
Behold the Lamb for sinners slain.
And thus in Thy great pity shield
Our soldiers on the battlefield.

4. And soon O blessed Prince of Peace
Bring in the day when wars shall cease
And men as brothers shall unite
To fill the world with love and light
Meanwhile in tender pity shield
Our soldiers on the battlefield.

This has been taken from the "Balkan News" sent by a Dawley soldier at Salonica.

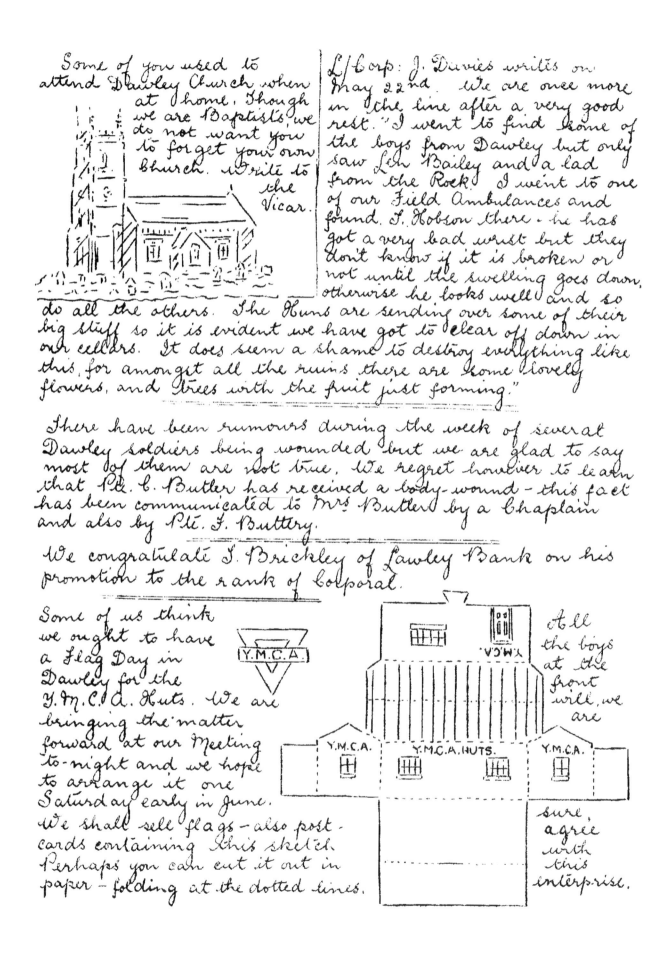

Some of you used to attend Dawley Church when at home. Though we are Baptists, we do not want you to forget your own church. Write to the Vicar.

L/Corp: J. Davies writes on May 22nd. We are once more in the line after a very good rest. "I went to find some of the boys from Dawley but only saw Len Bailey and a lad from the Rock. I went to one of our Field Ambulances and found S. Hobson there - he has got a very bad wrist but they don't know if it is broken or not until the swelling goes down, otherwise he looks well and so do all the others. The Huns are sending over some of their big stuff so it is evident we have got to clear off down in our cellars. It does seem a shame to destroy everything like this, for amongst all the ruins there are some lovely flowers, and trees with the fruit just forming."

There have been rumours during the week of several Dawley soldiers being wounded but we are glad to say most of them are not true. We regret however to learn that Pte. C. Butler has received a body-wound - this fact has been communicated to Mrs Butler by a Chaplain and also by Pte. F. Buttery.

We congratulate S. Brickley of Lawley Bank on his promotion to the rank of Corporal.

Some of us think we ought to have a Flag Day in Dawley for the Y.M.C.A. Huts. We are bringing the matter forward at our Meeting to-night and we hope to arrange it one Saturday early in June. We shall sell flags - also post-cards containing this sketch. Perhaps you can cut it out in paper - folding at the dotted lines.

Y.M.C.A.

Y.M.C.A.   Y.M.C.A. HUTS.   Y.M.C.A.

All the boys at the front will, we are sure, agree with this enterprise.

Gunner Garnet Fart writes on May 22nd:- "There is nothing much doing here at present. I am sorry to say we lost a Shropshire fellow last week named Lockl from Newport - he received a wound from which he died shortly afterwards."

Pte. J. Evans writes from Salonica district:- "We are doing no fighting, we are away up in the hills. The only fault is that we cannot buy anything, but our health and spirits are high."

Does 'P' write for 'H' or 'H' write for 'P' ?

We have received a letter from Salonica in one Dawley soldier's name but apparently written by another! A very good writer he is, but we don't want him to write letters for the whole Platoon! Never mind the shape of the letters nor the spelling, only write yourself, we can decipher them - we are writing experts!

"When You Boys Come Home."

One or two soldiers who have attempted to speak at our Tuesday meeting have got a bit nervous at the look of us!

"my dear friends, I'd sooner face the Germans than you"

"Whither depart the souls of the brave that die in the battle,
Die in the last hard fight for the cause that rests with them?
Are they upborne from the field on the slumbrous pinions of angels
Unto a far-off home, where the weary rest from their labour,
And the deep wounds are healed, and the bitter and burning moisture
Wiped from the generous eyes? Or do they linger, unhappy,
Pining and haunting the grave of their bygone hope and endeavour?
Whither depart the brave? God knows."

About 50 soldiers are working at the Hollingswood crusher, helping the local men to turn out vast quantities of ballast. They are billeted in Oakengates and St. Georges and are paraded each morning in Oakengates by their officer.

Sir Charles Henry, M.P. in the House of Commons the other day said that soldiers discharged from the Army owing to disease or wounds should receive a medal with a ribbon. The Under-Secretary for War said the Government were favourably considering this question.

By the death of Mr. William Taylor of Chapel Street Dawley Church people have lost one of their most useful lay-officials. He used to tell his friends he owed a great deal in early life to the influence of C. H. Spurgeon.

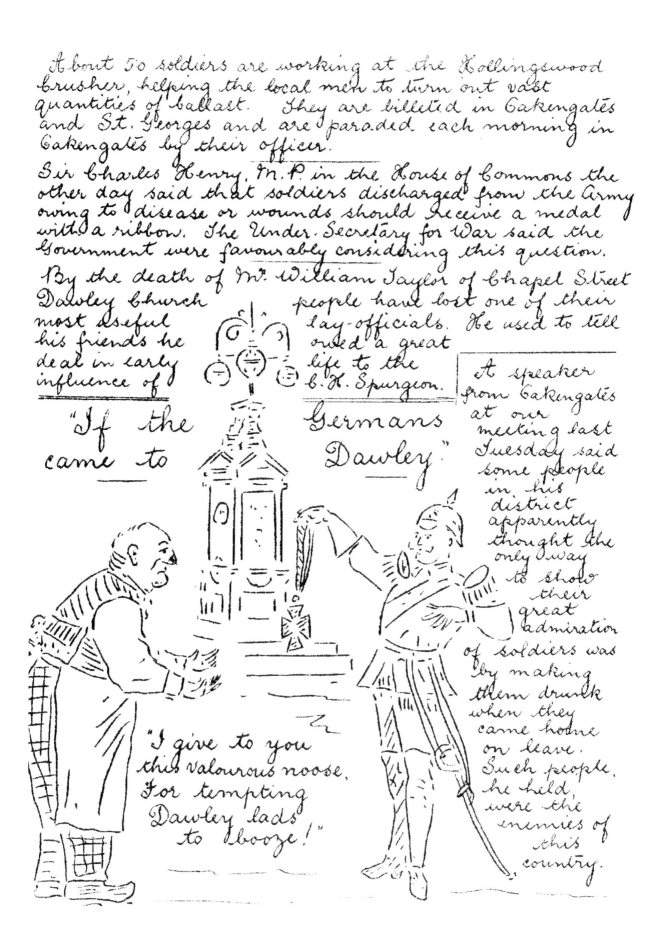

"If the Germans came to Dawley"

"I give to you this valourous noose, For tempting Dawley lads to booze!"

A speaker from Oakengates at our meeting last Tuesday said some people in his district apparently thought the only way to show their great admiration of soldiers was by making them drunk when they came home on leave. Such people, he held, were the enemies of this country.

92

Dawley was lively for a few hours last Saturday afternoon, when a Parade took place in aid of the Red Cross and Dawley Nursing Division Funds. The Friendly Societies had the management of the affair and it passed off very well. At four o'clock there was a fair muster in the Demonstration Field in King Street where a couple of speeches were made from the summit of a beer-barrel. Then a procession was formed

The Town Band led the way, followed by a ———————— representative of the Foresters and the Free Gardeners. Next came a few old soldiers in khaki from Lightmoor, then a good number of 'brothers' from various Societies in the glory of coloured regalia. Then came a large muster of Rechabites with their white sashes and a few Boy Scouts in the rear. All along the route the ladies of the local Nursing Division worked their collecting boxes. After the above triumphal march through the High Street a service was held in Dawley Church. This affair will probably be repeated for some other object.

Several suggestions have lately been made as to whether it is practicable to make arrangements to take a few wounded soldiers in Dawley? Some of us are anxious that the town should not be behind in good work.

Pte. S. Bird writes from France:- "The W.R. is a great credit to the people who are responsible for it. I saw something in one issue from Will Twings - he was one of my best chums - he seems to have travelled a great deal. I have only got as far as France yet and we are now in the trenches hence my short letter."

Pte. W. H. Barton of the R.A.M.C writes from a Hospital at Salonica:- "That sketch of the weather-cock which appears in the 'Report' I have just received, is found on the National Schools" (Quite right, you are the winner of the prize and a book is being sent to you this week) In appreciation of the 'W.R.' he sends a copy of the 'Balkan News' for Friday, April 21st - the newspaper issued for the British troops in the Salonica district. Curiously enough, there is reference to Rev. A. E. Gwen Jones, a Baptist minister who used to be at Whitchurch, preaching at the Greek Evangelistic Church at 62, Odus Constantinos Palaeologus, Salonica. We ask Dawley lads to find out Mr. Jones and ask him whether he remembers a walk in the Old Park years ago with Mr. Lester? That question will make the Chaplain laugh!

Pte. S. Davies writes from France on May 22nd:- "We are having some nice weather out here now and we are out of the trenches at present. I cannot tell you much war news as we are not allowed to and you really know as much as we do for you get the results in the daily papers."

Langley School
where some of you received many a whacking - heaven knows you deserved it!

Our Postage Fund.

We gratefully acknowledge the following for our Postage Fund:- Mrs J. S. Smith - 60 stamps; "The First money I ever Earned" - 18 stamps; "M & B's class" 6 stamps. May we remind our friends that this Fund must not be forgotten. The cost of the production of this little weekly is borne by those who attend our Tuesday meeting. but the expense of sending it out direct to soldiers in all parts of the world must be please shared by others

The Work of one of our Artists Somewhere in France."

Pte. I. Furber writes on May 21st:- "I am sorry you did not get my last letter there was a sketch in it and I suppose that is the reason it did not get through. I am sending you another, it is a ruined church "somewhere in France." I will send you

This sketch has been sent by Private I. Furber. (We have been compelled to reduce it somewhat in size)

the names and numbers of all the new Dawley boys who have recently arrived here, next time I write."

Pte. George Phillips writes from France :- I am pleased to say that I am going along alright and in good health. I was a little surprised to hear of the amount raised at the School Sermons - I only wish I could have been there in my old place. We are having some rather wet weather here at present - you would be surprised to see what a mess a drop of rain will make the trenches in. I hope this job will soon be over - we must hope for the best."

L/Corp: W. H. Oliver writes from Salonica:- "We are away in the hills and do not see much of the other Dawley boys. I should like to see the old place again since I was only there on three days leave in Nov: 1914 on my arrival from India before proceeding to France. Tell Mr. Lester the "Weekly Report" is thankfully received out here. When we get the mail in the boys shout "Has anyone got the Dawley Balkan News?" and they are all anxious to read it."

"I will try and make a few Sketches."

Pte. M. Cadman of the Royal Welsh Fusiliers writes:- The "W. R's have been following me here and you see by my address that I am now with the Egyptian Expeditionary Forces. I am sure you are doing what you can for the comfort of the soldiers. I will try and make a few sketches of this land of Egypt and send you when next I write. It is very hot here but I am glad to say it has not made me ill."

One of our artists at work in the land of the Pharaohs

Price One Penny.

This little paper is only sold to Dawley people who attend our Tuesday meeting. It is sent out to nearly 200 soldiers on foreign service each week. If any soldier, who hails from the Dawley district, now serving in the Army anywhere abroad does not receive it quite regularly, will he please communicate with us.

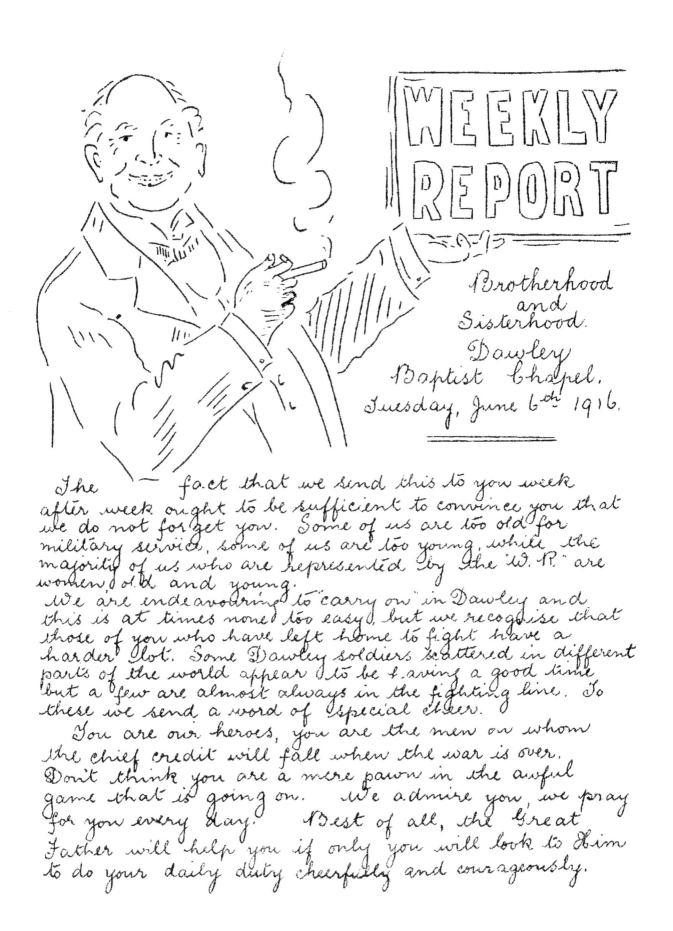

Brotherhood
and
Sisterhood.
Dawley
Baptist Chapel.
Tuesday, June 6th 1916.

The ⟨—⟩ fact that we send this to you week
after week ought to be sufficient to convince you that
we do not forget you. Some of us are too old for
military service, some of us are too young, while the
majority of us who are represented by the "W.R." are
women, old and young.

We are endeavouring to "carry on" in Dawley and
this is at times none too easy, but we recognise that
those of you who have left home to fight have a
harder lot. Some Dawley soldiers scattered in different
parts of the world appear to be having a good time
but a few are almost always in the fighting line. To
these we send a word of special cheer.

You are our heroes, you are the men on whom
the chief credit will fall when the war is over.
Don't think you are a mere pawn in the awful
game that is going on. We admire you, we pray
for you every day. Best of all, the Great
Father will help you if only you will look to Him
to do your daily duty cheerfully and courageously.

"Quite right, boss, half a mile to Lawley Bank Station"

"If the Germans came to Dawley"

They would "kommandeer" all public vehicles.

Local Tribunal.

Last Wednesday there were 37 appeals by men who think they can best serve the country by remaining at their work in Dawley than by soldiering. They were nearly all married men, three were managers of local works employing a number of workmen; others were tradespeople - a draper, a butcher, a greengrocer, a publican and others of this class. Surface workers at collieries now have to apply to local tribunals and one of these - a banksman - was given three months. Insurance agents, if there are no special circumstances exempting them will have to go and three months were given in two cases. An interesting case was that of two brothers who are employed in football-making. Documents produced showed they were making footballs for a Paris firm which supplied British and French troops, still it was felt one of these ought to join up and three months was allowed them to decide which. Short periods were granted to an infirm widow's only son in delicate health and to the only remaining son of a woman whose husband is ill, on the ground that three brothers are already serving. A large number of people were present in the Town Hall during these proceedings which occupied nearly three hours.

Dawley News of the Week.

£12 has been handed to the Red Cross as the result of the recent Parade arranged by the Friendly Societies and the Dawley Nursing Division.

The eldest daughter of Mr. H. Revell Phillips, the clerk to the Dawley Urban Council was married at Shifnal on Friday last.

Louis Mortier, aged 18½, the son of the Belgian Refugees in Lawley Bank is expecting to be called up to take his place in the Belgian Regiment which is training in England in order to take part in the operations in Belgium.

The Rev. Mr. Brentnall, who was the Primitive Methodist Minister in Dawley three or four years ago, preached the School Sermons for Dawley Wesleyans last Sunday. His visits to Shropshire from the town of Leicester are frequent as he has a son who is slowly dying at Shirlett Sanatorium.

The German Gun captured at Loos was paraded at Ironbridge on Saturday, and a collection was taken en route for wounded British soldiers.

A Soldier's Sermon.

One of our boys in a letter to the Brotherhood and Sisterhood gives his testimony to the value of religion to him, away in the Far East. We withhold his name but his letters reach us via Siberia. "You will be glad to know I am leading the better life. I gave my heart to God some time back and life is different now. I read the good old Book and it is wonderful what help you can get out of it when you are down-hearted. I think John 3:16 is a lovely verse – "God so loved .... that He gave His only begotten Son, that whosoever believeth might not perish". —

Pte. G. Roberts writes from Hong Kong on April 30th saying that he had just received the "W. R." and that the Key (of which he sends a sketch) is found at the Market Hall. He is rather late for a prize but as he is the first competitor from Hong Kong a book is being sent. (We have already given one prize to a soldier who sent the first postcard from France). Pte. Roberts in return sends us a puzzle. "This is a puzzle for you to solve" he says.

. . . .
P. S. T. P.

Can you make it out? If so, send an answer to him. We can! We had to pay 1d. extra for his communication to the Dawley post-girl, we therefore conclude that the answer to the Hong Kong Puzzle is:– "Postage Short, To Pay" or "Pay Something To Postman" or "Pay Smilingly This Postage"! If he means "Please Send the Prize" well we are doing so! No more Chinese puzzles of this sort, please George!

A ship in Hong Kong Harbour dressed and manned on a patriotic occasion sent by Pte. Roberts.

Honour to the Brave.

Everyone knows now of the great Naval Fight in the North Sea when our British Battle Squadron found and engaged the German High Seas Fleet. As far as can be seen the German losses were greater than ours but alas! we have lost several ships and what is more, some thousands of brave men! Up to the time of writing we can only hear of one of our Dawley lads who was in action – Noah Round. a boy-telegraphist on the Invincible. According to the information at present published, practically all lives on the Invincible have been lost and it is therefore possible that Noah Round may have gone. We have been asked by his step-mother and his little sister (aged 13) to make full enquiries and this we are doing but we fear for the worst

Noah Round was home only about three weeks ago and many Dawley people must have seen the sailor lad tearing about the streets on a bicycle. Before coming home he underwent a throat operation at the Mount Steward Hospital, hence his extended leave. He was on our B and S weekly list and received regular communications from us, which he appreciated. We have in front of us a letter – probably the last letter he wrote – from the Invincible dated May 17th, in the course of which he says he is looking forward to coming to Dawley again at Christmas.

Noah was 17 only last February. His father was killed in a coal-pit about three years ago. Two of his brothers are soldiers – Pte G. Round is in Serbia (we have often reproduced letters from him in the "W. R") and Pte Elias Round is now fighting in France. Another soldier-brother – Pte. Enoch Round – was killed in Gallipoli.

NOAH ROUND
BOY TELEGRAPHIST

We have rarely received so few letters from Dawley soldiers at the Front. Is the following note, taken from Monday night's paper, the explanation? "There has been desperate fighting on the British Front in France."

Pte. C. Butler, it appears, is not dangerously wounded though he is still confined to the hospital just behind the lines in France.

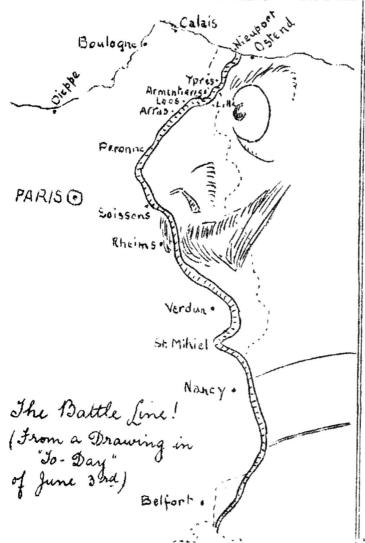

The Battle Line!
(From a Drawing in "To-Day" of June 3rd)

W. Hitchman of H.M.S. King George V writes he hopes to be home for Whitsuntide. (Not after the North Sea episode, my boy, they'll want you on your ship)

Among the local soldiers at home this week are Pte. A. Lloyd of the Finger and Pte. Jack Butler of Old Park. The latter looks very well – he regrets he has to return before our Meeting to-night.

Pte. Ernest Jackson (invalided from Salonica) writes he is now in No. 8 Ward, Worsley Hall Hospital, Worsley. Pte. J. T. Simmonds of Pool Hill has been invalided home and will probably get his discharge – he deserves it after the fearful experiences through which he has passed by being "gassed."

We have received 24 stamps in an anonymous letter for our Postage Fund for which we are grateful. We beg our friends to send us more money for this department of our work.

At our Meeting last Tuesday, Messrs S. T. Jones and E. Hatfield were appointed to audit the accounts of the Soldiers' Comforts Fund for the past 9 months.

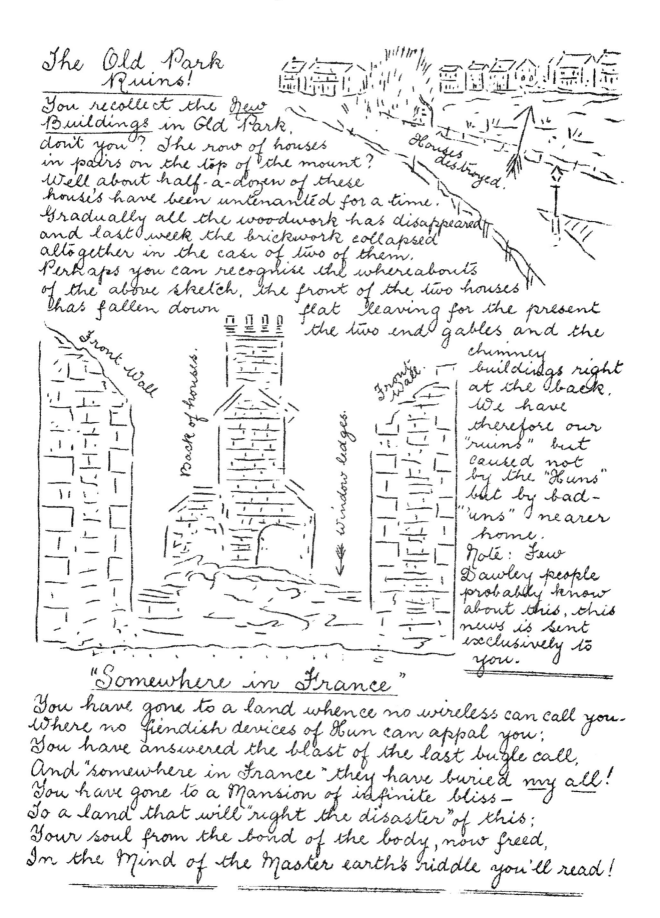

The Old Park Ruins!

You recollect the New Buildings in Old Park, don't you? The row of houses in pairs on the top of the mount? Well about half-a-dozen of these houses have been untenanted for a time. Gradually all the woodwork has disappeared and last week the brickwork collapsed altogether in the case of two of them. Perhaps you can recognise the whereabouts of the above sketch. The front of the two houses has fallen down flat leaving for the present the two end gables and the chimney buildings right at the back. We have therefore our "ruins" but caused not by the "Huns" but by bad-"uns" nearer home.

Note: Few Dawley people probably know about this, this news is sent exclusively to you.

Houses destroyed.

Front Wall

Back of houses.

Window ledges.

Front Wall

"Somewhere in France"

You have gone to a land whence no wireless can call you.
Where no fiendish devices of Hun can appal you;
You have answered the blast of the last bugle call,
And "somewhere in France" they have buried my all!
You have gone to a Mansion of infinite bliss—
To a land that will "right the disaster" of this;
Your soul from the bond of the body, now freed,
In the Mind of the Master earth's riddle you'll read!

"Imitation: A Form of Flattery."

We are receiving enquiries from various quarters as to our methods of work for soldiers and it is gratifying to think that other districts are beginning to do something for their own soldiers on our lines. This week a capable Wesleyan Minister in the neighbourhood of Wellington writes that his congregation have raised £25 for soldiers' comforts and wishes for some hints, etc. If soldiers from other districts wish to call the attention of their own people at home to our effort represented in the "W. R" we shall be glad to send them particulars.

Several funny stories were told by Mr. T. Withington of Dark Lane at our meeting last Tuesday. One was that of a transport van, containing some parcels for Old Park soldiers which got shelled in transit and one pork-pie reached its destination with a piece of German shrapnel in it. (This piece of "pork-pie" shrapnel is to be preserved in the Dark Lane Tabernacle) Another tale recounted was that of some Old Park lads who had gone to great trouble to secure, pluck and cook a fowl in anticipation of a nice supper when an enemy shell burst over the scene and scattered fire, cooking-pot and chickabiddy in all directions!

Price One Penny.

This paper is sent out to nearly 200 soldiers every week Only sold to Dawley people who attend our meetings.

The Plagues of Egypt keep the Shropshire Yeomanry in Constant Activity.

"The Flies and Mosquitoes are an awful pest."

Pte. W. E. Powell (1st Shropshire Yeomanry, A Squadron) writes from Egypt:- "I eagerly look forward to your "W. R"- we have no Dawley boys here but all the others like the paper, it is a great treat to get news of the Homeland. I am in camp on the banks of the Nile - we are not troubled like our friends in France with "charger" rats but with flies, mosquitoes, etc. While I am writing this I am so tormented that I shall have to put on my mosquito net. The heat is 118 degrees in the shade. You would not know us in our khaki drill and dark glasses. We have had two severe sandstorms while we have been here. The natives and their customs are very interesting, they dress just as they did in Bible times - they are just like the Bible pictures you see. They have their yoke of oxen and plough and thresh corn just in the same way as we read in the Bible.... Though I am not a Baptist I always made a point of attending your S. S. Anniversary and I am keeping your hymn-booklet as a little keep-sake. The old promise made to Moses somewhere in this region thousands of years ago is still true - "Certainly I will be with thee" and we have a right to believe that God will keep His Promises."

While our Front Page was in the Press news was received that the Rock School Treat had been put off – the picture therefore must be regarded as "intelligent anticipation" of an event still in the future.

All the shops were open and nearly all men were at work on Whit-Monday

Rev. S. Parmiter is coming to Doseley Church from Hull – he will be further away from the German raiders, won't he?

The Dawley Council Chamber is to have its windows cleaned and some fresh air let into it – it needs it!

The portrait of Rev. E. G. Gange appears in this year's Academy Exhibition in London. He writes saying "he's hanged at last."

An aeroplane was seen over Dawley last Saturday.

"When You Boys of the Air-Service Come Home"
We shall expect you to give our Sisters a ride on your Aeroplane.

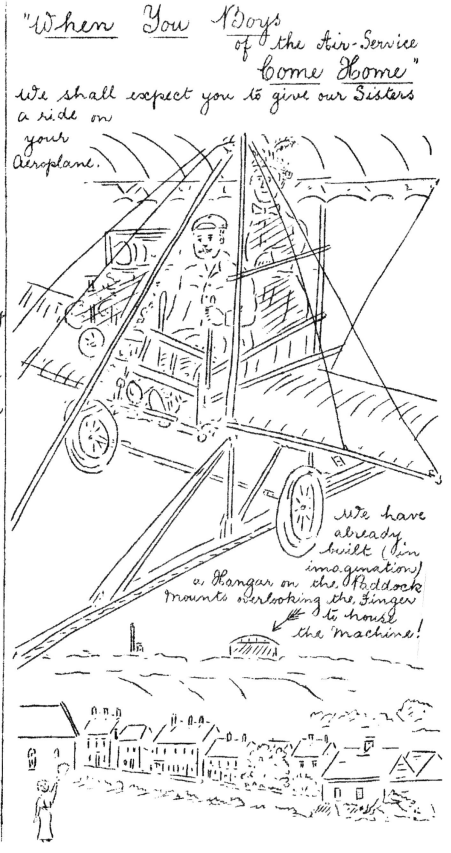

We have already built (in imagination) a Hangar on the Paddock mounts overlooking the Finger to house the machine!

Pte. L. L. Roberts of the British Mediterranean Expeditionary Force writes:- "Thank you for your Noble Little Paper which I have received many times. We have plenty to do even here.... We are sorry to read of the death of Eric Bailey but we are all willing to stand our chance for the good old country and its people for they are worth it."

Pte. J. Harley of the Salonica Forces writes on May 25th:- "I am receiving the "W. R" quite regularly. We soldiers here in Greece are wondering how long it will be before our turn comes to have a little leave at home so that we can come to your meeting!"

Pte. Harold Hollis (Old Park) writes from France:- "I am writing to you for the first time - I am tip - top. When the boys see the "W. R" they cheer. It is a bit rough out here but we must not grumble. I wish I was in the Sunday School class again but when we get back we will make up for it all. Wishing to be remembered to everyone - my address is:- Pte. H. Hollis - A Coy - 6th Batt: K. S. L. J. (1st Platoon). B. E. F."

"If the Germans Came to Dawley."

The Dover Memorial to Captain Webb of Dawley was unveiled on June 8th, 1910.

"Although our ship led the line of the big ships we came through without a scratch. I must say it was a grand sight to see our ship banging great shells at the Germans"

W. Hitchman (Barn Fold) writes from H.M.S. King George V on June 6th :- "I am writing to let you all know I am quite safe. I am at last partly satisfied, we have had a real scrap with the German Fleet and it was sharp work while it lasted.... I saw the "Invincible" go up and if Noah Round was on board I feel sorry for him. To see our big ship banging the shells was a grand sight. It was very good of them to let us come to grips with the cream of them and we have given old Tirpitz's successor a nasty blow. I enclose a copy of the Memorial Service which we held at the burial of some of our brave men last Sunday after the fight."... (Part of Will's letter has been cut out by the Ship's Censor, but we are much obliged to the gentleman for letting the above pass. Will says he hopes even now to get leave in a few days, if he comes we shall give him a welcome)

Official intimation has been received of the loss of the Boy. Telegraphist, Noah Round of the "Invincible".

We beg to acknowledge from "J.W." 12 stamps and from "Mrs. B". 6 stamps for our Postage Fund. We ask once again our friends at home to send us some help for this fund. We are spending nearly 10/- *every week* in postage and we shall not be able to continue unless more money is forthcoming. Next Tuesday, we are glad to say, friends from Wellington are coming to give an Entertainment including a Sketch. A collection will be taken on Entrance and if it is not sufficient another will be taken on Exit.

Pte. S. W. Archer (Scots Guards) writes from France:- "I was very pleased to spend that hour at your Meeting. Now that I am back in the trenches I look forward to the "W.R.": it is like an issue of rations. Jim Roberts from Lawley Bank has now joined my Battalion - he has lost a lot of weight since he came out but he is none the worse for that - I have been telling him about you good people at the Chapel. There was a big attack with the Huns a few days ago; we had to stand to ready to go up but we were not wanted.

Our Band is now out here - it is a treat to hear a bit of good music.... I am sorry I have no startling news to tell you but we have not had any big "biff" lately."

TO INCREASE YOUR WEIGHT USE "TOBY TICKLER'S JAM"

Pte. Albert Powell writes from Singapore:- "I had a very rough time of it on board ship - nothing to do and yet looking out all the time for German submarines. We had to keep our lifebelts on all the while even when we went to bed. I am with my brother Philip and both of us are in the best of health. Please send us some books as we have nothing to read, also some — for the heat is terrific. We do not get much money it is all in cents and you cannot keep it long, it is so small."

Pte. A. E. Corbett (Lawley Bank) writes from Hong Kong "We are grateful to you for the "W. R" and other papers we can see nothing hardly of the war from the Hong Kong papers. What a blessing it will be when it is over but as far as I can see it will not be yet. The name of the Dawley man I met in Australia is Fowles. When we come back we shall do what we can to tell you of our experiences in return for your trouble in sending us the 'W. R'."

Pte. I. Machin writes from France on May 27th:- "We have moved Ito France, I am glad to say after three months in Belgium. We have been at Ypres and I don't think there is a much worse place on the whole of the front. We have lost a lot of lives there.... We have had some stiff marching - we did fifteen miles in two hours less time than the Rifle Brigade the day previous. A good few had to fall out the last two miles, there was not a breath of air stirring. We are at present at drill behind the lines and it is not so bad.... I was glad to hear you had Albert Thomas at your meeting. I expect he would be rather timid."

We have undertaken to institute a search (through Red Cross and other people) for L/Cpl. W. Tart (of the Finger) 9537, 1st K. S. L. I. A Coy. He was last seen on Easter Sunday, since then he has been "missing". If any soldier has suggestions, please write to us.

Some "Sub"

"A bit of Dawley Talent!"

A sketch sent from France by Pte. Lovatt.

Pte. G. V. Lovatt (Pool Hill) writes from France:- "For some reason I have not had the 'W. R' for two weeks, please send it regularly. The gardens round here look beautiful, the people seem to live in their gardens - lots of the potatoes are in bloom. We heard the cuckoo at the end of April. I suppose all eligible Dawley men are now under orders."

Pte. A. Lloyd (The Finger) writes on June 2nd:—
"Many thanks for the "W.R" which I receive every week as regular as the clock. I have been on pass but I was sorry I did not get the chance of attending your meeting, the time was so short. There is no country like England to us and I enjoyed myself while I was there: I was pleased to know you did so well at your Anniversary—I am keeping the hymns by me for there is one I have proved very much. No.8. "God is everywhere". If He hadn't have been it would have been all over with us."

Pte. George Jackson writes from Alder-Hey Hospital, West Derby, Liverpool. "I have arrived in old England at last and I hope to see you soon. How nice to get out of that dirty place called Greece — it is the dirtiest place that ever I saw."

"I didna think it would serve thee like that!"

"All in our Ward have had a read at your "Weekly Report." (Extract from a Dawley soldier's letter written in a hospital situated on the East Coast.)

Price One Penny.
We issue this little weekly for Dawley soldiers on foreign service — there are nearly 200 of them. Dawley people can only purchase a copy by attending our Tuesday meeting.

Weekly Report

"Hello, hello, are you No 3. Dawley? Is that Mr. Wooding? You can tell Mr. Lester I've just landed in England and I shall be at your meeting next Tuesday!"

OUR TELEPHONE NUMBER IS "3 DAWLEY, SALOP"

Brotherhood and Sisterhood.
Dawley Baptist Chapel.
June 20th 1916.

"Allow me to thank you for sending out to me more socks and cigarettes" writes Lance-Corporal G. Frost from Singapore. "I am sure it is very good of you and may God give you His blessing so that you may continue to encourage Dawley soldiers scattered all over the world till peace-once more reigns. Some new men arrived here from England last week — they looked very tired after their long journey by sea but we are glad to have a few more good old Shropshires among us. I hope they will make themselves contented and do their duty here as we are trying to do."

To A Soldier at the Front.

If you have never written to us in reply to the weekly receipt of this little paper please do so! We in Dawley need cheering up just as you do. Don't tell us war-secrets but about your daily doings — if you can sketch so much the better!

Pte. J. W. Price of the Cameron Highlanders is now in the V. A. D. Hospital, Shrewsbury. He writes saying he is sorry to hear of the death of the Boy-Telegraphist Noah Round with whom he had a chat in Dawley only a few weeks ago. He says he is not much better in health but the nurses are very good and the Shrewsbury people give them a good time free motor-rides, etc.

"One at a Time Please"

A Quarter-Master-Sergeant's Worries after his Company has been in an Engagement. A sketch sent from France by Serg: J. H. Price.

The other day he was taken to Leighton Hall where he went to see the horses of the Remount Dept: they have there.

We have been able to glean further information respecting the death of Sergeant A. Eric Bailey. One of the five soldiers who were with him at the time has visited Dawley — Private Boycott of Coalmoor. They were together on a firing-platform in the trenches when a German shell came and buried all five of them. When Sergeant Bailey was extricated he was lifeless, though he wore a steel helmet death was evidently instantaneous. One of his College Chums who is in the London Regiment has put up a rough wooden cross of which he sends a sketch. We expect in a week or so to have from France a photograph of his grave which will be here reproduced in outline.

We gratefully acknowledge the following for our Postage Fund. Pte. W. L. Perry 36 stamps; "Welsh Woman" 24 stamps. Mrs Pugh (School House) 6 stamps. If friends who wish to share in the upkeep and the cost of posting the "W. R" to soldiers care to help us we shall be glad to acknowledge their donations next week.

At our meeting last week we had with us Pte. W. J. Perry of the Australian Auxiliary Forces. Pte. Perry, it will be remembered went to Australia about five years ago with an uncle. After war broke out he joined a regiment in Adelaide. After 3 months training he went to Egypt for another 3 months. Then he was fighting for about 4 months with the Australians in Gallipoli. For the past 3 months he has been in the trenches in France, obtaining a short leave to visit his

"If the Germans Came to Dawley"

ELEPHANT AND CASTLE

We should soon dispose of them if one or two of you boys happened to be on leave. (Quite a number of men have been home from the Front lately)

relatives here at Dawley Bank. He is very well and is greatly interested in our work to which he has generously subscribed.

We are expecting a number of friends from Wellington to carry out the programme of our meeting to-night which is to include a Sketch. We have asked one of our artists to be present to make a drawing of one scene in it.

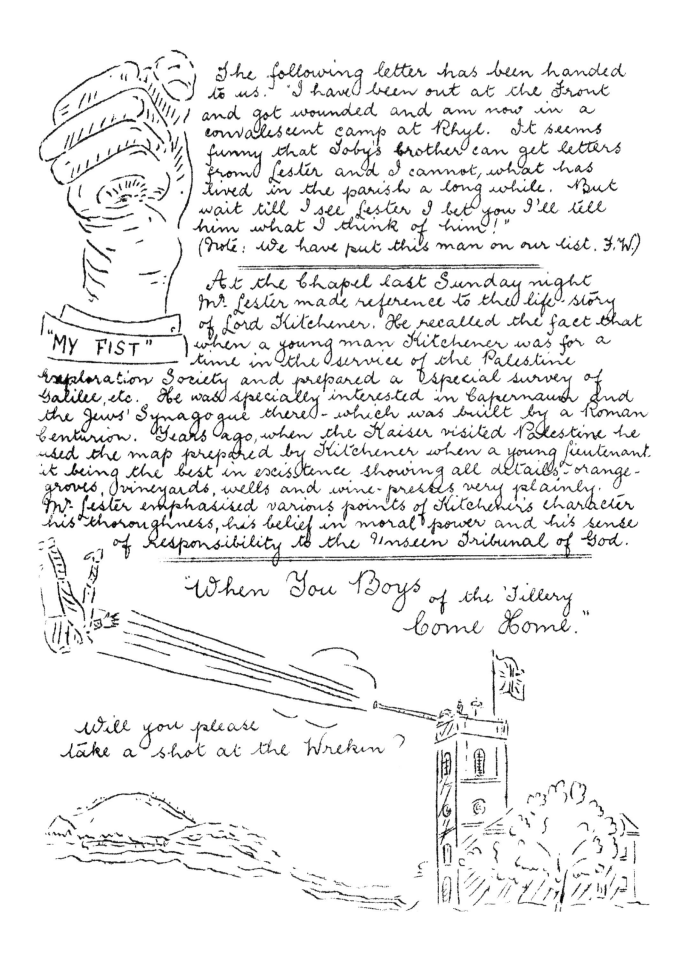

The following letter has been handed to us. "I have been out at the Front and got wounded and am now in a convalescent camp at Rhyl. It seems funny that Toby's brother can get letters from Lester and I cannot, what has lived in the parish a long while. But wait till I see Lester I bet you I'll tell him what I think of him!"
(Note: We have put this man on our list. F.W.)

At the Chapel last Sunday night Mr. Lester made reference to the life story of Lord Kitchener. He recalled the fact that when a young man Kitchener was for a time in the service of the Palestine Exploration Society and prepared a special survey of Galilee, etc. He was specially interested in Capernaum and the Jews' Synagogue there - which was built by a Roman Centurion. Years ago, when the Kaiser visited Palestine he used the map prepared by Kitchener when a young lieutenant. it being the best in existence showing all details - orange-groves, vineyards, wells and wine-presses very plainly. Mr. Lester emphasised various points of Kitchener's character his thoroughness, his belief in moral power and his sense of Responsibility to the Unseen Tribunal of God.

"When You Boys of the Tillery Come Home."

Will you please take a shot at the Wrekin?

"MY FIST"

The owners of the Dancing Bear (see last page) are Roumanians. Their caravan has been located amid the mounts at Charleshay. All sorts of stories have been started about these people — that they were spies, etc etc. The police say that before coming into the town the man brought his passports, identification papers, &c for inspection. The people are quite harmless. Further, you may be relieved of any anxiety when we tell you they were due to leave the district last night, taking the Bear with them!

There was a small Fair in Gwen's Field, Oakengates during the week-end and it was not very well patronised — so they say.

M. Deleus of Horsehay, a Belgian Refugee, it is said is joining the Army this week in response to the call throughout the country for Belgians of military age to go into training in England, in order to take their share when the time comes in driving the Germans out of Belgium. The case of Louis Lawley Bank eldest Belgian boy living in under age. has been looked into — he is still

Surgeon Guy Woodhouse, a nephew of Mr. F. Wooding who was on the "Malaya" one of the bigger ships which went into action under Beatty against the Germans in the North Sea has visited Dawley during the week. ———— Will Hitchman of the King George V is to have a little present at our Tuesday meeting following his arrival at Lawley Bank at the end of the month. ———— Another visitor expected shortly is Chaplain Perry, of the Australian Auxiliary Forces — a son of Rev. Enoch Perry who went out from Dawley to Australia many years ago.

If the summer weather really comes we are hoping to arrange some garden meetings on Tuesdays following the meeting next week. We are open to receive invitations out!

Driver C. Woolgar writes:-
"We were all pleased to hear of the German Fleet coming out - we only wished it had stopped to fight to a finish then it would have been no more! They are cowards, like the men in the trenches they are alright under cover but as soon as you have got them they shout for mercy. The sketch is what remains of a lovely church which the Huns have taken a liking to and they have not finished with it yet for they are gradually making it less and less. I don't think the war will last much longer - but we have got to get a victory if it takes ten years to do it. I never see any Dawley boys but I met Sergeant Langford from Horsehay Flat about a month ago and we had a good talk about the old place. Thank you very much for the "W. R". P.S. I hope you are enjoying the Daylight Saving Bill."

A sketch (slightly altered by request) sent by Driver Cyril Woolgar from "Somewhere in France."

Lance-Corporal F. Buttery writes from France:- "The "W. R" I received on Whit-Monday at 2.a.m. for which I thank you very much. I am very sorry to hear about R. Round as he was such a nice boy but I hope he is better off. I often see his brother George when we are out of the trenches also a lot more of our Dawley boys and we generally speak about our small town when we get together and also about the people there. I am sure Dawley is doing its share to win this awful war if not more, according to its size. I have been out in this country 19 months now and I have been one of the lucky ones for which I thank my Heavenly Father, as I ask Him night and morning to keep me safe beneath His Almighty Wings... We are having some awful weather just at present but that is caused by the heavy bombardments which are still in progress as it has been very lively around our place these last 14 days."

Summary of Soldiers' Comforts Fund (Nov: to June) Receipts £23-18-7. Expenditure £21-5-1. (Balance £2-13-6 paid by Miss Breeze to General Funds of B and S — (Treasurer Mrs Lavender) out of which Comforts, etc. are now being provided.

Expenditure.	£	s	d
Shirts, socks etc	6	5	9
Various Comforts	5	13	11
Carriage on Parcels	4	5	10
Cigarettes	1	12	0
Wool	1	6	0
Stationery, Food, etc	2	1	7
	£ 21	5	1

Proceeds of Collections, Donations, etc — £ 23-18-7

We are sending a complete balance-sheet I audited by Messrs S. T. Jones and E. Hatfield to about 100 friends in a few days This Fund will be re-opened at the beginning of the winter.

The above statement does not include large gifts of goods, cigarettes, stationery etc which have been donated to us by various friends, nor any part of expenditure on "W. R" or postage which is a separate account and which will be audited in due course.

Penance!

Some time ago signing himself "One from Dawley" a soldier upset some of our readers. This good fellow now writes:— "I am extremely sorry and I assure you all and also our gallant comrades that it was not intended in the light they took it. As anyone might have seen who has been in the trenches, it was nothing more than a joke — a big enlargement of the life spent here. I can assure my critics I have seen more of the war than the average but in any case I wish you to publish this apology and forgive the humour."

VIRESCIT VULNERE VIRTUS!

VIRTUE

SHRINE OF UNDILUTED TRUTH (NO HUMOUR ALLOWED)

A Dancing Bear
visited Dawley and Lawley Bank
on Wednesday evening last to the
delight of all the women-folk.
All business, all traffic was
temporarily stopped - everybody gave
themselves up to the enjoyment of what
was undoubtedly the sensation of the week!

Sergeant J. Farr
writes from France:-
"I am glad to hear
the boys at home
are not taking
any Whit-holiday.
we must all work
together now. we
don't get much
news of the war
out here, what
there is gets cooked.
Our old patients
are better"(Sergeant
Farr is attached
to the Veterinary
Department and
has to do with
horses)"and we
have some new
patients in which
require our attention.
We were all sorry
to lose our great
Commander "H of K":
it is very bad.
I wonder if it
was some spy's
work or whether
as they say, a
mine. I am
glad there is
prospect of a good
harvest at home.
We all think the
"W. K" is lovely."

Price:
One Penny.
This little paper
is sent out to
nearly 200 soldiers
every week. It
is only sold to
Dawley people who
attend our meetings.

WEEKLY · REPORT

JUNE 27th 1916.

Brotherhood and Sisterhood.
Dawley Baptist Chapel.

A soldier of the R. E (who shall be nameless!) writes to someone (who shall also be nameless!) "I am still despatch-riding at the Head.quarters and I am doing a lot of miles per day. I've worn one machine out and now I've got a new one - a beauty! Oh, if you could sit on the back! If only you could come out with me for one day you would realise what war means. To see the towns all in ruins - big towns too - not a shop standing and graves all over the place."

Price One Penny.

This little paper is produced chiefly for Dawley soldiers now out of England and is sent to nearly 200 of them every week. We are anxious to keep going for the greater part of the holiday season, for our brave fellows in the fighting-line are as much in need of encouragement as ever they were. We ask them to write to us in return. The "Weekly Report" is only sold to Dawley people who attend our Tuesday meetings.

Our artist was so convulsed with laughter that he was incapable of producing anything else but the following!

"A Quiet Cup of Tea"

"Mrs Featherly"

"Captain Bouncer R.A"

"Mrs Mount chestnut"

"Dr Dickenson"

"Clara"

The Prompter (behind the Piano)

We are deeply obliged to our friends from Wellington for the help they gave us on Tuesday last when 36/- was collected for the Postage Fund. Mr. and Mrs. E. G. March Mr. and Mrs. W. Pritchard, Miss G. Waterton, Miss A. King and Mr. K. Davies rendered excellent service and the sketch will not readily be forgotten by those present - they laughed, and that in these dull days is a good thing - especially for people who take serious views of their work as most of us at the Tuesday meeting do.

2nd Corporal J. Smith of No 1. Siege Co. R.M.R.E - B.E.F. France writes:- "I appreciate the "W. R." very much and so do most of the men of my corps. I will send you some sketches when I have time for we have lots of material to work on We are not a fighting corps but we are equipped like an infantry soldier with a rifle and bayonet and all that is necessary for a fighting man but up to the present we have not been called upon to use them. We are engaged upon important work - the nature of which we are not allowed to say. - I had a near shave about a fortnight ago for I got a bullet bang in my back, but thank God, as it was spent it left me with no more than a bruise. I am writing this by the light of a candle in a dug-out which we have made - a German shell exploded on top the other day but it only blew the earth off - so much for the strength of the work of the R. E."

Pte. H. L. Brown writes from France:- "Thanks for your breezy little paper – you say there is a dearth of news from your end, well it is the same this end. We are not allowed to tell you what we should like to - perhaps it is as well. Dawley was bad enough before the war for being sleepy, it must be very boring to be there now "(Come, come, Brown, you don't know how lively we are on a Tuesday night!) "I suppose Horsehay Works are mostly on war materials. Thank the B and S for the little paper."

Pte. J. Holmes of the Balkan Expeditionary Force says:- "Thank you for the cigarettes and "W.R" I received quite safely. We are having some lovely weather here just now but it is rather too hot. I can venture to say we shall be as brown as berries when we get back to dear old Dawley. All the boys are keeping well out here."

"If the Germans Came to Dawley"

They would certainly examine the vaults under the Elementary Schools.

A manager of a school recently boasted in public of the amount of money saved by his children during the year!

The Sunday School services are now nearly all over – the collections as a rule have been larger than last year. The Methodists are trying to arrange their Sunday School Demonstration again this year but the officers say there is increasing difficulty in doing so.

If you could have been at the Public Tribunal in the Town Hall on Friday last you would have seen that men only get exemption from military service when they can show good reason for it. Among those whose appeals were refused was that of a farmer – represented by a Wellington solicitor – who has three sons of military age at home – on behalf of one son. Another man who pleaded the care of an aged aunt was required to make other arrangements for a home for his relative. Another was a house-painter, who was only allowed till the end of September in order to close up his business. Among those who secured temporary exemption were several men employed at the new Brandlee Colliery.

One of the Dawley boys in Hong Kong says:- "The English people out here won't look at a soldier – we often have to "tell some of them off" and ask them why they do not join the Army – that is the reason they don't like us."

We acknowledge with many thanks the following contributions to our Postage Fund. "A reader of the W.R." 132 stamps; "M.E.B's" Class – 6 stamps. The collection on Tuesday last at the "Quiet Cup of Tea" etc. enables us to purchase 432 stamps. We are grateful for this help, as our expenses are very heavy.

"When You Boys of the Navy Come Home"

STATION LANDING STAGE

CO-OP

PRIDE OF THE POOL

You'll be expected to start a Ferry across Horsehay Pool.

Pte. Ernest Jackson is invalided home – almost the first of the men to return to Lawley Bank from Greece. — A letter was received from Jim Alford yesterday saying he is still in hospital in Germany and that he gets his parcels alright. Some people in Oswestry are specially kind to him.

The Toy-Factory in Wellington is gradually growing – about 60 girls are now employed, making Teddy Bears and other soft goods which formerly came from Germany. Several Dawley girls work there – others hope to do so.

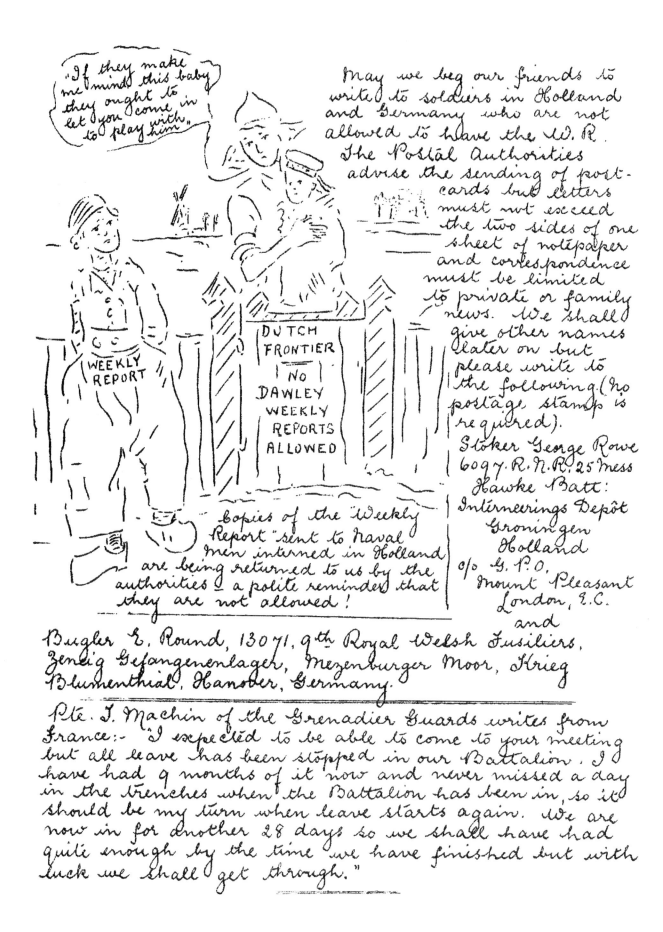

May we beg our friends to write to soldiers in Holland and Germany who are not allowed to have the W.R. The Postal Authorities advise the sending of postcards but letters must not exceed the two sides of one sheet of notepaper and correspondence must be limited to private or family news. We shall give other names later on but please write to the following (No postage stamp is required).

Stoker George Rowe 6097. R.N.R. 25 mess Hawke Batt: Interneerings Depôt Groningen Holland c/o G.P.O. Mount Pleasant London, E.C. and

Bugler E. Round, 13071, 9th Royal Welsh Fusiliers, Zeneig Gefangenenlager, Mezenburger Moor, Krieg Blumenthial, Hanover, Germany.

Pte. J. Machin of the Grenadier Guards writes from France:- "I expected to be able to come to your meeting but all leave has been stopped in our Battalion. I have had 9 months of it now and never missed a day in the trenches when the Battalion has been in, so it should be my turn when leave starts again. We are now in for another 28 days so we shall have had quite enough by the time we have finished but with luck we shall get through."

L/Corp: E. Taylor writes from Convalescent Camp, Blackpool:- "We are having a long stay here but I don't object - we have close on 2,000 wounded soldiers in at present, some leave every week on a ten days' furlough home and then back to their units if they are fit, if not they go back to hospital. The "W.R" is a fine little book - you can always see some of your old pals' names in it.... I don't know what our poor lads out at the Front would do without the B and S. I remember the very first parcel I had from them, at a place called Bois Grenier, just off the La Bassée Road, where we had a rough time of it."

Pte. S. Furber writing from France, says:- "It is eleven months since I left England but I don't know when I shall get leave home. Thank you for all you are doing for us Dawley boys - your letters put new life into us."

The Bungalow of Harold Rowe (from the soldier's own sketch).

Driver H. Rowe writes from France:- I think the "W. R's" are getting more interesting, your 'German' sketches are very amusing - I don't think they'll get to Dawley yet..... I have been looking forward to a furlough for a long time but I expect the war will be over before I get one - if so, that will be all the better. We are stationed in the grounds of a big English residence here in France and I am writing this letter in my little Bungalow which I have made my place of abode - it consists of asphalt walls and a tarpaulin roof - you will see by the sketch it is like a big dog-kennel but I have made it very comfortable with straw and shelves all round. The table has to be outside at the foot of a big fir tree, so you see I am in a healthy spot."

Barbed Wire.

1. We have a Captain brave
   and bold.
   Who's really worth his weight in
   gold.
   His only fault, if you enquire
   Is putting out of Barbed Wire.

2. He looks around near every night,
   Again he comes by time it's light,
   Only one thing he will enquire
   "Have you put out
   your barbed wire?"

3. He asks you
   "Have you any men?"
   And when you answer,
   "Yes, sir, ten."
   He'll tell you "Those
   I shall require
   To put out twenty
   rolls of wire."

4. Next morning
   just about "Stand to",
   The periscope he will
   look through,
   But not the landscape
   to admire,
   He really looks at the barbed
   wire.

5. Our Colonel, who is quite a 'toff"
   Exclaims "The men have done
   enough"
   But the Captain answers him,
   "No, sire,
   Another fifty rolls of wire."

6. I tell you, when he goes to sleep
   In midst of slumbers he must
   creep
   Round the dug-outs, near the fire
   Searching, dreaming of barbed
   wire.

7. The G.O.C. one day came round
   And quickly said, "Well, I'll
   be bound.
   The ruined church's broken spire
   You've hidden with
   your barbed wire!"

8. We've put out
   twenty thousand rolls
   Enough to reach to
   both the Poles
   And as it mounts
   up higher and
   higher
   The "boss" keeps
   saying "More
   wire, more wire."

9. We've rifles,
   mortars, bombs and guns,
   "But these", he says "won't
   beat the Huns
   The only thing that I
   require
   Is old Lloyd George to
   send me "wire."

VERSE 10

10. Perhaps, some day a shell
    will come,
    And blow him straight to
    Kingdom Come
    And the Crown for which he does
    aspire
    Will not be gold or thorns but WIRE.

The above "ode" has been specially written for this paper by an Old Park soldier. He has dedicated it to an officer — whose name the Censor has obliterated. We therefore do not give the name of the author - can you guess it?

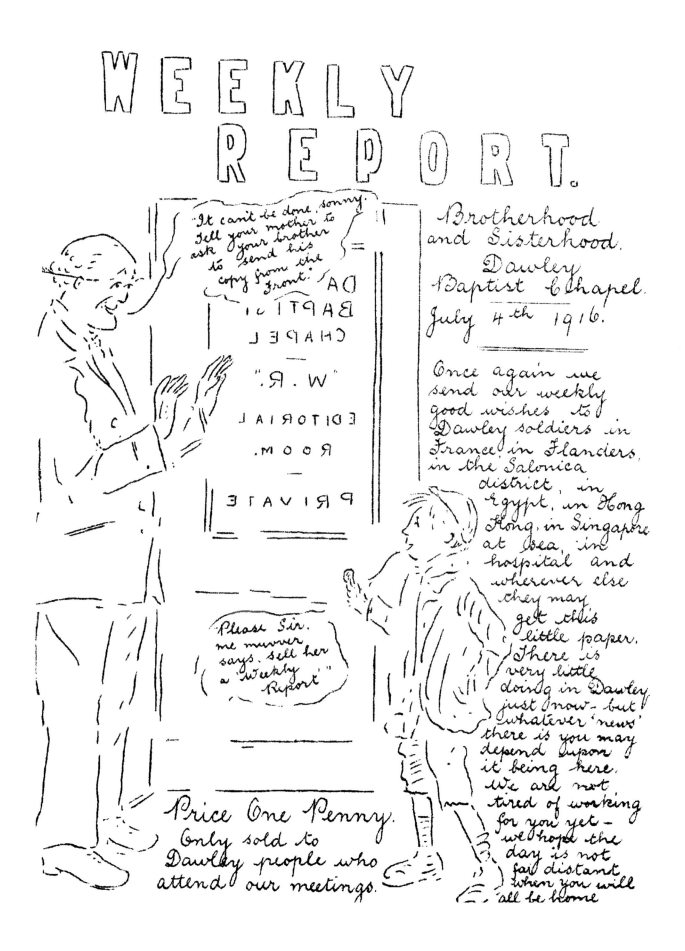

We are all more or less excited in Dawley now, in spite of the cold rains at the news of the beginning of the great "Push on the Somme. We hope and pray that all our men may come through safely – each will do his duty, we know.

One puddler at Haybridge and two young men at Sinclair's Works, Ketley were summoned at Wellington Police Court on Monday and fined for neglecting their work – the first £5 and the other two 10/- each.

The soldiers in khaki-overalls employed at the Hollinswood Crusher may be seen any day in Oakengates or St. Georges – they are paraded at the beginning and the close of the day under Lieutenant C. J. Ruffle.

A number of wounded soldiers are now in Wellington in the houses provided by Mr John Bayley. It is said there are 200 hospital-beds provided at the Wellington Union House, in case they are needed.

"When You Boys
Come Home"

Shall we arrange with
our Ice-Cream
merchant to stock
"Toby Ticklers Jam"
in

the
High
Street
on
a
Saturday
night?

TICKLER'S JAM.

IMPORTED FROM FRANCE.

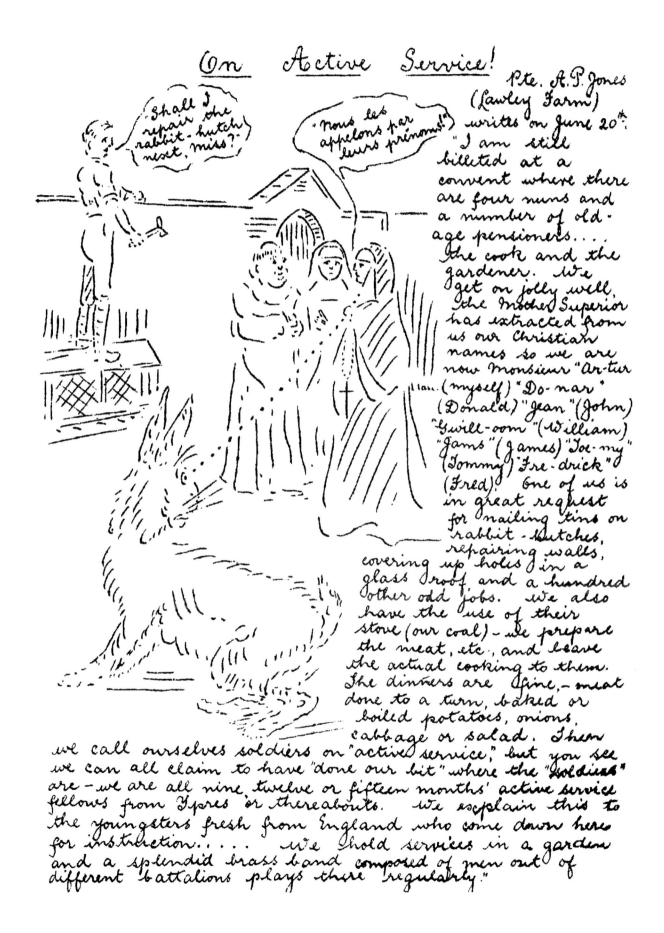

On Active Service!

"Shall I repair the rabbit-hutch nest, miss?"

"nous les appelons par leurs prénoms!"

Pte. A.P. Jones (Lawley Farm) writes on June 20th. "I am still billeted at a convent where there are four nuns and a number of old-age pensioners.... the cook and the gardener. We get on jolly well. The Mother Superior has extracted from us our Christian names so we are now monsieur "Ar-tur" (myself) "Do-nar" (Donald) "jean" (John) "Gwill-oom" (William) "James" (James) "Toe-my" (Tommy) "Fre-drick" (Fred). One of us is in great request for nailing tins on rabbit-hutches, repairing walls, covering up holes in a glass roof and a hundred other odd jobs. We also have the use of their stove (our coal) — we prepare the meat, etc., and leave the actual cooking to them. The dinners are fine, — meat done to a turn, baked or boiled potatoes, onions, cabbage or salad. Then we call ourselves soldiers on "active service", but you see we can all claim to have "done our bit" where the "soldiers" are — we are all nine, twelve or fifteen months' active service fellows from Ypres or thereabouts. We explain this to the youngsters fresh from England who come down here for instruction..... we hold services in a garden and a splendid brass band composed of men out of different battalions plays there regularly."

At the Baptist Chapel on Monday afternoon lance-Corporal Geo. Collis was married to Miss S. J. Bishop in the presence of a large congregation of friends and neighb Pte. Bert. Bishop, who is in training in Bedfordshir acted as "best-man." L/Cpl. Collis is an old soldier of 2nd K.S.L.I and wears a ribbon. At the beginning of the war he fought in France and later was sent to Salonica district. He is now acting as an Instructor a Pembroke Dock but is, of course, quite uncertain as to future movements. Miss Bishop has been a worker connection with our Tuesday meeting right from the commencement of our efforts for soldiers.

Steps are being taken to arrange a house-to house and other collections in Dawley for Red Cross Funds. This latest venture is being taken up by people connected with the County Agricultural Committee. While it is true that several efforts have previously been made for Red Cross Funds it is felt that only a comparatively small sum has so far been given by Dawley people. We hope therefore to redeem our characters shortly in this respect.

During the past week we have only received 18 stamps for our Postage Fund – 12 from Mr Round (Meadow Rd) and 6 from Mrs Pugh (School House). We shall be glad of other kind contributions this week.

"If the Germans

The Baptist Girl Guides would know deal with

(A favourite youngsters of to douse one water from th front of the

Among the censored letters received during the week is one from Rev. Alfred. S. Nickless, B.D, the minister of Albany Park Presbyterian Church, Chicago. He went to America some years ago and has done very well – passing through McCormick Seminary Chicago and getting a theological degree. He says:- "I want very much to see Dawley again. I sometimes think I ought to be at home doing my bit for my country. You may be sure England has many friends out here in her struggle. There are 750,000 Germans in this city. I have quite a number in my Church, some of them being born in Germany. But for all that many of us think our President has been a little slow in letting Germany know where the U.S.A. does stand." — He also tells us of Mr. W. S. Hall, who is now in Chicago.

Corporal J. Bullock writes from Hong Kong:- "I get the "W.R" week by week and it is very kind of you to bring back our thoughts to the dear Home-land we have left so many miles behind. I can assure you the "W. R" sets us all talking about you – though we are away in an Eastern Land it does not seem far to Dawley Bank. You should see how our comrades crowd round us to hear us read them out to them. We hope it won't be long before we return and then we will try and give you an account of our Eastern experiences." (Thanks, but we shall be pleased to have written experiences for this little paper)

e to Dawley"

to

ion of the
ey Bank is
d with
drant in
el.

One of the 1st Grenadier Guards Recalls Old Times at Ketley and King's Palace.

Pte. J. Machin writes from France:- "I am pleased to say I am still quite well. I was sorry to hear of the death of Noah Round. he worked for me more than once at Ketley Iron Works and I can honestly say he was a very good lad. I would like to know the number and battalion of J. W. Archer and J. Roberts (Lawley Bank) of the Scots Guards as I expect I should be able to find them out quite easily. I would like to march behind our Band again to Buckingham Palace the same as I have had the pleasure of doing while in London. I would like everybody in Dawley to see the Guard mount in Buckingham Palace - it would be the finest sight they had seen for a long time. You can't help feeling smart with so many people watching you. You had a very good sketch indeed of "Toby Tichler's Jam" - I wish a good many Dawley people had some of it as Tommy throws a lot away! A chap out here the other day said he was pleased we did not go in the trenches he wanted to know what we had done with our horses - that's after nine months of trench duty!"

Pte. G. V. Lovatt (Pool Hill) sends us a picture-postcard of Evian-les-Bains and reports they had a bit of a typhoon a few days ago which was strong enough to give them the impression they were about to leave Mother Earth altogether and at short notice! "Happily we survived, which is more than the trees can say."

As will be noticed in this "Report" we have received very few letters from the French Front this week. We all know the reason why! The following letter from Pte. S. Davies dated June 26th is the latest we have received. "Thank you very much for the Report. It is very hot here now but I cannot tell you where we are. I think we are about at the turning-point and in a short time now the Germans will have had enough – we are hoping to get the best of them this time. I am glad to see your work is going on so well."

X X X X X X X X X X X X X X X X X X X X

More things are wrought by prayer
Than this world dreams of! Wherefore, let thy voice
Rise like a fountain for me, night and day.
For what are men better than sheep or goats
That nourish a blind life within the brain
If, knowing God, they lift not hands of prayer
Both for themselves and those who call
                                                them friend.

x x x x x x x x x x x x x + x x x x x x x

We are glad that our Chapel has had some share in the erection of the new Institute which is to be opened in July. We have received an invitation to attend the opening. Says a daily paper "The new soldiers' home, built by the Baptist Union at Aldershot, which Mr. Lloyd George (who is of course a Baptist) will open on July 14th is the most up-to-date institution of its kind. The concert-hall is the largest of its type in Aldershot. It has a fairly large billiard-room, containing two tables, and there are games and reading-rooms. Its canteen, in which no alcoholic liquors are sold, is divided from the kitchen by a wall, the food coming through a buttery hatch, so that the soldier is free from the varied odours which too often pervade his regimental supper-bar. There are washing-baths and shower-baths also a drying-chamber, where a soldier soaked from parade or route march can deposit his overcoat or tunic and can tackle his tea or supper knowing that the garment will be dry by the time he has finished.

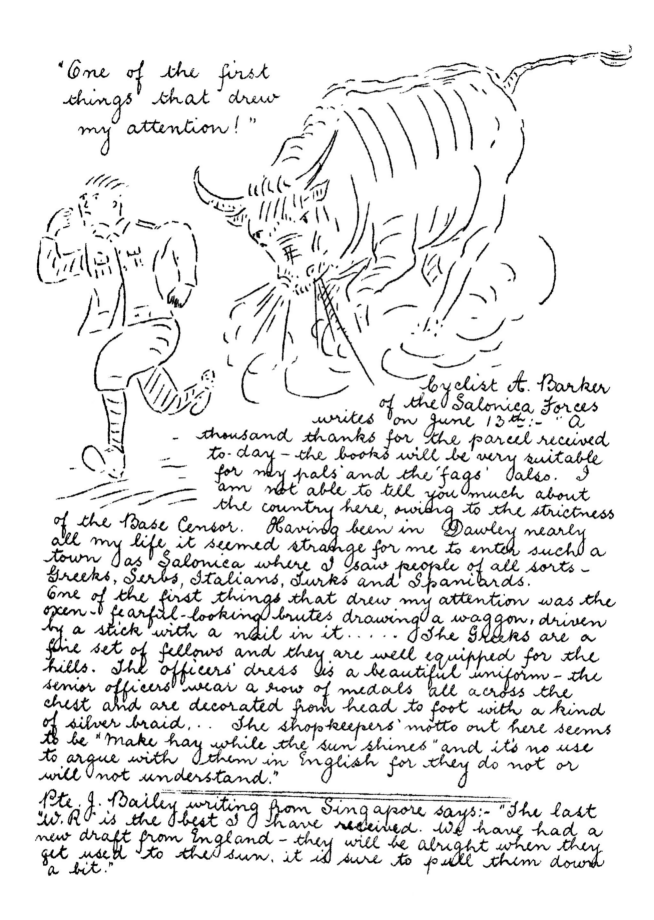

"One of the first things that drew my attention!"

Cyclist A. Barker of the Salonica Forces writes on June 13th:- "A thousand thanks for the parcel received to-day – the books will be very suitable for my pals and the 'fags' also. I am not able to tell you much about the country here, owing to the strictness of the Base Censor. Having been in Dawley nearly all my life it seemed strange for me to enter such a town as Salonica where I saw people of all sorts – Greeks, Serbs, Italians, Turks and Spaniards. One of the first things that drew my attention was the oxen – fearful-looking brutes drawing a waggon, driven by a stick with a nail in it..... The Greeks are a fine set of fellows and they are well equipped for the hills. The officers' dress is a beautiful uniform – the senior officers wear a row of medals all across the chest and are decorated from head to foot with a kind of silver braid... The shop keepers' motto out here seems to be "Make hay while the sun shines" and it's no use to argue with them in English for they do not or will not understand."

Pte. J. Bailey writing from Singapore says:- "The last "W.R" is the best I have received. We have had a new draft from England – they will be alright when they get used to the sun. it is sure to pull them down a bit."

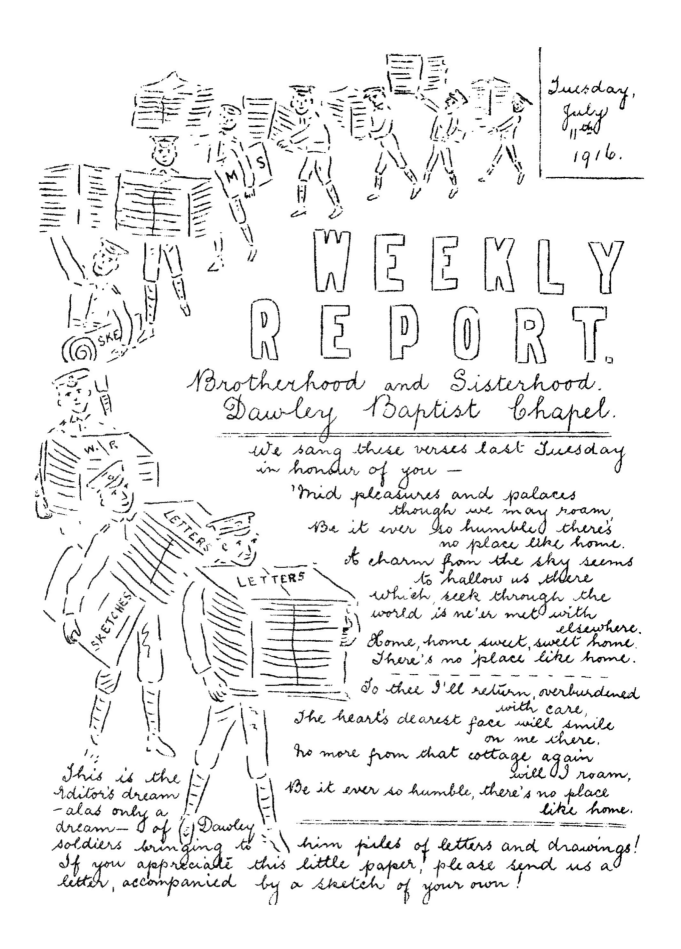

Tuesday,
July 11th
1916.

WEEKLY REPORT.

Brotherhood and Sisterhood.
Dawley Baptist Chapel.

We sang these verses last Tuesday
in honour of you —

'Mid pleasures and palaces
  though we may roam,
Be it ever so humble there's
  no place like home.
A charm from the sky seems
  to hallow us there
Which, seek through the
world is ne'er met with
  elsewhere.
Home, home sweet, sweet home.
There's no 'place like home.

To thee I'll return, overburdened
  with care,
The heart's dearest face will smile
  on me there.
No more from that cottage again
  will I roam,
Be it ever so humble, there's no place
  like home.

This is the
Editor's dream
– alas only a
dream— of Dawley
soldiers bringing to him piles of letters and drawings!
If you appreciate this little paper, please send us a
letter, accompanied by a sketch of your own!

"Some at home may think" writes a British officer at the Front "that the war is blinking the morality of our soldiers, but let that thought be banished, for if there is one thing beautiful in this incessant battle it is the moral elevation of the men who have come out to give their all. Men who have never known religion have found it, selfish men have become charitable, and life-long drunkards have become sober. Every man who lives to see our victory will be a moral gain to England, and every man who dies will be better prepared for death than he otherwise would have been."

Another writes from the Front:- "How the fellows sing at the services held and enjoy the hymns; perhaps we get a bit flat at times, but that does not matter, the heart is there that counts."

Jim Alford at Giessen.

Two postcards have been received from Jim Alford dated June 12th - one a picture p.c. from which this sketch is taken. He says:- "I received a nice long letter from Mr. Hatfield of the B and S. Give them all my best respects and tell them I am still going along mending, but slow." As will be seen, the Prisoners' Camp appears to be pleasantly situated and our friends are invited to write to him :- 10754, Pte. J. Alford, 5th K.S.L.I. 9 Coy. Baraque A. Lazaret, Giessen, Germany. Giessen is a nice town, very pleasantly situated about 40 miles north of Frankfort-on-the-Maine, in population about the size of Shrewsbury, 33,000. It is about 100 miles inside Germany as the crow flies - perhaps 130 in a direct line bending slightly to the south from Liège in Belgium. (You can easily find it on a map).

The 23 year old son of Rev. I. Brentnall, Primitive Methodist Minister at Dawley a few years ago, died at Shirlett Sanatorium last week and is to be interred in the Baptist Cemetery, Dawley Bank.

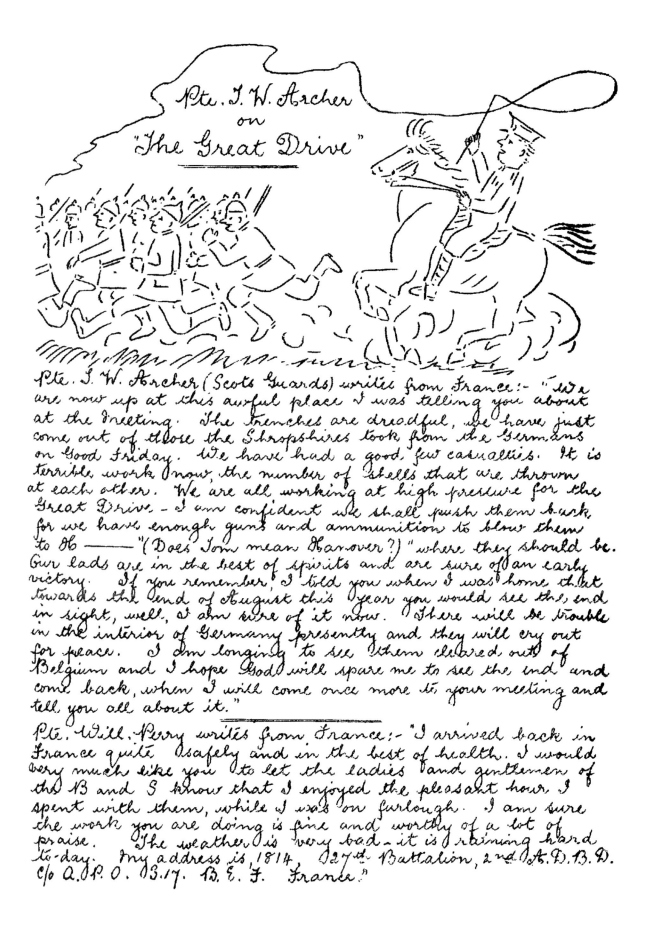

Pte. I. W. Archer
on
"The Great Drive"

Pte. I. W. Archer (Scots Guards) writes from France:- "We are now up at this awful place I was telling you about at the Meeting. The trenches are dreadful, we have just come out of those the Shropshires took from the Germans on Good Friday. We have had a good few casualties. It is terrible work now, the number of shells that are thrown at each other. We are all working at high pressure for the Great Drive. — I am confident we shall push them back, for we have enough guns and ammunition to blow them to H —— "(Does Tom mean Hanover?) "where they should be. Our lads are in the best of spirits and are sure of an early victory. If you remember, I told you when I was home that towards the end of August this year you would see the end in sight, well, I am sure of it now. There will be trouble in the interior of Germany presently and they will cry out for peace. I am longing to see them cleared out of Belgium and I hope God will spare me to see the end and come back, when I will come once more to your meeting and tell you all about it."

Pte. Will. Perry writes from France:- "I arrived back in France quite safely and in the best of health. I would very much like you to let the ladies and gentlemen of the B and S know that I enjoyed the pleasant hour I spent with them, while I was on furlough. I am sure the work you are doing is fine and worthy of a lot of praise. The weather is very bad - it is raining hard to-day. My address is, 1814, 327th Battalion, 2nd A.D.B.D. c/o Q.P.O. B.17. B.E.F. France."

"If the Germans came to Dawley" by 'Zepp.

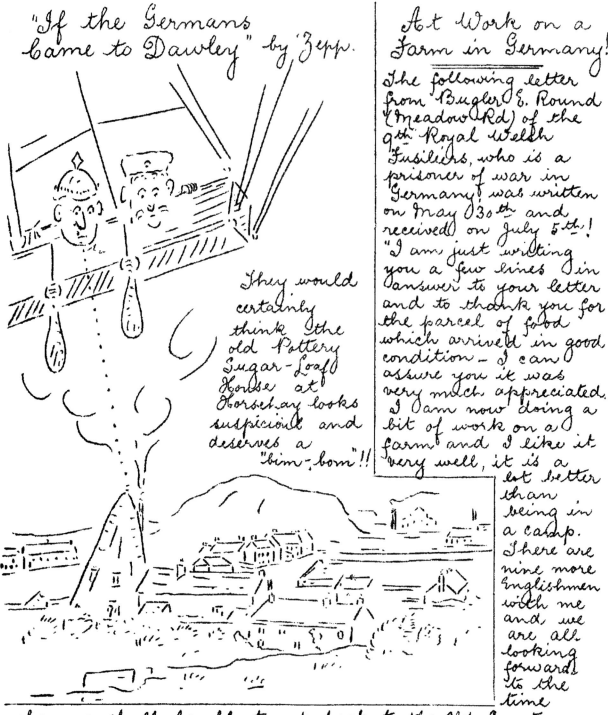

They would certainly think the old Pottery Sugar-Loaf House at Horsehay looks suspicious and deserves a "bim-bom"!!

At Work on a Farm in Germany!

The following letter from Bugler E. Round (Meadow Rd) of the 9th Royal Welsh Fusiliers, who is a prisoner of war in Germany, was written on May 30th and received on July 5th! "I am just writing you a few lines in answer to your letter and to thank you for the parcel of food which arrived in good condition – I can assure you it was very much appreciated. I am now doing a bit of work on a farm and I like it very well, it is a lot better than being in a camp. There are nine more Englishmen with me and we are all looking forward to the time when we shall be able to get back to the Old Country again. We often sing "There's a Silver Lining to the Dark Cloud Shining". We are getting some lovely weather here and our surroundings are fine."

(We invite our friends in different parts of the world to write to this soldier – no war-news or it will not pass the Censor. Ask Mr Wooding for his address)

L/Cpl. J. Davies writes from France "I am pleased to know that Dawley is going on alright if it is quiet but I expect they will liven it up a bit on August Monday, all being well. What a startling affair you had the other day – I can imagine the children following that bear and monkey about and the enjoyment it would give them. We are back for a week's rest and we want it badly for we have had a tough 24 days of it. A little rest helps us to pull ourselves together a bit, and we have a fine cinema that we can go to at night – it all helps to change the mind to brighter things and to forget the war for the time being. You would be surprised to see how a letter from home cheers us up even if it is only a short one."

Pte. E. Pitchford (son of the late Mr. E. Pitchford of Red Lake) a member of the Canadian Exped'y Force in France is "missing."

"When You Boys Come Home"

Will you please attend a Special Thanksgiving in the Chapel?

(A united Service of Intercession is being arranged at the end of July.)

Rev. F. A. Smith, late vicar of Doseley Church, preached the School Sermons there last Sunday.

Rev. H. M. Brook, B.Sc., the Wesleyan Minister leaves Dawley in August for Circuit work in Eastbourne.

A group-photograph of the soldiers of the Durham Regiment (who are employed at the Hollinswood Crusher,) appeared in the "Wellington Journal" last week.

The Rock School Treat is to take place on a Saturday, soon — they have now decided to have no Procession and no Band this year on the score of expense.

The buildings at Day's Works are slowly being dismantled and the gentleman with the pick-axe is about the only bit of life to be seen in this miniature wilderness of bricks — the stacks are not down yet.

"I'd sooner put up a place in Dawley than pull it down."

There are several local soldiers now at home, discharged through illness or wounds, J. Grice, W. Icke, N. Jones, J. B. Simmons. We are glad soldiers in their position will be able to wear a badge of distinction but the recently-issued Army Order does not appear to apply to men in mufti — the gold braid is only for use on uniform.

Pte. J. Furber writes from France:- "Thank you for the 'W. R.' which I receive every week. All the boys in my Platoon look out for it - they think it is fine. We are still at the trenches and the weather is getting better, one good job, as it is rough out here now."

Mr. F. J. Wooding has handed to us for the upkeep of this little paper £1, being the proceeds of the sale of envelopes bearing the Army "Field Post-mark." For our Postage Fund we have received the following: Miss Tranter. 30 stamps; Miss "P. B", 12 stamps. We shall be pleased to receive other contributions.

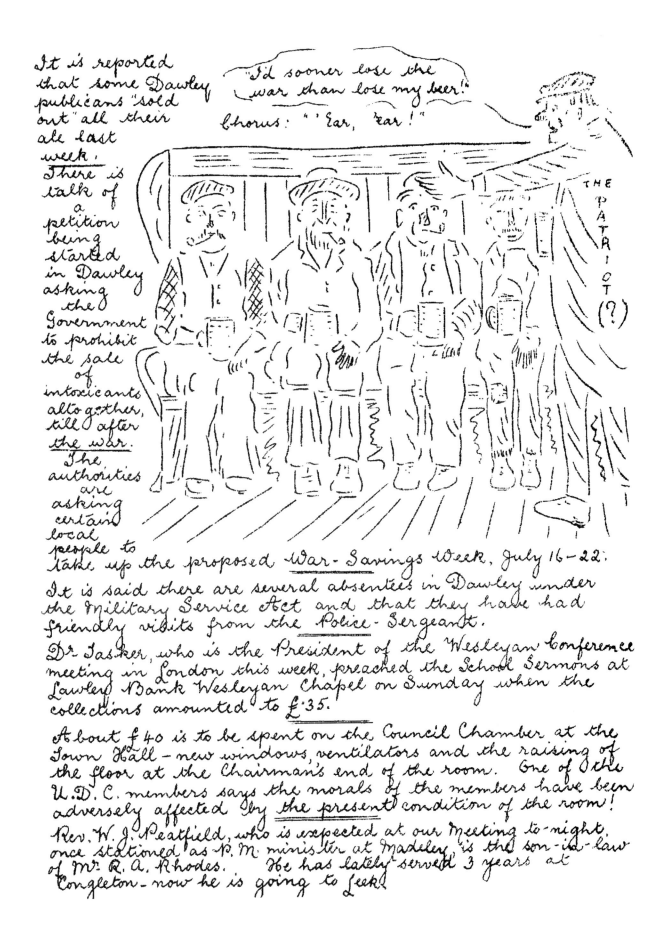

It is reported that some Dawley publicans "sold out" all their ale last week.

There is talk of a petition being started in Dawley asking the Government to prohibit the sale of intoxicants altogether, till after the war.

The authorities are asking certain local people to take up the proposed <u>War-Savings Week, July 16-22.</u>

It is said there are several absentees in Dawley under the Military Service Act and that they have had friendly visits from the Police-Sergeant.

Dr. Tasker, who is the President of the Wesleyan Conference meeting in London this week, preached the School Sermons at Dawley Bank Wesleyan Chapel on Sunday when the collections amounted to £35.

About £40 is to be spent on the Council Chamber at the Town Hall — new windows, ventilators and the raising of the floor at the Chairman's end of the room. One of the U.D.C. members says the morals of the members have been adversely affected by the <u>present</u> condition of the room!

Rev. W. J. Peatfield, who is expected at our Meeting to-night, once stationed as P.M. minister at Madeley, is the son-in-law of Mr. R. A. Rhodes. He has lately served 3 years at Congleton — now he is going to Leek.

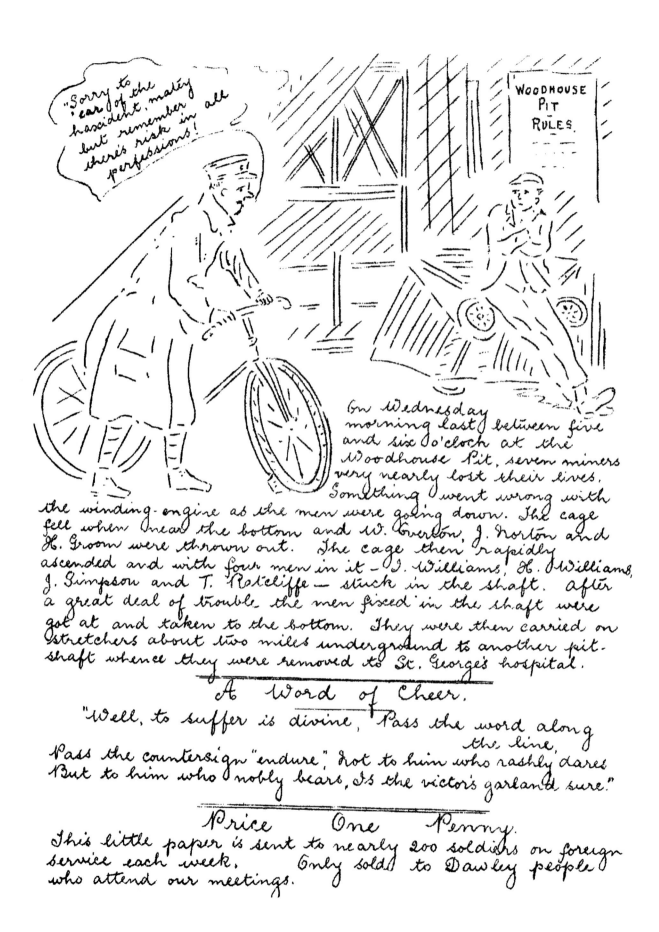

On Wednesday morning last between five and six o'clock at the Woodhouse Pit, seven miners very nearly lost their lives. Something went wrong with the winding-engine as the men were going down. The cage fell when near the bottom and W. Overton, J. Norton and H. Groom were thrown out. The cage then rapidly ascended and with four men in it – J. Williams, H. Williams, J. Simpson and T. Ratcliffe – stuck in the shaft. After a great deal of trouble the men fixed in the shaft were got at and taken to the bottom. They were then carried on stretchers about two miles underground to another pit-shaft whence they were removed to St. George's hospital.

A Word of Cheer.

"Well, to suffer is divine, Pass the word along the line,
Pass the countersign "endure"; Not to him who rashly dares
But to him who nobly bears, Is the victor's garland sure."

Price One Penny.

This little paper is sent to nearly 200 soldiers on foreign service each week. Only sold to Dawley people who attend our meetings.

Brotherhood and Sisterhood.
Dawley Baptist Chapel.
July 18th 1916.

Sergeant T. E. Davies of 46 Coy, Machine Gun Section writes from France on July 10th:— "Many thanks for the "W. R"— I can assure you it is well appreciated not only by myself but by friends of mine out here who have never seen Dawley. I think the work you are doing is fine and I wish you every success. We are too busy now to write long letters — we have a lot of work on hand."

"From cheerful English homes they came
From Irish cabin, Scottish hill:
They had no quarrel with the world,
No hate within, no lust to kill.

Yet here they died. For naught? the praise
When nations shall be born again,
And righteousness and peace shall kiss,
Be theirs, the army of the slain!

For every mound of Flemish earth
Shall witness bear, as men go by,
That greater things than life and death
Are Truth and Right, which cannot die."

Among soldiers recently reported to be "missing" is Corporal Norman Jones, younger son of the late Mr. Thomas Jones of Lawley Bank. Before enlisting he was in Lloyd's Bank, and joined the Berkshire Regiment.

"It's hard lines to work on August Monday but it's for the lads at the Front so I don't mind."

The decision to work on the first Monday in August has upset many holiday arrangements. Some local Sunday School Treats will take place on that day but the usual Methodist Demonstration, with procession through the streets, may be held on the previous Saturday.

On Sunday night Mr. Lester drew attention to the appeal which is being made to people to help to end the war by Saving and by purchasing War-Savings Certificates. At our Meeting to-night the Government plan is being explained. Anyone can help by buying a Certificate for 15/6 for which anyone who holds it will get £1 in 5 years time! If the money is needed before that time it can be withdrawn with interest. If 15/6 cannot be paid at once a War Savings Card can be procured at the Post Office on which 6d stamps can be stuck. The Card has 31 spaces and when it is full it will be exchanged for a War-Savings Certificate. Soldiers at the Front should urge their people at home to save in this way - it would be a good thing to find a bit in the Bank when you come home, wouldn't it?

"If the Germans came to Dawley"

Some of us might wish Big Billy Ball back!

The Horsehay Giant.

A wonderful picture-postcard is on sale in Dawley telling of the once famous William Ball, who was born at Horsehay on July 8th 1795. He worked for 40 years as Puddler and Shingler at the Coalbrookdale Co's works then located at Horsehay.

"The weight of this "Shropshire Giant" exceeded 40 stone. His dimensions were alleged to be Neck, 23½ inches, Arms, 27 inches, Breast, 70 inches, Calf of Leg, 25 inches, etc!"

Pte. W. H. Parton, R.A.M.C. writes from Salonica on June 30th thanking us for the book-prize and the cigarettes. "I found the Rev. A. E. Gwen Jones who was mentioned in the "W.R." - he is the Free Church Chaplain at the Salonica Hospital, he remembers Mr Lester and when I reminded him he had a good laugh about his walk in the Old Park years ago"

Before the Tribunal.

About 15 cases were dealt with at Dawley Town Hall on Friday last – two or three men were there under the Military Service Act – that is, they did not attest – they were not willing to do so. to serve until compelled These men are liable to less consideration, as a rule, than attested men.

Several farmers appealed for their men – they could not work their farms without them, they said. One small-holder asked for a few weeks for his man till he could get his hay in. "When will that be?" asked the Chairman. "Heaven only knows" was the reply – then he added "when the rain stops!"

A grocer's sub-manager was given a period, grocers' and bakers' assistants who deliver goods, only a short time – the idea being they must be replaced by others, if the war goes on. Quite lately, wheelwrights and boot and shoe repairers have been placed in the list of "certified occupations" and long periods were given to two men on these grounds. one month only. A farm-worker for whom an appeal was made declared he didn't know how old he was! His shaggy, antediluvian appearance was very interesting – the unanimous opinion of the Tribunal was he better remain in Dawley! A woman appealed for a son on the ground that he helped her more than either of her three other sons at home – this man was refused exemption as also was the son of a swing-boat proprietor. A man of 40 with 9 children, at work on explosives secured conditional exemption. It is acknowledged that the members often have a difficult task to decide fairly and squarely on the merits of a case.

Pte. J. Machin writes from France:- "Thank you for the "Reports" I receive so regularly. I laughed about that poetry on "Barbed Wire"- we were on a "wiring" expedition not many nights ago and when we got in next morning the "W. R" was waiting for me. The one who wrote it was not far out by what he said, for it's none too pleasant a job.... There's no one now in my Battalion from round about Dawley but still there are plenty of good lads here and we always try to help one another as much as possible. I saw one of my old mates yesterday - J. Yapp of Little Dawley. I am sorry A. W. Jones of Madeley has been wounded - he was a chum of mine at the Depôt. Glad the weather is finer - we have had plenty of rain of late."

We at home follow all the incidents report from the Fro____ in France with great interest. One item which stirred Dawley people on Monday morning was the report of a Cavalry Action in a corn-field. This is our artist's idea of it!

We are expecting to see at our Meeting to-night Corporal Underwood and Private Spencer of the Durham Regiment's Working Party engaged at Hollinswood, who will contribute to our programme. Also Will Hitchman, of the King George V - from the Battle of Jutland — to whom a little memento will be given. A collection is being taken on behalf of our General Funds, for which help is needed.

Pte. J. Bailey writes from Tanglin Barracks, Singapore:- "I pass the 'W.R' on to my friends to read and they do laugh at the sketches... We have had a new draft come out to us - C. Burns; J. Jonks and a few more from Dawley. They will get used to this country in time, the heat is very trying at first"

Pte. I. Furber writes to us frequently from France. In his letter received this week he says:- "I get your grand little paper every week - many thanks for it. We are still in the trenches, the weather has not been so bad lately I am glad to say. I was sorry to hear of N. Round, he was a pal of mine - we used to work together before the war."

"When You Boys Come Home"

Perhaps the Dawley U.D.C. will allow you to "camp out" in the Park. (Some men who come home on leave say it will be difficult for them to take to indoor life again)

Writing from Singapore L/Cpl. G. Frost says:- "We are all eager to know how our comrades are going on in different places and also the doings of our native town. We soldiers out in the East so many thousands of miles away, often think about you all at Dawley. We are all in the best of health and hope to keep so."

We shall be very glad if soldiers will write to us - many in France are now very busy, we know but some others may have leisure.

We do well to appoint seasons for prayer and to keep them. But in addition to this we should go through our work constantly praying. We should be saying, "Lord, help me," "Lord, bless me," "Lord, keep me," "Lord, forgive me." At every turn this dart may be thrown upward. Throw it when you are handling the letter which may contain bad news. Throw it when the image of some loved one grows clear to your mind. Throw it when you are solely tempted to passion or pride or dispair or in danger of death."

We acknowledge with thanks the following donations to our Postage Fund – "A Sisterhood Member" 48 stamps; "Crispin" 30 stamps; Mrs Brown, 4 stamps.

L/Cpl. A. Brittle writes from Hong Kong:– "I don't know when we are going to shift from this place but they tell us we are doing our bit out here. We should all like to go to the front."

The members of the K.S.L.I stationed at Hong Kong and Singapore complain of the torture of being kept there – with nothing to do!

An old form of Chinese punish-ment was to keep a culprit in the same position, with his hands tied.

During the week we have had a visit from an old Dawley soldier who served in the South African War and who offered his services at the outbreak of the present war, for home-service. For certain reasons it is best neither to give his name nor the places where he has been engaged. He began by serving at a German Internment Camp, then he was transferred to guard munition works, then to explosive stores, next to a German Prisoners-of-War Camp and finally to a place where Irishmen concerned in the recent rising in Ireland are detained.

Chorus "mercy, camarads!"

Driver H. Rowe writes from France:- "The great Push has commenced. On July 1st we were in the firing-line and we did our best. You can talk about a bombardment, the Germans can't touch our lads. Our chaps have only to get up on the parapet and the Germans jolly soon put up their hands. It does not say half in the papers what our lads are doing but they will soon put the finishing touch on the Germans now. I can't tell you all but the war can't last many more weeks. We are now sent back for a short, well-earned rest."

Price One Penny.

The "Weekly Report" is sent to nearly 200 soldiers on foreign service every week. It is only sold to Dawley people who attend our weekly meetings.

Weekly Report.

Tuesday,
July
25th
1916.

Brotherhood and Sisterhood.
Dawley Baptist Chapel.

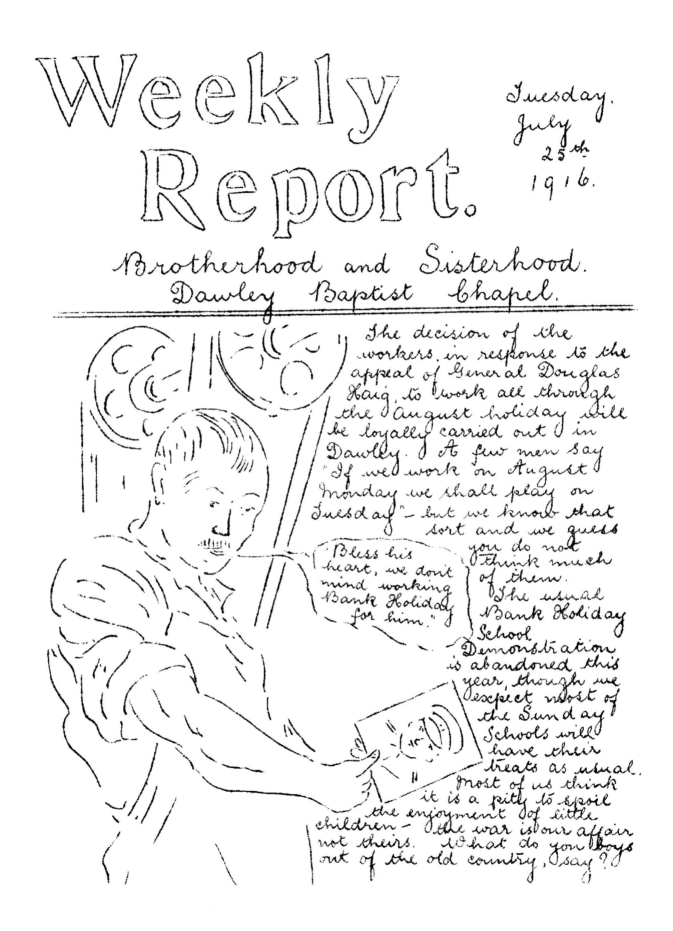

The decision of the workers, in response to the appeal of General Douglas Haig, to work all through the August holiday will be loyally carried out in Dawley. A few men say "If we work on August Monday we shall play on Tuesday" – but we know that sort and we guess you do not think much of them.

The usual Bank Holiday School Demonstration is abandoned this year, though we expect most of the Sunday Schools will have their treats as usual. Most of us think it is a pity to spoil the enjoyment of little children – the war is our affair not theirs. What do you boys out of the old country, I say?

"Bless his heart, we don't mind working Bank Holiday for him."

Pte. J. W. Price of the Cameron Highlanders writes from Sherwardine Hall, Market Drayton. "Before I left the Hospital I was showing the Night Sister the "Reports" and she asked me if I would mind lending them to her to read. I said "With pleasure" and when she brought them back she said she had had a good laugh over them. They went all round the Hospital – I think they have been through about a hundred hands.... This Convalescent Home is about six miles from Market Drayton, right in the country. We have plenty of games – bowls, tennis, football and cricket and the other day we were helping to pick the fruit as they are very short-handed just now."

The Night Nurse wanted to see them!

Will Hitchman of H.M.S. King George V called to see us on Thursday last when in the name of our meeting he was handed a useful Pocket-Book as a memento of the Jutland Battle in which his ship was willing to take part, but didn't! He has written the following letter. "Thank you very much indeed for the Pocket-Book which you have given me. I was sorry I could not get to your meeting last Tuesday but I was detained in Shrewsbury and I have to be on board again by Saturday morning" He says he thinks the most laughable thing he has to do is his washing and we have asked him to send us a sketch of this later on!

Rev. Colin. A. Roberts, a native of Dawley and who is remembered by many of our men, is a Wesleyan Chaplain at Aldershot. At a recent Sunday School meeting in the South of England he drew attention to the need of a stricter censorship over picture palaces attended by children.

Among the men who have recently been called up are W. V. Phillips (Variety Stores) and W. Bott (Horsehay). Both of them are in the R.G.A – the former at Winchester, the latter at Southsea. Mr. S. Phillips, the postman, has 'joined up' and his work is being done by a young lady.

"Beware of embarking on rough seas in inadequate cockle-shells."

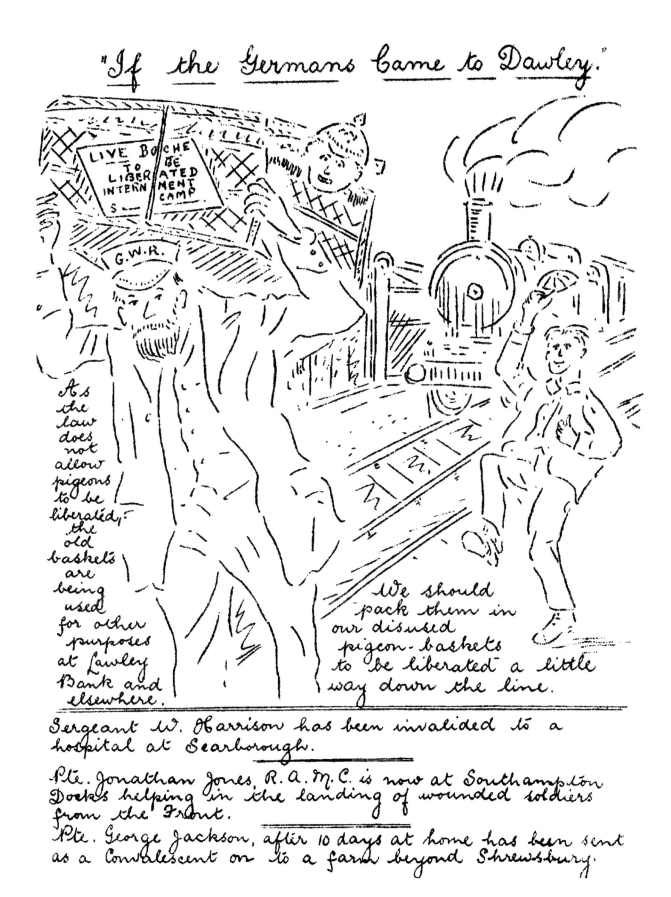

"If the Germans Came to Dawley."

As the law does not allow pigeons to be liberated, the old baskets are being used for other purposes at Lawley Bank and elsewhere.

We should pack them in our disused pigeon-baskets to be liberated a little way down the line.

Sergeant W. Harrison has been invalided to a hospital at Scarborough.

Pte. Jonathan Jones, R.A.M.C. is now at Southampton Docks helping in the landing of wounded soldiers from the Front.

Pte. George Jackson, after 10 days at home has been sent as a Convalescent on to a farm beyond Shrewsbury.

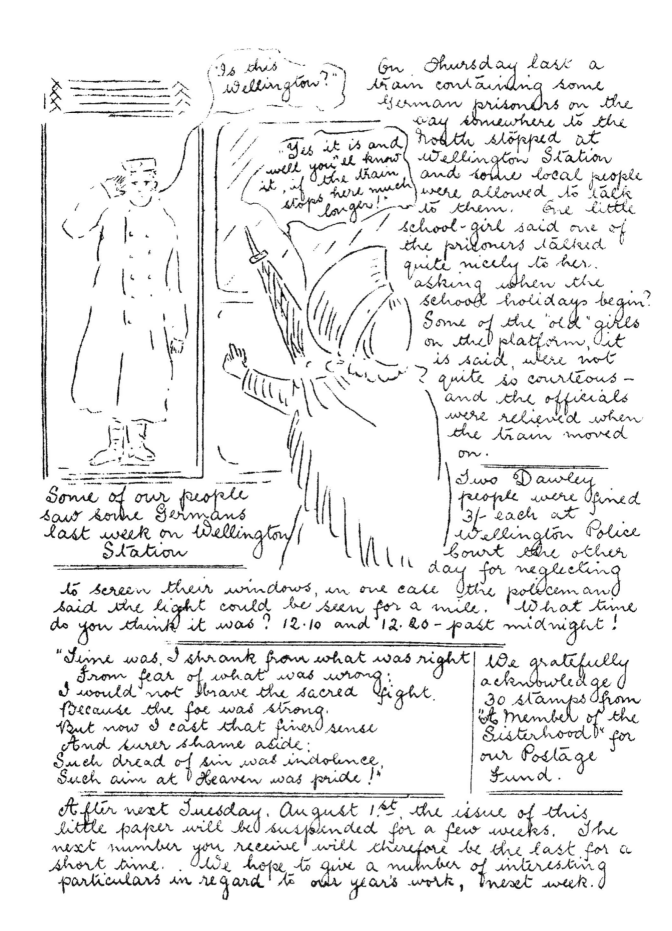

"Is this Wellington?"

"Yes it is and well you'll know it, if the train stops here much longer!"

Some of our people saw some Germans last week on Wellington Station

On Thursday last a train containing some German prisoners on the way somewhere to the north stopped at Wellington Station and some local people were allowed to talk to them. One little school-girl said one of the prisoners talked quite nicely to her. asking when the school holidays begin? Some of the "old" girls on the platform, it is said, were not quite so courteous – and the officials were relieved when the train moved on.

Two Dawley people were fined 3/- each at Wellington Police Court the other day for neglecting to screen their windows, in one case the policeman said the light could be seen for a mile. What time do you think it was? 12.10 and 12.20 – past midnight!

"Time was, I shrank from what was right
  From fear of what was wrong:
I would not brave the sacred fight.
Because the foe was strong.
But now I cast that finer sense
And surer shame aside:
Such dread of sin was indolence,
Such aim at Heaven was pride!"

We gratefully acknowledge 30 stamps from "A Member of the Sisterhood" for our Postage Fund.

After next Tuesday. August 1st, the issue of this little paper will be suspended for a few weeks. The next number you receive will therefore be the last for a short time. We hope to give a number of interesting particulars in regard to our year's work, next week.

At our meeting last week we were disappointed at the non-appearance of some who were expected, but in spite of that we had one of the best meetings of the season. On the previous evening there arrived in Lawley Bank Rev. Chas. Perry — son of the late Rev. Isaiah Perry who went out from Lawley Bank to Australia many years ago — on a visit to his aged grandmother. He is about 30 years of age and after a College course of 4 years he entered the Methodist ministry at Adelaide, whence he enlisted as a Chaplain to the Australian Expeditionary Forces. Leaving Adelaide about Christmas time, he and the men of his division went to Egypt for training, arriving in this country only a few days ago. Chaplain Perry expects to leave for France at any time to fill any vacancy which may occur. His address was very interesting, reminiscent of the freedom and brightness of Australian life. One of his stories concerning a soldier on the ship on the voyage from Australia stopping a gramophone record "His Mother's Prayer" "because he couldn't stand it" will not be readily forgotten by those present.

"When You Boys Come Home."

Next August Bank-Holiday Monday

Perhaps you'll want to go to Buildwas Abbey.

The "Weekly Report" in the Hands of the Censor!

("Please Mr. Censor, forgive us the following bit of fun — don't cross out any more than you can help — we are very careful what we put in our little paper.")

"We must not allow the Germans to assume they will get to Dawley!"

English Censor.

IF THE GERMANS CAME TO DAWLEY

Stoker George Rowe of the R.N.R. interned at Groningen, Holland, writes after a long silence saying he has been seriously ill but is now better and at the camp again. We are pleased to hear he is receiving the "W.R." (we imagined the authorities were not allowing it to pass) — but he says his copies are censored — the soldiers' names and addresses are crossed out.

In the course of his letter Stoker Rowe says:- "The 'Reports' are very good - even if they are censored and when I was ill they came alright. I was sorry to read of the death of Eric Bailey... I was pleased to see that my brother Sidney had been giving an address at the meeting - I wish

"Good Heavens! We must not allow the R.N.R. men to think they are ever going home."

Dutch Censor.

"WHEN YOU BUYS COME HOME."

I could have been there to hear it. Things are much the same here, we have a new Recreation Hall in place of the one that was burnt down at the beginning of the year, but I hope we shall not require it for long. I put the wet weather out here down to the 'Gun-firing'."

Pte. R. Huggins, after being ill two or three times in the course of training has been appointed to the Remount Department, Bush Camp, Pembroke Dock.

Among local soldiers who have recently landed in France are L/Cpl. George Collis and Pte. Seth Baugh, eldest son of Mr. Mark Baugh, Old Park.

At the Dawley end of the town the sensation of the week has been the fall of the tall chimney-stack on the now almost vacant site of Day's Works. It took place on Saturday last, when many local celebrities were present.

"It fell — and great was the fall of it"

Owing to increased cost of paper and alleged scarcity the "Wellington Journal" has been reduced to eight pages. For a few evenings the "Express and Star" stated that one penny would be charged for it, but on Saturday it was announced that it would still be a halfpenny — they think it better to keep it 1/2d if they wish to keep their customers. And the "W.R" remains the same size & same price!

Pte. E. Baxter writes from the Balkans on July 3rd. "Your "W. R" I receive every week, the last one was dated June 13th. You must excuse me for not writing before but we have been a bit busy lately. Everybody in my Platoon likes to have a look at the "Report" - they say how neat and pretty it is all combined together. I don't know when we boys out here are coming home but when we do we shall have some things to tell you about the Balkans.

The old Jews believed Beelzebub was the god of flies - has he a bungalow in the Balkans, Baxter?

"The flies out here are something dreadful. millions of them tormenting one day and night, there are about 100 on my hand while I am writing this letter."

I am sorry one of my chums. L/Cpl. W. Sart of the Finger is missing.

Pte. Harold Hollis writes from France:- "Thank you for your letters and "Reports". We have got a few Dawley boys with us now and we often talk about old times. We have had some awful weather just lately but that is caused by the heavy bombardment which is still in progress."

Pte. E. Jackson, after 10 days at home has gone to a convalescent camp at Buxton. His brother Herbert - another member of the Baptist congregation, has recently joined the Army.

Price One Penny.

This little paper is sent by post to about 200 Dawley soldiers on foreign service every week. It is only sold to Dawley people who attend our meetings

The demolition of the chimney stack at Day's Works on July 22, 1916.

Dawley High Street, probably shortly before World War One. The town's Market Hall is on the right.

The Horsehay Works was one of the major employers in the Dawley area, while the Round House - part of an area known as Horsehay Potteries - and nearby cinder hill, were distinctive features on the landscape.

WEEKLY REPORT.

Tuesday,
August 1st
1916.

Brotherhood and Sisterhood.
Dawley Baptist Chapel.

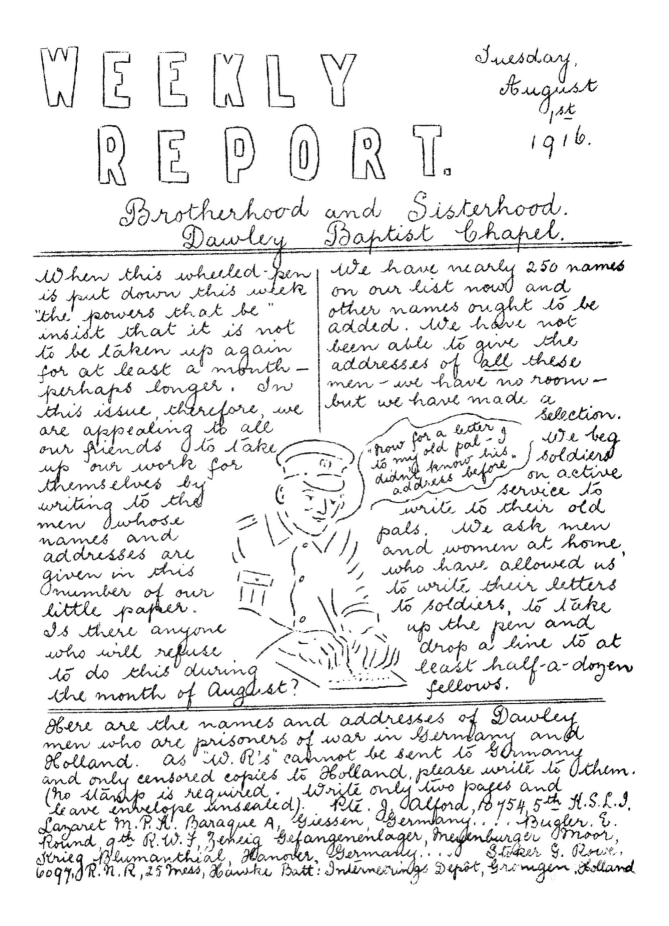

When this wheeled-pen is put down this week "the powers that be" insist that it is not to be taken up again for at least a month — perhaps longer. In this issue, therefore, we are appealing to all our friends to take up our work for themselves by writing to the men whose names and addresses are given in this number of our little paper. Is there anyone who will refuse to do this during the month of August?

We have nearly 250 names on our list now and other names ought to be added. We have not been able to give the addresses of all these men — we have no room — but we have made a selection.

"Now for a letter to my old pal - I didn't know his address before."

We beg soldiers on active service to write to their old pals. We ask men and women at home, who have allowed us to write their letters to soldiers, to take up the pen and drop a line to at least half-a-dozen fellows.

Here are the names and addresses of Dawley men who are prisoners of war in Germany and Holland. As "W. R's" cannot be sent to Germany and only censored copies to Holland, please write to them. (No stamp is required. Write only two pages and leave envelope unsealed). Pte. J. Alford, 10754, 5th. K.S.L.I. Lazaret M.P.K. Baraque A, Giessen, Germany..... Bugler. E. Round, 9th R.W.F, Zweig Gefangenenlager, Mecklenburger Moor, Krieg Blumanthial, Hanover, Germany..... Stoker G. Rowe, 6097, R.N.R, 25 mess, Hawke Batt: Interneerings Depôt, Gromgen, Holland

Remember lots of you who are interested in our work have been content to let us write for you for a year, now its your turn — will you fail the brave men abroad?

"True, I've sent dozens of "W. R's" but now I've got to write some personal letters. Shall I, or shall I not sign my name to them?"

Pte. Bert Archer, 15423 6th K.S.L.I 20th Div. I.B.D. A.P.O. S/17. B.E.F.

Pte. J. Bailey 1926, E. Coy, 4th K.S.L.I Singapore S.S

Cyclist A. Barker, 22nd Div. Cyclist Corps, Salonica Forces Greece.

Pte. E. Baxter 16651 C Coy 8th K.S.L.I. B.E.F. c/o G.P.O.

Pte. S. Bird, 5586 No 2 Section. 69 M.G. Coy. M.G. Corps, B.E.F.

Pte. J. Bishop, 15438, 8th K.S.L.I B.E.F. c/o G.P.O.

Sergt Frank Bott, 28675 2nd Cavalry Division, Aux. Horse Transport Coy, B.E.F.

Pte. W. A. Brooks 18927, B. Coy. 5th K.S.L.I. B.E.F.

Corporal J. Bullock, 4th K.S.L.I Hong Kong. China

Pte. T. Butler 19140, D Coy, Sappers Platoon, 2nd South Staffs, B.E.F.

Pte. M. Cadman 3816 g, B. Coy. 2nd Garr: Batt: R.W. Fusiliers, Egyptian Forces.

Pte. H. Corbett, 5588 69 Machine Gun Co., 69 Brigade M.G. Corps, B.E.F.

Driver E. Edwards, 105658 No 1 Sec. P.A.C. 12 F.A., 9th Division B.E.F.

Pte. W. Ewings, 12441, B. Coy. 6 Platoon, 8th K.S.L.I, B.E.F. c/o G.P.O.

Bombardier R. Harley 20457 1st Siege Battery, R.G.A., B.E.F.

Sapper R. James, 43564 82 Field Coy R.E., B.E.F.

Pte. E. Archer 15444, 8th K.S.L.I. B.E.F. c/o G.P.O.

Sergt. J. Arden Headquarters Co. 12 Div. Train A.S.C. B.E.F.

Pte. Chas. Ayres, 10543, A Coy 3 Platoon, 1st King's L'pool Regt. B.E.F.

Pte. Seth Baugh, 22046, A Coy, 6th, K.S.L.I B.E.F. c/o G.P.O.

Gunner Bodkin, 43065 C. Coy, 1st Canadian Contingent Divisional Artillery, 1st Heavy Battery, 1st Group, B.E.F.

Sapper H. L. Brown, 74435, 3rd Sig: Squadron 3rd Cavalry Div: B.E.F.

Pte. Jack Butler, 10753, 14 Div. Training Co. New Zealand T.C. B.E.F.

Pte. F. Buttery, 6563, B Coy, 5 Platoon, 1st K.S.L.I. B.E.F.

Pte. A. E. Corbett, 1912. A Coy, 4th K.S.L.I. Hong Kong, China.

Sergt. J. Farr, 34711, No 1 Car — Vet. Hospital. Le Havre France

L/Cpl. G. Frost 1451 E. Coy. 4th K.S.L.I. Singapore

Pte. Herbert Bailey 118.76, A Coy, 6th K.S.L.I. B.E.F.

Pte. C. A. Ball, 23509, 6th K.S.L.I. 20th Divⁿ S/14 Inf: Base Depôt, A.P.O. B.E.F.

Pte. E. P. Brown, 1639, C. Coy., 4th K.S.L.I. Hong Kong.

Pte. C. T. Collier 13337, D Coy: 14 Platoon, 8th K.S.L.I. B.E.F. c/o G.P.O.

Pte. E. Deakin, 20297, A Coy., 1st K.S.L.I. 6th Inf: Div: B.E.F.

Pte. A. Harriman, 11946, B. Coy., 6th K.S.L.I. B.E.F.

Pte. Percy Howells 17139, Machine Gunner 2nd Northumberland Fusiliers B.E.F.

Sergt. W. Hughes, 47378, 4th Garr: Batt: R.W.F. A.P.O. S/8 B.E.F.

Sergt. F. Langford, 7133, D Coy. 5th K.S.L.I. B.E.F.

Pte. Alf. Lloyd 14656, A Coy., 7th K.S.L.I. B.E.F.

Pte. H. Mason, 6238, 2nd K.S.L.I. 27th Inf: Base Depôt Rouen, France.

Staff-Sergt. H. Morris, A.S.C. 32/016339, 9 Field Bakery. B.E.F.

Ptes. J. & W. Oakley, 4th K.S.L.I. Hong Kong.

Pte. O. Phillips 15364, B. Coy., 8th K.S.L.I. B.E.F. c/o G.P.O.

Driver A. Round 79419, 459 Battery, R.F.A 1 Canⁿ Divⁿ B.E.F.

Sergt. Skelton 1556, B Coy., 4th K.S.L.I. Singapore S.S.

Pte. F. E. Tart, 2052, A Coy., 4th K.S.L.I. Hong Kong

Pte. Jack Williams, 10760, 177 Coy., R.E. B.E.F.

Pte. W. Williams, 17190, A Coy., 4 Platoon 2nd South Staffs. B.E.F.

Pte. L. Bailey, 15440, A Coy, 6th K.S.L.I. B.E.F.

Sergt. C. P. Ball A. Coy., 4th K.S.L.I. Hong Kong, China.

Cpl. E. Candlin, 10105, A Coy. 3 Platoon, 4th K.S.L.I. B.E.F.

L/Cpl. H. Dacre, 12566, C. Coy., 12 Platoon, 2nd South Staffords, B.E.F.

Pte. John Holmes, 15757, A Coy., 8th K.S.L.I. B.E.F. c/o G.P.O.

Pte. J. Kelsey, 1574, 4th K.S.L.I. Hong Kong.

Pte. J. Bailey 18532, 1st K.S.L.I. 6th Inf: Base Depôt B.E.F.

Cpl. J. Brickley. 6599, C Coy., 1st K.S.L.I. B.E.F.

Pte. W. Crocker, 22367, D Coy., 3rd K.S.L.I. B.E.F.

Pte. L. Halford 16646, 2 Platoon 8th K.S.L.I. B.E.F. c/o G.P.O.

Pte. A. Holbrook, 8847–9 Coy., 3rd K.S.L.I. B.E.F.

Pte. A. Kelsey, 15070, Z Coy., 2nd K.S.L.I. B.E.F. c/o G.P.O.

Pte. A. Morton, 15043, 14 Divⁿ Mining Co. c/o New Zealand Tunnelling Co. B.E.F.

L/Cpl. W. Oliver, 9829, Y Coy, 2nd K.S.L.I. Salonica Forces.

Pte. H. Purcell 1453, E. Coy. 4th K.S.L.I. Singapore, S.S.

Pte. G. Roberts, 1575, C Coy., 4th K.S.L.I. Hong Kong.

Pte. Jos. Shepherd, 12515 R.A.M.C. L.M.S. Letitia, c/o G.P.O. London.

Pte. James Sherwood, 2976, 4th K.S.L.I. Hong Kong.

Pte. H. Skelton, 2045 C Coy., 4th K.S.L.I. Hong Kong.

L/Cpl. L. Tart 1542, B. Coy., 4th K.S.L.I. Singapore, S.S.

Driver C. Woolger, 147 M.M.L. Section 3. 46 Divisional Ammunition Colⁿ B.E.F.

"True, I've given a subscription but I've never written a letter myself, but here goes, it's a pity the thing should stop."

Aren't these men, who are far from home, worth writing to?

"Keep the home-fires burning
While your hearts are yearning,
Though the lads are far away
They dream of home.
There's a silver lining
Through the dark cloud shining.
Turn the dark cloud inside out
Till the Boys Come Home"

We are deeply obliged to Miss F. Blocksidge (Madeley) for the excellent entertainment she arranged for us last Tuesday. A very enjoyable evening was spent – songs, piano and violin items and the two sketches were appreciated by all. Miss Lowe (Oakengates) sang "Little Grey Home in the West" and "Till the Boys Come Home – both of which created great enthusiasm. The other artistes did equally well and we hope to see several of them again at our meetings later on.

Pte. Howard Brothwood, 15219, 6th K.S.L.I. A. Coy, B.E.F. writes:– "We have lately been moved, and no one knows only we who are out here, what it is like. If it had not been for our artillery we should have been cut up."

Miss Winnie Lowe asked the people at last Tuesday's meeting to join in the Chorus – and they did!

Pte. S. Davies. 15504, B. Coy. 10th Worcester Regt. B.E.F. writes:– "I am pleased to say I am going on well, considering the rough time we have had lately. We are still advancing but if you could see the places the Germans have been holding you would think they would never be moved. They were in cellars 20 or 30 feet down and as soon as our big guns would stop they would come out of their nest with their machine-guns and start banging away. But we got the best of them, some running away and others shouting for mercy."

Pte. T. Furber, 12221, B. Coy. 6th K.S.L.I. B.E.F. says he saw Pte. J. W. Archer in the camp the other day but he did not speak to him as he does not know him personally.

Pte. W. J. Harrison, 12069, C. Coy., 6th K.S.L.I. Headquarters, B.E.F. writes:- "I daresay you were all very pleased to hear the good news which is going round at present. But there will be even better news, I hope, before long. I wish to tender my heartfelt thanks to all who participate in your good work at Dawley."

Pte. J. W. Archer, 3215 C. F. Coy, 2nd Scots Guards, B.E.F. says:- "I am writing this in my dug-out. There is heavy firing on both sides but I hope they do not hit us, for I have got a bit of Dawley cake for tea.... Things are looking brighter all round. I met some Dawley lads a few days ago - young Soames, Herb. Bailey and Bert Archer."

Holidays at Home.

... a few people, I suppose, are

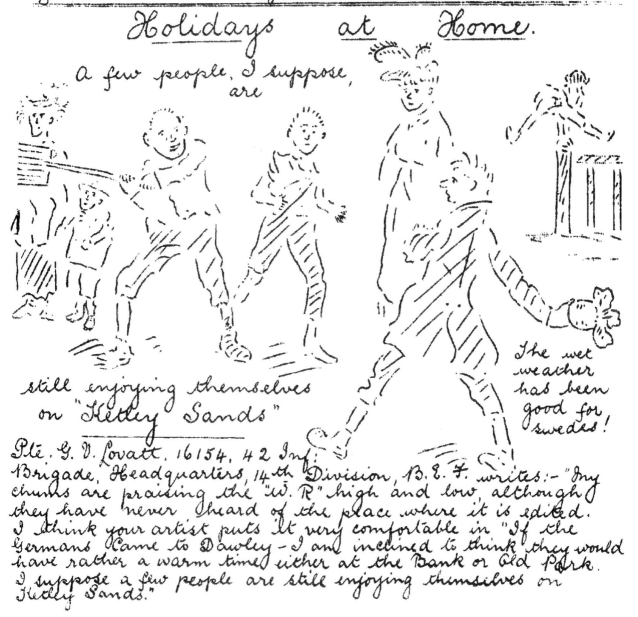

still enjoying themselves on "Ketley Sands"

The wet weather has been good for swedes!

Pte. G. V. Lovatt, 16154, 42 Inf. Brigade, Headquarters, 14th Division, B.E.F. writes:- "My chums are praising the "W.R." high and low, although they have never heard of the place where it is edited. I think your artist puts it very comfortable in "If the Germans Came to Dawley - I am inclined to think they would have rather a warm time either at the Bank or Old Park. I suppose a few people are still enjoying themselves on Ketley Sands."

At the outbreak of war, now nearly two years ago, our men's and women's meeting was merged into one and practically all the energies of the meeting devoted to work for Dawley soldiers out of this country. The second year which is now closing, has been fairly successful and we appreciate the help which has been rendered by many friends.

First and foremost comes the name of Mr. F.T. Wooding, who has had charge of the Register of Soldiers, has seen to the despatch of all parcels and the preparation of (lately) nearly 200 envelopes for letters, etc. each week. Miss May Rowe has given valuable clerical help to Mr. Wooding. Mrs Lavender, Miss Breeze and Miss Walker have acted as treasurers to various funds.

The meetings have been well-attended and we express our thanks to scores of people who have assisted us in them. Messrs C.H. Taylor, E. Brookes, H. Chilton, J. Tranter and C. Tranter and several lady friends have done good service.

The "Weekly Report" during the year, has become an important branch of our service. The first number was issued on Sept: 28th - just a reproduction of soldiers' letters, the demand for it has grown steadily until we are now producing 200 copies a week. Many people buy them at the meeting and after reading them post them in our envelopes to soldiers. Where soldiers are not likely to get a copy we send them direct - sometimes we have to send 100 and more. In the sales and posting we are indebted to Mrs. H. Chilton, Mrs Roberts, Miss Bill Miss Roberts and others.

The work of preparing the "W.R" is considerable - no matter how quickly the reader worked he or she could not do it in less than 20 - 24 hours each week! We have used up about 10,000 sheets of paper - which means that 40,000 pages have had to be printed with a hand-roller. We wish some good friend would give or lend us a machine until the close of the war so that we could produce up to, say 500 copies a week. We shall need them.

Postage Fund. We acknowledge with thanks the following:- Miss "P.B". 12 stamps; "Mr. E. B's" Class, 6 stamps. (Since the opening of this Fund in March last, 2,288 penny stamps have been contributed)

Sergt. W. Hughes writes from France on July 26th:- "I have just a few minutes leisure so felt I must write a line to thank you for your cheery little booklet. I had been told to expect it but when it arrived it quite surprised me as you know what a soldier would expect to receive - something dry! My comrades were much interested in the sketches and wanted to know if William Ball happened to be any relation to John Bull! I am sorry I cannot tell you much news - it would only be censored if I did, but if you care to have a few picture - postcards I shall be pleased to send them."

A House-to-house Collection has been made in Dawley during this last week on behalf of the Red Cross.

L/Cpl J. Davies, 45284, 84 Field Coy. R.E. B.E.F.

Pte. Stephen Davies, 15823, 8th K.S.L.I., B.E.F. c/o G.P.O.

Sergt. J.E. Davies, 3319, 46 Coy. Machine Gun Corps. B.E.F.

Rifleman J.A. Davies, 7483, B. Coy, 8 Platoon, 1st King's Royal Rifles, B.E.F.

Pte. J. Evans, 6333, 2nd K.S.L.I. B.E.F. c/o G.P.O.

Pte. A.P. Jones, 16940, D Group Observation Section, 2nd Field Survey Coy, Anzac H.A., B.E.F.

Pte. W. Jones, 15419 B Coy, 5 Platoon, 8th K.S.L.I. B.E.F. c/o G.P.O.

Sergt. P. Morgan, D Coy, 5th K.S.L.I. B.E.F. c/o G.P.O.

L/Cpl Geo. Phillips, 19845, 42nd Brigade Machine Gun Coy, 14th Light Division. B.E.F.

Pte. Philip Powell, 1479, E. Coy, 4th K.S.L.I. Singapore, S.S.

Sergt. J.H. Price, 10518, A Coy 5th K.S.L.I. B.E.F.

Pte. A.R. Pugh, 700, C Coy 15th Service Batt. Royal Warwick Regt B.E.F.

Signaller E. Lloyd Roberts, 12841, B. Coy, 8th K.S.L.I. Signalling Section. B.E.F. c/o G.P.O.

When you write you need not use a pin with a wheel on the tip as we have to do in producing the W.R. Do you notice all our lines and curves are a series of little dots? The teeth of the wheel cut little holes in a stencil sheet from which 200 copies are made.

Sergt. S. Hardman, 4509, B. Battery, 61 (How) Brigade, R.F.A Guards Div B.E.F.

Pte. John Harley, 15197, A Coy, 3 Platoon, 8th K.S.L.I., B.E.F. c/o G.P.O.

W. Hitchman. Cook's Mate, 59 Mess, H.M.S King George V, c/o G.P.O. London.

Signaller Thos. Hobson, 7251, A Coy, 6th K.S.L.I. B.E.F.

Pte. H. Hollis, 18926, A Coy, 1 Platoon 6th K.S.L.I. B.E.F.

Pte. T.H. Jones, 7736, X Coy, 2nd K.S.L.I. B.E.F. c/o G.P.O.

Pte. Noah Jones, 1501, E.Coy, 4th K.S.L.I. Singapore, S.S.

Pte. J. Machin, 21724 No.2 Coy, 6 Platoon 1st Grenadier Guards, B.E.F.

Pte. Merrington, 16391, Y Coy 2nd K.S.L.I, Salonica Forces.

Pte. W.H. Parton 61957 R.A.M.C, 21st Stationary Hospital, Salonica Forces. c/o G.P.O.

Pte. W.L. Perry, 1814, 27th Batt. 2nd A.D. B.D. c/o G.P.O 3/17. B.E.F.

Sergt. T. Pitchford, A Coy. 3 Platoon, 8th K.S.L.I B.E.F. c/o G.P.O.

Pte. W.E. Powell 2596, 1/1 Shropshire Yeomanry British Medit.n Forces.

L/Cpl R.G. Richards, 14306, D. Coy, 7th K.S.L.I. B.E.F.

Pte. L. Roberts 13338. D Coy, 8th K.S.L.I. B.E.F. c/o G.P.O.

Gunner Sart, 112 Battery, R.F.A. B.E.F.

Gunner E. Round, 77353, 21st Div. R.F.A 94 Brigade, 6 Battery, Medit.n Exped.y Force

Pte. G. Round, 8938. A Coy, 1st K.S.L.I. B.E.F.

Driver H. Rowe, T/027803, 63rd Field Ambulance, 21st Div. Train R.A.M.C. c/o G.P.O, London.

Cpl. J. Smith, No 1 Siege Co. R.M.R.E. B.E.F.

Pte. G. Taylor 16645, C Coy, 10 Platoon, 8th K.S.L.I. B.E.F. c/o G.P.O.

Pte. S. Small, 58273. 142 F. Ambulance Corps. B.E.F.

Pte. L Taylor 15223 6th K.S.L.I. B.E.F.

Pte. P. Tonks, 12229, C. Coy. 6th K.S.L.I B.E.F.

Pte. T. Tranter, 15416, C. Coy. 10 Platoon, 8th K.S.L.I B.E.F. c/o G.P.O

Pte. T. Tranter 1911. A coy, 4th K.S.L.I Hong Kong China

Our thanks are due to many soldiers who have written us, appreciating our work during the year. without these tokens of the worth of our endeavour we certainly should not have gone on.

We regret we have so little space for soldiers' letters this week but all received up to this evening are being read at to-night's meeting, which is of an informal character.

If, during the next month, soldiers care to write to us will they please address their letters - "W.R" c/o (Miss) G. Lester, General Post Office, Aylesbury, Bucks. We shall be specially pleased to receive foreign picture-postcards of places in which Dawley soldiers are interested, particularly if a few words of description can be added. Some of these post-cards may be used in future issues of the "W.R."

It is generally acknowledged that the Y.M.C.A is doing a splendid work in different parts of the world where our soldiers are located and some of us are anxious to take part in its practical work.

Some of the labour hitherto put into the production of this little paper may now be put into Y.M.C.A work in a big camp in England, about 120 miles away from Dawley, where 20,000 soldiers are in training. There's nothing like seeing things as they really are!

Price One Penny.

This is sent to about 200 soldiers now out of this country. No other issue will be prepared till our meetings re-commence in September.

Dawley News

For Soldiers Abroad.

September 19th 1916.

Brotherhood and Sisterhood
Dawley Baptist Chapel.

Once more we commence the issue of our little weekly paper, which has ceased since August 1st. We have received many letters from our friends to which we are quite unable to reply. One soldier asks bluntly why we should have taken a rest while so many others are fighting or working? Another soldier says he is glad we have had a holiday because we needed "renovating"!

The people who have most to do with the production of this paper have taken some part in social and religious work in a Y.M.C.A. Hut in a large Training Camp somewhere in England during their holidays.

Hurrah! Here we are again! The old "W.R" with a new name!

They have looked night after night into the faces of hundreds of Suffolks, Norfolks, Cambridgeshires and R.A.M.C men, and they have brought home from the Camp among other things, some of the songs the soldiers sing.

Having begun here at Dawley Bank we hope to continue. We are trying to send this to at least 200 Dawley soldiers who are out of this country every week. If it is found Dawley soldiers do not receive it we shall be very glad of their names and addresses. On the other hand, we hope all soldiers who receive this will write to us and send sketches — original, please!

Dacre in Delville Wood.

L/Cpl H. Dacre writes from No 4 Ward, Mill Road Infirmary, Liverpool. "I have been wounded in Delville wood in close quarters with the famous German Crown Prince's Army - the Brandenburger's, and we had the time of our lives. Our respected Colonel issued orders and you may guess we did what we were told. I have had the bullets taken out and I have them as a keep-sake - the doctor told me they were a good souvenir of the Great Push. When they ask me what I did in the Great War I shall be able to say I stopped two German bullets - but I am proud to be alive, for it is the third time I have been wounded. Please send me your little paper again."

Stoker George Rowe (interned in Holland) says:- "Holland is not a very bright place for a prisoner of war but we try to make ourselves as comfortable as possible under the circumstances. We all have our troubles at this crisis and I have had mine, but I am better in health now."

Several aeroplanes have visited the district lately. One settled down for a few hours within easy reach of the Finger on Sunday evening week to the great interest of people in the locality. Another came to the ground near Madeley last week owing to engine trouble, and remained there several days.

"That's right, mate, make yourself acquainted with the look of Dawley."

Cyclist A. Barker writes from Malta "I have been in a hospital in Salonica but am now booked for England. Our men seem to be introducing themselves to the Bulgars, for a few wounded came into Malta the other day... I don't wish to do any more cycling in the Balkans, I should like to do the rest of my soldiering in France."

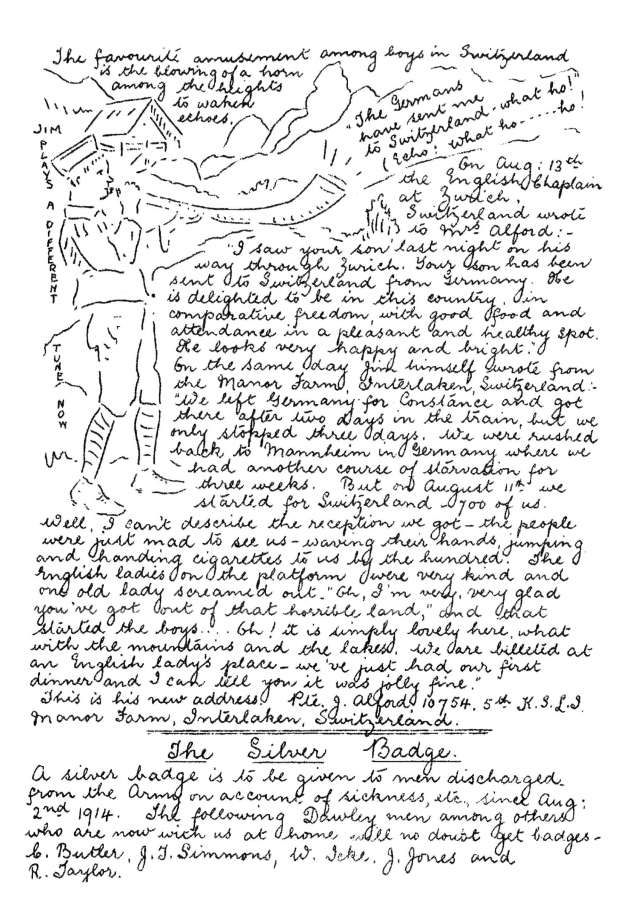

The favourite amusement among boys in Switzerland is the blowing of a horn among the heights to waken echoes.

JIM PLAYS A DIFFERENT TUNE NOW

"The Germans have sent me to Switzerland. what ho!" (Echo: what ho----ho!)

On Aug: 13th the English Chaplain at Zurich, Switzerland wrote to Mrs Alford:-

"I saw your son last night on his way through Zurich. Your son has been sent to Switzerland from Germany. He is delighted to be in this country, in comparative freedom, with good food and attendance in a pleasant and healthy spot. He looks very happy and bright."

On the same day Jim himself wrote from the Manor Farm, Interlaken, Switzerland:- "We left Germany for Constance and got there after two days in the train, but we only stopped three days. We were rushed back to Mannheim in Germany where we had another course of starvation for three weeks. But on August 11th we started for Switzerland –700 of us.

Well, I can't describe the reception we got – the people were just mad to see us – waving their hands, jumping and handing cigarettes to us by the hundred. The English ladies on the platform were very kind and one old lady screamed out."Oh, I'm very, very glad you've got out of that horrible land," And that started the boys....Oh! it is simply lovely here, what with the mountains and the lakes. We are billeted at an English lady's place – we've just had our first dinner and I can tell you it was jolly fine."

This is his new address. Pte. J. Alford 10754. 5th K.S.L.I. Manor Farm, Interlaken, Switzerland.

The Silver Badge.

A silver badge is to be given to men discharged from the Army on account of sickness, etc., since Aug: 2nd 1914. The following Dawley men among others who are now with us at home will no doubt get badges. C. Butler, J.J. Simmons, W. Icke, J. Jones and R. Taylor.

Yesterday morning, Mr A. Teece, 18 Church Rd received word that his son, Pte. H. Ashley was killed in action about two months ago. He was previously reported "missing" and we have been making enquiries about this soldier.

Sergeant Tom Davies (Lawley Bank) wounded in action has had his leg and thigh amputated in a French hospital. He is now at Netley.

Sergeant W. Hughes (Chapel St) writes appreciatively of this little paper. He says they have had much to put up with from flies and dust. He suggests Dawley Urban Council should send out its water cart for use on their dusty roads, torn up by the heavy traffic.

Pte A. P. Jones (Lawley Farm) says he has now left the French convent and "the congenial company of the friendly nuns" and once again become "one of those who live in dens and caves, in holes and caverns of the earth."

"It's a Long Long Trail" from this place to Dawley.

A p.p.c. has been sent by a Dawley soldier but the name of the place has been deleted.

A book-prize will be sent to the first Dawley soldier abroad who identifies this place in his letter. He must not be stationed there, however.

At our meeting to-night we are expecting Dr. Woodhouse, Misses Eva Clay and Winnie Lowe. A collection is being taken for the family of the late Pte. S. Small, R.A.M.C.

We sing this every Tuesday now
"Be with all the loved ones
whom we miss to-night
In the hours of danger
Keep them calm and bright.
From the camp and trenches,
From the battle-plain,
From the mine-sown ocean
Bring them safe again.

Remember, you are never out of our thoughts, never forgotten in our prayers.

German prisoners-of war are now working at Priorslee and Donnington at cinder-heaps, but the general public are not allowed to see them.

The whole front of the Lord Hill has been recently painted and the Webb Fountain cleaned and painted which has quite brightened up that part of the High Street.

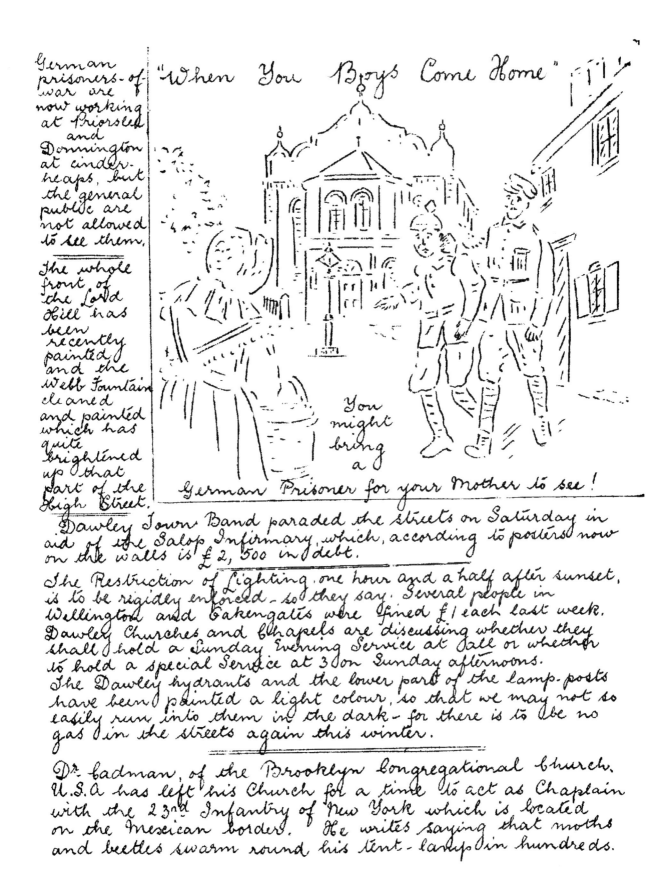

"When You Boys Come Home"

You might bring a German Prisoner for your Mother to see!

Dawley Town Band paraded the streets on Saturday in aid of the Salop Infirmary, which, according to posters now on the walls is £2,500 in debt.

The Restriction of Lighting one hour and a half after sunset, is to be rigidly enforced - so they say. Several people in Wellington and Oakengates were fined £1 each last week. Dawley Churches and Chapels are discussing whether they shall hold a Sunday Evening Service at all or whether to hold a special Service at 3 on Sunday afternoons. The Dawley hydrants and the lower part of the lamp-posts have been painted a light colour, so that we may not so easily run into them in the dark - for there is to be no gas in the streets again this winter.

Dr. Cadman, of the Brooklyn Congregational Church, U.S.A has left his Church for a time to act as Chaplain with the 23rd Infantry of New York which is located on the Mexican border. He writes saying that moths and beetles swarm round his tent-lamp in hundreds.

We deeply regret to have to announce the death of the following soldiers. each of whom was well-known by Dawley men. Sergeant R.E.B.H. Soame-elder son of Sir. C.B.H. Soame, who died in hospital as the result of wounds received in action.

Pte. Raymond Ketley of the Lincolnshire Regt. who was killed in action on July 2nd. Gunner W. Baugh of Horsehay of a Machine Gun Section who was killed in action in July.

Pte Alfred Bowers who was killed at Albert, France on Aug: 18th while carrying in a wounded man. He only enlisted on March 24th - He was in training at Pembroke Dock for 15 weeks only.

Pte. F. W. Bowers of the 1st K.S.L.I (an elder brother of Pte A. Bowers) has also died of wounds received in action on Aug: 24th, leaving a wife and five children at the Finger, Dawley.

Also, Pte George Baugh (Aqueduct) of the 5th K.S.L.I who worked for the Madeley Wood Company.

We wish we had space to give some account of each of these brave men but we feel we must mention in more detail the death of Pte. Albert Ball of Church Rd. His sister, (with whom we deeply sympathise) as her mother before her, has been one of our hardest workers for soldiers. Albert enlisted the day after his mother's funeral, having been employed at Hadley and he had been out at the Front less than 3 months. Captain J. Latham writes about him as follows on Sept 9th "He was killed in action by a German shell. He was engaged in carrying wiring material to put up entanglements in front of a newly-captured position. He was buried with three others near the spot where he fell - it was done spontaneously by his comrades at the imminent risk of their lives. The place is marked and the body will be moved to a military cemetery as soon as possible and you will be given the particulars."

The day following the intimation of his death came letters from Pte. H. Hollis saying he was with him when he was killed and from Pte. J. Davies, who helped to bury him.

We also deeply regret to announce the death of Pte. Samuel Small, a member of the old Brotherhood, who died on July 24th. He attended the Ambulance classes in Dawley, and at the outbreak of war volunteered first for Hetley and later on for the Front. It is understood he was killed in the very act of attending to a wounded comrade. The following letter was received by his wife (née Bertha Corbett) who is left with three little boys:—

"On behalf of the Ambulance and myself I wish to tender our sincere sympathies to you in the loss of your husband. As his Sgt-Major I can honestly assure you he was a good soldier, willing and respectful and a great favourite with all ranks and I am deeply sorry to lose him. He did not suffer at all as he was killed instantaneously by the bursting of a shell while doing his duty on the field tending the wounded. We are all called upon to make sacrifices at this terrible time and God called upon him to make the supreme sacrifice of laying down his life for his King and Country. Our sympathies go out to you at this terrible loss and I hope God will give you strength to bear up at this time.

Respectfully Yours
C. W. Telling
Sgt-Major,
142, Field
Ambulance
B.E.F."

Mr. Lester on writing for further particulars received the following:

"I will endeavour to give you what particulars I can of Pte S. Small's death. I am not allowed to tell you where he was killed but no doubt you will hear in time. He was killed instantaneously by the bursting of a shell on July 24th at about 11 o'clock in the morning. He was buried in the evening in the British cemetery with military honours by a Church of England clergyman, but I do not know his name. His grave is registered and a wooden cross is above it. This is all I can tell you."

"In the very act of tending a wounded man."

Pte Jonathan Jones, R.A.M.C writes from Southampton. "The King sent us a letter recently congratulating us on the splendid way we have performed our duty, breaking all records in unloading hospital ships. Many of my old chums have gone to Egypt — my word, they did get a send-off when they went, about 200 of us lined up at the side of the ship and we didn't half cheer them. But after all, it was touching to be parted from fellows with whom you have worked for two years."

About twenty cases were dealt with at the meeting of the Dawley Tribunal on Sept: 1st. The call from the Army is still "more men" and every appeal for exemption was very carefully considered. Cloggers and shoe-repairers have recently been placed among the reserved occupations and this has relieved at least two local men from service. There is some local feeling about insurance agents — a few appeals from men of this class have been refused; where time has been granted there is generally some private reason of which outsiders know nothing. One or two men have been granted temporary exemption in order to help invalid fathers who have sent, in one case, two and in another, three sons to the war already. There is still an idea abroad that some of the local works might spare more men than they have done, but with this process of "combing-out" the local Tribunal has of course nothing to do.

Men we Exempt!

The Shoe-Mender.

Price One Penny.

This little paper is only sold at our Tuesday meetings. On account of the large demand for it among soldiers out of this country, we are not now able to supply friends who ask for it except on condition that they undertake to send each copy, when they have read it, to some soldier either in this country or out of it.

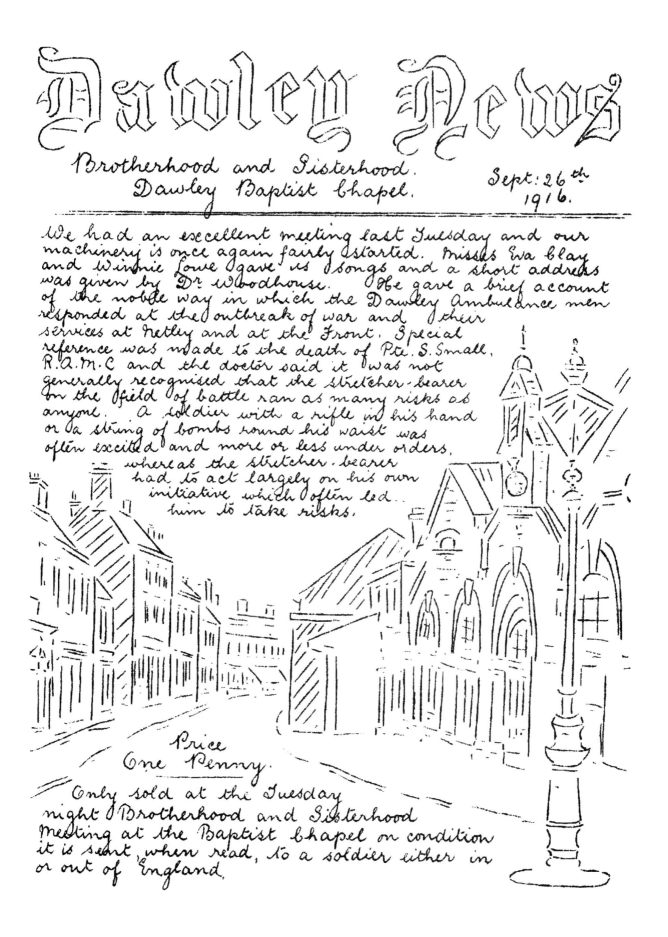

Dawley News

Brotherhood and Sisterhood.
Dawley Baptist Chapel.

Sept: 26th 1916.

We had an excellent meeting last Tuesday and our machinery is once again fairly started. Misses Eva Clay and Winnie Lowe gave us songs and a short address was given by Dr. Woodhouse. He gave a brief account of the noble way in which the Dawley Ambulance men responded at the outbreak of war and their services at Netley and at the Front. Special reference was made to the death of Pte. S. Small, R.A.M.C and the doctor said it was not generally recognised that the stretcher-bearer on the field of battle ran as many risks as anyone. A soldier with a rifle in his hand or a string of bombs round his waist was often excited and more or less under orders, whereas the stretcher-bearer had to act largely on his own initiative which often led him to take risks.

Price One Penny.

Only sold at the Tuesday night Brotherhood and Sisterhood meeting at the Baptist Chapel on condition it is sent, when read, to a soldier either in or out of England.

At the Primitive Methodist Harvest Service last Sunday afternoon a Communion Table was unveiled which has been placed there in memory of the late Mr. John Oakley, a staunch supporter of the Chapel for many years.

Pte Stephen Davies writes from Salonica on Sept: 7th asking us to alter his address "as the "W.R" has been delayed something awful." A member of this man's family last week journeyed from Dawley to Netley to see Sergt. J. Davies, who is in Hospital there — he is going on fairly well but terribly maimed.

The Local Soldiers at ——

Our visit to — recently has convinced us that there is need of our help there. They are old soldiers for the most part, right away from friends. We want good, fresh books and magazines for these men and we have appointed Messrs Hubert Bailey and A. Thorn to pay a visit to the place once a week on our behalf. Will our friends kindly bring to the Tuesday meeting books and magazines — not more than a month old? All gifts will be acknowledged here. We shall be glad to send parcels they may have for disposal if they will kindly let us know.

Like other people in England we in Dawley were interested last week in the first exploits of the "Tanks" at the Front — the new steel-land-ships, "the dust-coloured tortoises which belch out fire and spit death at the enemy." Some engaged in work at home are particularly interested in rivetting-work of this character. We are suggesting that in their spare hours they should show us what they can really do in this direction. A few pieces of rivetted-armour-plate would be useful, for instance, to fowls which apparently live in other people's gardens at Lawley Bank. There are also a great many puppies "under six months old" in Dawley just now, which might be protected against sticks and kicks to which they are liable in their playful attacks on passers-by!

On Saturday last at the Finger there was a Rally of Boy-Scouts, several troops from neighbouring places being represented. For an hour or two the old place was quite lively with their drum and bugle band.

Practically all the corn-harvest is now in. On a piece of ground in the old Park a crop of maize is growing – shortly to be used, it is understood, as fodder for cattle.

One or two places of worship are deciding to hold their main service at 3 o'clock on Sunday afternoons, most of the others are darkening their windows in order to hold the service at 6 as usual. In one case, the gas is being laid on in a school so that it may be used instead of the Chapel, during the winter.

Next Saturday night all clocks have to be put back one hour – in accord with winter-time arrangements. One may be sure, some will fail to do this. Imagine people at their Church or Chapel doors, one hour before time next Sunday! Or tipplers, standing one extra hour outside their favourite "pub"!

Pte A. E. Powell (Lawley Bank) writes from Singapore :- "I now take the pleasure of writing these few lines to you hoping you are going on alright. All the boys at Singapore from Dawley are quite well at the present time but they would like to receive a line or two about Shropshire and Philip and me would like to receive the "Weekly Report" to see how you are going on with the work you are carrying on for the soldiers and sailors. We have got a few Germans here and we have got to keep guard over them – they are not very nice people. Some of our boys took all men who were able to work to Australia so as to release some young men who are wanting to fight. I hope the Brotherhood and Sisterhood will keep it up because it cheers the soldiers up. Friends, I should like to have a few cigarettes if you have got the money to spare to buy them because these out here are not very good to smoke."

"Old Remembrances are Thro' my memory Thronging" Alright! Where's this place?

A book-prize will be sent by post to the first soldier out of England from whom a post-card is received identifying this place. The post-card must be marked "Old Remembrances, No. 1."

When It's Over.

Me and Bill and Ginger
Sailed away to France
Said good-bye to Farver,
Landed back at Harver:
Didn't have no chance
To parley-vous at Harver or
go upon the spree.
But started touring Flanders-
Ginger, Bill and me.
Since that time we've travelled -
Ginger, me and Bill -
Seen what's left of Wipers,
Dodged the German snipers
Under Vimy hill,
Rested in the valley where
Somme goes out to sea
And strafed the Boche
at Montauban -
Ginger, Bill and me.
When the War is over,
When we're done with guns,
We three means to go, Sir,
Where we do not know, Sir,
But far from any Huns,
And run a farm or
something, as cosy as could be
And no more France or
Flanders!
For Ginger, Bill, and me!

"W. G."

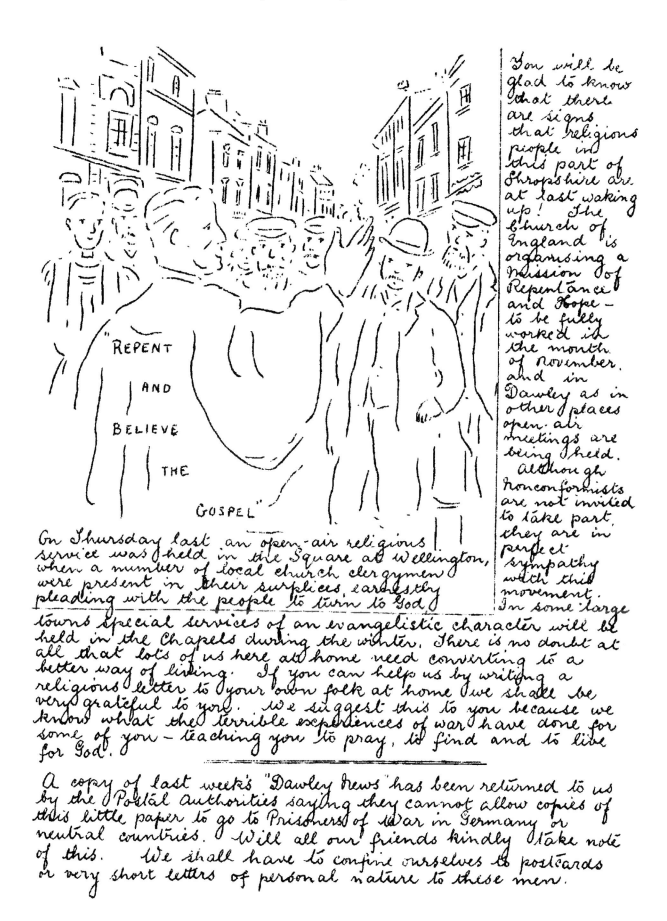

"REPENT

AND

BELIEVE

THE

GOSPEL"

On Thursday last an open-air religious service was held in the Square at Wellington, when a number of local church clergymen were present in their surplices, earnestly pleading with the people to turn to God.

You will be glad to know that there are signs that religious people in this part of Shropshire are at last waking up! The Church of England is organising a Mission of Repentance and Hope — to be fully worked in the month of November, and in Dawley as in other places open-air meetings are being held. Although nonconformists are not invited to take part, they are in perfect sympathy with this movement.

In some large towns special services of an evangelistic character will be held in the Chapels during the winter. There is no doubt at all that lots of us here at home need converting to a better way of living. If you can help us by writing a religious letter to your own folk at home we shall be very grateful to you. We suggest this to you because we know what the terrible experiences of war have done for some of you — teaching you to pray, to find and to live for God.

A copy of last week's "Dawley News" has been returned to us by the Postal Authorities saying they cannot allow copies of this little paper to go to Prisoners of War in Germany or neutral countries. Will all our friends kindly take note of this. We shall have to confine ourselves to postcards or very short letters of personal nature to these men.

Dawley Military Tribunal.

At a meeting in the Town Hall last Friday about 20 cases were heard — the proceedings lasting nearly three hours. The two first cases were those of workmen employed by a local firm, who had been recently unbadged. Several members of the Tribunal asked the representative of the firm whether, in view of the military necessities of the country they thought they ought to continue to hold every man at present in their employ, to which answer was made that every man they appealed for was considered essential. Dealing with the two cases before them the one case was postponed for the production of a birth-certificate, as the man was alleged to be only 16; in the other one month only was allowed. A master-house-painter (married) was granted three months exemption to go before the Army Medical Board before any further application. A master-printer appealed for the younger of two employees — one month was allowed. The cases of several Insurance Agents were dealt with — one case was adjourned for re examination by the medical Board another, 40 years of age next month, just recovering from illness was granted further time, while a third now employed in making shell-nozzles was granted one month in order to produce a badge as a war worker. A local Sanitary Pipe Company appealed for two men — one, an engine-driver was granted a further period, the other was refused. Two farmers, engaged in agriculture, secured temporary exemption, as also did a baker and a grocer's foreman. A man engaged in a coal and clay pit was referred to the miners' Tribunal.

By the courtesy of his friends we here give a sketch of the monument which has been affixed to the grave of the late Sergeant A.E. Bailey in the French military Cemetery at Ecoivres

We have this week received information that the body of the late Private Samuel Small was buried in the North-West Corner of Bernafay Wood, near Longueval on July 24th. We are securing a photograph and in due course a sketch of the grave will be reproduced here.

For a day or two there was some little uncertainty as to the death of Pte A. Ball and during this period we wrote to Captain Latham asking if he would kindly look into the matter again, as no one at home ever knew Albert as a stretcher-bearer. The following reply was received on Sunday last:- "I regret to say that there is no possible doubt as to the identity of the man killed about 200 yards beyond Trones Wood. His pockets were searched

"now that the little paper has started again I must certainly send a few lines."

Please notice how few letters we have received from the Front. No doubt this is due to the fact that we only re-started our little paper last week. Please write to us now – all the 200 of you!

by Lieutenant Allen, our M.G. Officer who found on him it is true, no identity disc, but the pay-book and a packet of letters addressed to Pte A. Ball. He was buried by his comrades who knew him well under Sergt. Barclay. Pte. Ball went through a 10 days' course of stretcher-bearing recently and had only just taken on the duties of S.B. to fill a vacancy. The pay-book and letters have been sent home and will arrive in due course."

The collection at the close of last week's meeting for the wife of the late Pte. S. Small amounted to £3-1-0 – a letter of acknowledgement will be read to-night.

We shall now be very glad to acknowledge contributions in aid of our various funds. For our General Fund, for our Soldiers' Comforts Fund, for the "D.N." Fund and for the Postage Fund. Four funds look formidable but experience teaches us that some of our friends prefer to give to one fund while others are specially interested in another. We gratefully acknowledge the gift of £1 towards the upkeep of this paper, which with the concurrence of the donor has been spent in the purchase of additional reproducing apparatus. Dr. Woodhouse has kindly donated 5/- to the same fund. For our Postage Fund we received last week – "King Street" 2/- and "W.L." 2/-. Our good friends will not forget our needs, will they?

Pte. E. Baxter writes from the Macedonian region:- Every soldier appreciates the little paper and says it is very good of you to keep in touch with us. It is awfully hot out here and the flies are something dreadful! We shall be glad when the war is over so that we can come and have some pleasant evenings at the Chapel.

He's Got His Wish!

"I should have liked a cocoanut shie or two at the Wakes."

Pte Harold Hollis writes from France:- "I am sorry to have missed the Oakengates Wakes. I should have liked a cocoanut shie or two but never mind, we are living in hope of a safe return and a jolly good time when all the boys come home. I wish I could come to the Chapel again to hear the Choir and Mr. Gange – he is a fine preacher and I have often had a good lesson from him."

Pte. A. R. Candlin writes from Salonica:- "All the boys in my platoon thank you for your paper and others wish they were lucky enough to have something like it. The weather has been very hot but we are ready to meet the enemy with a heart as strong as ever."

Our War Information Bureau.

As announced at our meeting last Tuesday we have opened a new department which experience has found to be necessary. It often happens that people lose touch with soldiers, when are reported "missing" or the ordinary Regimental Records Offices are unable to give information. We find that by making enquiries direct to N.C.O's on the field or from men of a particular Platoon we are able to secure information weeks before the official notification comes through and often of a more detailed character. Again, if a soldier is ill in hospital abroad or at home it is extremely difficult for friends to find out where – unless the man is well enough to write – whereas we are often able to help.

Mr. W. Preece is in charge of this new section, but all enquiries, etc, must be made of him at the close of the Tuesday meeting.

Station Road, Dawley, in the early 20th century. Note the old spoil mounds which were – and still are – a feature of the Dawley landscape.

Finger Road, perhaps around 1908. This area of Dawley, called The Finger, was named after a pub in the area called Peter's Finger – the name came from a biblical reference.

Two unidentified Dawley area soldiers.

William Ball, "the Shropshire Giant".

Billy Lloyd, left, at only 4ft 4ins was a well-known Dawley character.

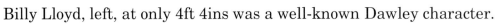

October
3rd
1916.

We have put back the Town Clock one hour. Will it keep correct time all the winter ???????!

Bugler E. Round (Meadow Road) who is a Prisoner of War somewhere in Hanover, Germany writes on Sept: 19th "I thank you all for your kindness in writing, it is cheering to get a letter from the old town as time hangs so heavily on our hands. I trust I shall have the pleasure of hearing from you again."

Unfortunately we cannot send the "D.N" to Germany or to neutral countries the Postal Authorities forbid us. We therefore beg our friends to ask for the addresses of these Prisoners of War so that they may send them letters.

Price One Penny.

Only sold to people who attend the Brotherhood and Sisterhood Meeting at Dawley Baptist Chapel on condition it is sent, when read, to a soldier either in or out of England.

Sergeant W. Leigh Thomason of the Australian Forces writes from the "Trenches Somewhere in France":- "I received the copy of the Dawley News" you so kindly sent me and I am much interested; I trust you will continue to send me a copy. I should say the name of the place which bears the heading "It's a Long, Long Trail from this place to Dawley is the Citadel, Cairo, Egypt - am I right? We have occupied the same trenches as the boys from Dawley. I just missed seeing them as I was on guard at the time but had a pleasant surprise when I got there and was handed a copy of your paper which had been left behind in the cook-house in the firing line. You may wonder why it was handed to me, it may be that I'm never tired of praising my native haunts. I expect to get leave shortly when I hope to have the pleasure of a chat with you. Thank you once more for the "Dawley News."

A Soldier's Sketch.

The Village Pump.

L/Cpl. W. H. Oliver writes from Salonica:- "I see that women in Shropshire are taking over some of the men's farm-work, I therefore send you this sketch for the paper...... I am in touch with the boys of the K.S.L.I. out here and have had a talk with Ptes. G. Merrington and Rushton."

Pte. P. Tonks writes on Sept: 24th from France;- "I have received the "D. N" safely and am pleased you have started it again as we have missed the old paper very much. There was quite a rush among the boys when it came to-day. We have been very busy this last week or two and have had plenty of rain. We shall soon have winter here - I was hoping we should be home again as it is not very nice out here in winter."

Pte Jack Nickless (Rough Ground) says: no one can realise what it is, we have to work like niggers and we are standing in water. I shall never forget my first night in the firing line. There are only three of the boys from our town just about here, two Morgans and myself. I have still a good pal of mine with me, one from the Madeley Colliers..... I think it's a bit rotten separating mates."

"I've been in the trenches nine days now -

Mr. Thomas Payne of Dark Lane who passed away early on Wednesday morning last was for years a member of the Dawley Urban Council and Madeley Board of Guardians, also one of the chief supporters of the Dark Lane Primitive Methodist Tabernacle.

Several of the local works closed on Wednesday night or Thursday in order to give the men a holiday instead of the Whitsuntide and August holidays. By this time, however, practically all are at their work again – working all the harder, we hope, for the brief rest and change.

Jobs For Germans in Dawley.

It has been suggested that instead of employing German prisoners at —— we might use one or two of them in Dawley on work of greater interest and local advantage! Very good! We therefore bring one (in imagination) into the town to-day – can you suggest the job he should be set first to do?

The "Lawley Bank" Belgian Refugee family is on the point of removing from this district. Mr. J. Mortier, his wife and four children came to Lawley Bank exactly two years ago this week but lately Mr. Mortier's work and health have been so uncertain that it has been thought desirable to advise him to accept a place offered him in Messrs. Cadbury's Cocoa Factory at Bournville Birmingham. He will be there with other Belgians as a general hand in the Chocolate packing department. If Mr. Lester can make arrangements for the clearing-up of their affairs they will leave Lawley Bank for good at the end of this week. We take this opportunity of thanking our friends for the help they have so ungrudgingly given for the relief of these Belgians. There now remain only Mr. and Mrs. Deleus with their 5 children at Horsehay. The man is employed at the Horsehay Works and is so badged, otherwise he would be called up for Belgian Military Service.

Men We Exempt.

The Sugar-Seller.

Small shop-keepers in Dawley complain of the difficulty they experience in getting their supplies of sugar — what if we, who have a "sweet tooth" should be driven to Tickler's Jam!

A Dawley shop-keeper was fined £1 at Wellington Police Court last week for neglecting to obscure the lights in his window. This is the first local case — will it be the last?

Several of the older soldiers on our list are in hospital — this little paper is being returned to us marked to that effect but address not known. Please remember we shall be glad to send this to our wounded heroes in hospital in England or abroad if only their friends or pals will kindly tell us where they are.

We have received for our Postage Fund during the week — Nothing — not even the value of one penny stamp!

"It's A Long, Long Trail from this place to Dawley."

A Picture-Postcard has been sent to us by a Dawley soldier but the name of the place has been deleted. The first Dawley soldier abroad (not now at this place) who identifies it in his letter will receive a book-prize from us.

We are sending a book-prize to-day to Sgt W. L. Thomason for the first correct answer to a previous picture :- "The Citadel, Cairo."

The Anniversary Services took place at the Chapel on Sunday last, when Rev. E. J. Gange (whom many of you have heard in past years) preached. The Collections amounted to £ 35.10.10 for the Chapel funds. There were excellent congregations - the only disadvantage was you were away. It is a relief to us that the financial result was so good as it relieves us from some anxiety in order that we may be able to do "the extra bit" which the "D. N" and in fact the whole of our Tuesday effort represents.

We are sorry to have so much bad news to report to you this week. If we do not as a rule say much about Religion here, we beg you to remember that we constantly pray for you and commend you to the care of the Great Comrade, the Friend "that sticketh closer than a brother."

"Faint not, nor fear, His arms are near. He changeth not and thou, art dear, Only believe and thou shalt see That Christ is all in all to thee"

(a passage from a hymn we sang at Special Services on Sunday.)

TO THE
HONOUR
OF
A
BRAVE
MAN,
NOW
DEAD

Old Park Soldier Recommended for the D.C.M.

We deeply regret to say that Private W. J. Harrison died of his wounds in a hospital at Rouen in France on Sept 26th. He was 22 years of age only and in civil life worked at Kemberton. Attached to the 6th K.S.L.I he was wounded in action a few days ago and though the best was done for him he succumbed to the severe gun-shot wounds he received in the back. His Colonel has recommended him to the Brigadier-General for the D.C.M. Under heavy shell-fire a few days ago he went out into "No Man's Land" and brought in his wounded Sergeant-Major on his back. His family hope shortly to receive the official recognition of his brave deed.

His father, Sergeant Harrison, who won the D.C.M in the South African War is invalided home for a short while. After service in the trenches he was appointed an Instructor in a School at Rouen where he has met many Dawley boys on their arrival in France from England. Sergeant Harrison leaves home again for Pembroke Dock this week, where he hopes to secure a post in connection with the Barracks there.

Among the local men officially reported wounded recently is Pte. Harry Bryce, who has several brothers here in Dawley. He belongs to the 5th K.S.L.I. He was put out of action six weeks ago and is in hospital somewhere in France, — at the request of his friends we are trying to find out where. If any soldier can send any information we shall be glad.

Rev. G. Parmeter, who was instituted as the new Vicar of Doseley Church by the Bishop of Lichfield on Thursday last, began his ministerial career in 1893. For some years he worked in Leicestershire and since 1913 in Hull.

Rev. J. B. Morgan is being again invited to the pastorate of Wellington Baptist Church — he was previously the minister from 1880-1885 and has since held charges at Crewe, Chester and Bradford.

Pte. J. Davies (Church Rd West) writes:- "I am sorry to tell you that Pte. Len Bailey (Stony Fold) is wounded badly. We were in a Bombing-post and he got a bullet in the head, but he appeared to be going on as well as could be expected when he was taken away — where to I do not know. We are having a rough time of it now as we are in the "B.P."— but it is all bringing the war to a finish, I hope."

On Sunday morning the following was received by Pte. L. Bailey's family:- "I have the sad duty to tell you that Pte. L. Bailey died of a bullet wound in the head he received on 17th September. He was holding a bombing-post in the most advanced position in the newly-won trenches and the Germans were attempting to gain their lost ground and were being repelled with great loss by our bombers. Although the Non-Commissioned Officer on the bombing-post had been killed the little section of bombers stuck to their post and so inflicted a great defeat on the attacking Germans…. Corporal Edwards speaks highly of him. He was an exceptionally good bomber and that is why he succeeded in beating off the German attack." Len Bailey was 25 years of age and worked at the Stafford Pits. His mother and brothers live in Stony Fold, Lawley Bank - he has another brother in the 1st K.S.L.I at the Front.

Pte. Len Rufus (Crown St) has been wounded and brought to a hospital in Derby where he is going on well.

The Egg Collection in Dawley for wounded soldiers and hospital use is still going ahead - nearly 1900 having been forwarded during the past month.

We deeply regret to say that on Wednesday morning last Mr. and Mrs. Taylor (Powis Fold, Lawley Bank) received a letter from the Sergeant of his platoon that their son, Private Len Taylor was killed in France by a shell on Sept: 18th. He appears to have been badly wounded and the ambulance men went out under heavy fire to do what they could for him in dressing his wounds but all to no avail. He was buried just behind the lines and we shall communicate with the authorities asking for the removal of the body to one of the Military Cemeteries later on. The boy was only 18 years of age last August. He was a member of the Baptist Sunday School. He has three brothers in the Army — Ted, a member of the original Expeditionary Force, is now at Blackpool Camp, Will and George are both at Salonica.

We had a good meeting on Tuesday last when the schoolroom was almost full. An evangelistic address was given by Mr. J. Meredith and two songs were sung by Miss Lottie Roden. Letters from soldiers in France and elsewhere were read by Mr. J. J. Wolding and Mr. W. Preece was present, answering questions and giving any information asked for. Mr. Lester, in presiding, said the old Savings-Funds are discontinued — a branch of the National War-Savings Association to take their place, as soon as the services of a secretary could be secured.

A Dawley soldier who is a Prisoner of War in Germany asks for a Bible.

Will someone from the Chapel kindly send him one? Name and address will be given privately on application.

Dawley News

Tuesday, October 10th 1916.

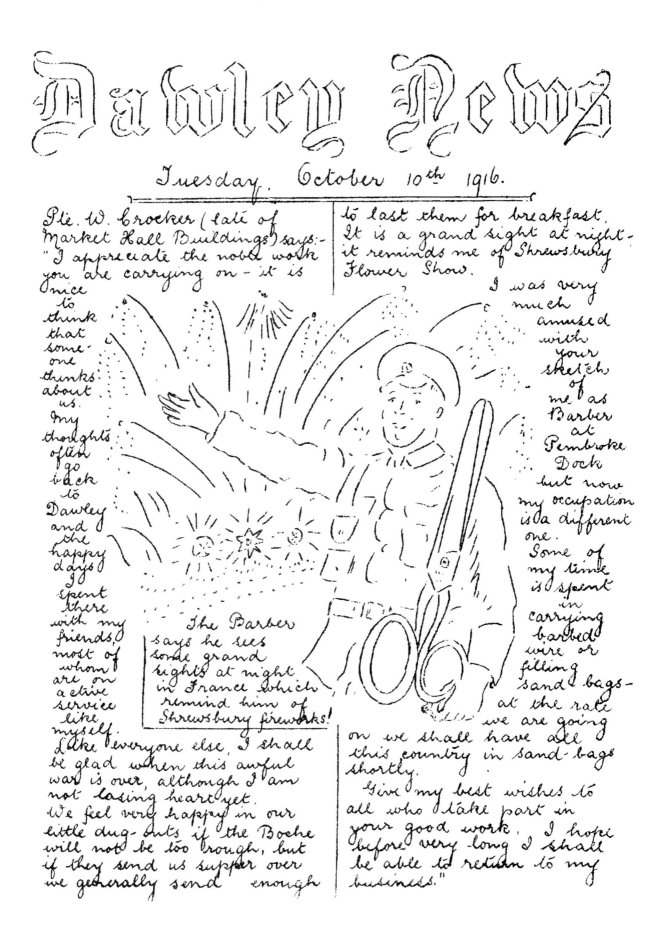

Pte. W. Crocker (late of Market Hall Buildings) says:- "I appreciate the noble work you are carrying on - it is nice to think that some one thinks about us. My thoughts often go back to Dawley and the happy days I spent there with my friends, most of whom are on active service like myself.

Like everyone else, I shall be glad when this awful war is over, although I am not losing heart yet. We feel very happy in our little dug-outs if the Boche will not be too rough, but if they send us supper over we generally send enough

to last them for breakfast. It is a grand sight at night - it reminds me of Shrewsbury Flower Show.

I was very much amused with your sketch of me as Barber at Pembroke Dock but now my occupation is a different one. Some of my time is spent in carrying barbed wire or filling sand bags - at the rate we are going on we shall have all this country in sand-bags shortly.

Give my best wishes to all who take part in your good work. I hope before very long I shall be able to return to my business."

The Barber says he sees some grand sights at night in France which remind him of Shrewsbury fireworks!

If by any chance this copy gets into the hands of someone who is not proposing to send it to a soldier we beg that friend to apply to Mr Wooding for an addressed envelope   We have this week produced 225 copies of this paper – we cannot do more on a hand machine. Last week 25 Dawley soldiers out of this country were deprived of their copies: we shall have to remedy this, and there appears to be only one way, viz: by only selling it to friends who take an envelope

A large audience was present last Tuesday when Mr R. Deakin gave an excellent talk on "Penmanship" with black board illustrations Mr R. Ward gave us two songs and the meeting altogether was a great success.

"If England Only Knew"

(Rev. T. W. Hart (late Baptist Minister at Shrewsbury) who preached our School Sermons some years ago and is now a Chaplain at the Front was last week awarded the Military Cross)

There's many a man has won the Cross
Which but the few may wear
High fame will come to such but some
must be denied their share
The greatest prize in human eyes
Is that which is most rare

Good luck to those who gain the Cross
It is their right and due.
Yet 'tis no test of all the rest
For heroes are not few
And many a grave holds one as brave
If England only knew.

There's many a man has given his
life
A noble gift and free –
To shield his friend unto the end
When none was there to see
But those who passed with him at
last
Into Eternity

Honour to those who wear the Cross!
But 'neath a brighter sun
A hero band one day shall stand
When earth's brief race is run
And shall rejoice to hear His
voice:
"Soldiers of God well done!"

"D. M"

Abide with me: fast falls
the eventide
The darkness deepens: Lord
with me abide
When other helpers fail
and comforts flee
Help of the helpless, O
abide with me.

The new address of the Mortier family - the Belgian Refugees who are now leaving Lawley Bank - is 13, Anderton Road, Sparkbrook, Birmingham, the nearest Railway Station being Smallbrook and Sparkbrook, G. W. R.

We have made enquiries of the India Store Dept, Belvedere Road, Lambeth, S. E. respecting a new order which allows parcels of comforts over 11 lbs. in weight to be sent carriage free from London to soldiers in India, Egypt, Salonica and Mesopotamia – We are glad to say the authorities give us permission to send similar comforts to our soldiers in Hong Kong and Singapore. There

Jobs for Germans in Dawley.

We might put one on the second Delivery of Letters to Lawley Bank which, as reported at the Urban District Council Meeting on Tuesday last, the Post-Master-General declines to reinstate.

(It may be remembered, we brought (in imagination) a German prisoner from his occupation at — to Dawley last week, in order to employ him on work of local advantage.)

are certain conditions, however, to be complied with, which Mr. W. Preece will be glad to explain.

Sergeant J. H. Price (Old Park) writes:– "Please accept my thanks for the old 'Report' under its new title. It is a treat to get it once again. I must bear out what our old friend L/Cpl Dacre says about that place he mentioned in his letter. I saw a lot of fighting there and can assure you it was a warm place. Perhaps Dacre will be pleased to know that in the big advance of Sept: 15th in which my Regiment took part we pushed our line over three thousand yards beyond that spot. Excuse me further."

Someone has had to write the whole of this little paper for you — will you in return write a short letter to us?

The Dawley Church Harvest Festival was held on Sunday last — at the evening service the place was crowded.

Several of the local chapels have been improving their property lately — the Old Park Primitives have placed a door to their front porch and have cemented the outside pathway.

Several of the local shop-keepers now shut up their establishments during the dinner-hour; in addition to closing for the night at seven o'clock.

The lock-up shop in the Market Hall Buildings, vacant since the enlistment of Pte Crocker, has been let by the Council to Mr. Evans, the draper.

On the last Sunday in October, instead of our Monthly Church Collection we are taking a Hospital Collection — two-thirds to be sent to the Salop Infirmary and one-third to the Wellington Cottage Hospital, where a number of wounded soldiers are being treated.

Mr Samuel Phillips, who was called up for Military Service a few weeks ago has been discharged on the grounds of ill-health and has returned to his duties as postman, but on a different district.

A story runs that a number of youths who used to jeer at German prisoners en route for their work at — have been threatened with a fine of 2/6 if the offence is repeated.

Steps are being taken towards an Infant Welfare Centre in Dawley. A few Dawley women take their children to the Wrekin Hall, Wellington each week for consultation and advice

The floor of the Council Chamber has been recently elevated at the Chairman's end. Why shouldn't we go further and erect a proper magisterial bench? — it is a great nuisance to have to go to Wellington or Madeley for all our excitements!

but many people who know the district feel there is just as much need for a Centre here. Dr. Wheatley has promised to come and survey the land and we are hoping that he will consent to a start being made.

When you write home tell your people you receive this from us and advise them to attend our Tuesday meeting — it will help them!

We experience great difficulty in getting our letters or books through to our Prisoners of War in Germany and Switzerland. One letter was last week written on the back of a circular containing Mr. Gange's portrait — it has been returned to us with the intimation that "correspondence written on paper bearing any pictorial illustration is stopped by the Censor" —

therefore Mr. Gange's portrait is debarred from going into Germany. A book recently sent by one of our friends has also been returned with the intimation that only the publishers of books are allowed to send volumes, which means that in future a P.O and an address must be sent to the publishers.

Soldiers stationed at Hong Kong are being taken off our list temporarily — a special letter is being sent to them which we hope will receive due attention.

We are searching for Pte Harry Bryce who is now officially posted as "missing." Pte Howard Brothwood (who was in the same charge at the front and was wounded) is now home for a few days, but he knows nothing.

The announcement that women may be employed at Hadley, attracted a crowd of applicants of all sorts and sizes to the Works at the latter end of last week.

Sgt Wesley Vaughan writes that Pte Bryce was seen after the battle on the way to the dressing-station but we are awaiting confirmation of this. If any soldier can send us information we shall be glad.

We acknowledge with many thanks the following donations to our Postage Fund :- "W. H. D" 10/-; "H. R. P" 5/-; A member of the Sisterhood "2/6; "Reporter" 2/-; "Every Little Helps" 3d

Cook's Mate W. Hitchman writes from H.M.S. King George V:- "The weather here at present is ripping and you would hardly credit that we are at war. I should like you to be with us for a few days just to see our splendid Fleet and it's might. There's nothing so inspiring as the sight of the ships ploughing their way across the ocean - it seems to give one the courage of andorras(?). For myself, I can say that I'm jolly glad I joined the Navy and am more than proud I belong to the Senior Service. I am pleased that the meetings at the Chapel have re-commenced and I shall expect to hear from someone now. I suppose Dawley is still as quiet as ever - I see they are weeding out a great many from the Works.

Dawley Military Tribunal.

In public interest the last meeting in the Town Hall easily eclipsed all others. A number of men employed at Horsehay Works have recently been unbadged by the Ministry of Munitions and after hearing a statement in private from representatives of the Company the Tribunal adjourned all these cases for further consultation with the Ministry of Munitions. Butchers and bakers were exempted from service for the present, also several farm-hands. Several men - including a grocer - were ordered to submit themselves to Army medical examination. A public-house-keeper was offered exemption for a period if he went into a local munition works. A house-painter, a pleasure-brake driver, a carter and a clay-getter were refused exemption. If you could be present as one of the public you would appreciate the difficulties the members of the Tribunal often have in coming to a fair decision.

"There's my case, gentlemen, and if you consider the lad will serve the Country better in the army, I've no more to say - only remember, I put up the shutters if he goes."

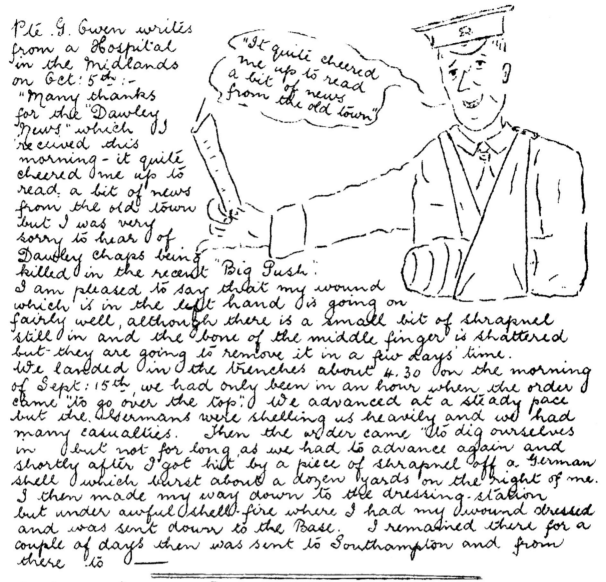

Pte. G. Owen writes from a Hospital in the Midlands on Oct: 5th :-

"Many thanks for the "Dawley News" which I received this morning - it quite cheered me up to read a bit of news from the old town but I was very sorry to hear of Dawley chaps being killed in the recent "Big Push". I am pleased to say that my wound which is in the left hand is going on fairly well, although there is a small bit of shrapnel still in and the bone of the middle finger is shattered but they are going to remove it in a few days' time.

We landed in the trenches about 4.30 on the morning of Sept: 15th, we had only been in an hour when the order came "to go over the top". We advanced at a steady pace but the Germans were shelling us heavily and we had many casualties. Then the order came "to dig ourselves in" but not for long, as we had to advance again and shortly after I got hit by a piece of shrapnel off a German shell which burst about a dozen yards on the right of me. I then made my way down to the dressing-station but under awful shell-fire where I had my wound dressed and was sent down to the Base. I remained there for a couple of days then was sent to Southampton and from there to _____

Owing to Lighting Restrictions etc, it has been decided to try the experiment of a Sunday afternoon Service at the Chapel from 3.15 to 4.15, beginning next Sunday. It was hoped to be able to get all Churches and Chapels into line so that all services were held at the same hour but this is impossible. Half of the Churches and Chapels will have a service on Sunday evening next as usual, while the other half are arranging it in the afternoon, abandoning the evening service.

No one can really tell what will be the result until the experiment of an afternoon service has been tried and this has now to be done. At the same time Mr. Lester is of opinion that if any number of Chapels are closed on Sunday evenings an Evangelistic service will have to be started - if not at Lawley Bank, then elsewhere.

The wintry weather is coming on, my boy and we are beginning to think what it will be like in the trenches then! We are this week hoping to start once again our Soldiers' Comforts Fund to provide such necessary little comforts as we are able to send to you. We have now so many men on our list that it is almost impossible for us to treat all alike. Nor is it necessary, for some soldiers have many more friends at home than others. We are particularly anxious to help the man who has few friends, or where people are indifferent to his needs. If this sort of man is known to you -

"Old Remembrances are Thronging, Thro' My Memory." Alright! Where's this place?

A book-prize will be sent to the first soldier out of England from whom a postcard is received identifying this place. The postcard would be marked:-

"Old Remembrances" No 2.

the Dawley man who never gets an extra pair of socks or a muffler, who never gets a packet of "fags" from anyone at home we shall be pleased if you will send us his name, number, etc. You need not fear

that we shall give his name in this paper or announce it at our meetings. If you do not need help but are able to subscribe to this fund we shall be glad of money, which will be acknowledged by the Treasurers. Remember, we do not ask you to subscribe - people at home will do that - but some soldiers have been glad to help us in this way - to help others.

Price   One   Penny.

Only sold at the Brotherhood and Sisterhood Meeting at Dawley Baptist Chapel on condition it is sent, when read, to a soldier.

Our Portraits (?) of Women Applicants for work at Hadley, last week, did not meet with universal admiration! The same people in munition overalls, however, look different, winning the affection of everyone, particularly wounded Tommies!

Following our note on the front page (which holds a reference to a sketch which appeared last week) it may be said that at Hadley only middle aged women are to be employed at present.

The Shropshire Provident Society last week decided to pay death-benefits to members killed in the war — a satisfactory alteration which will be of advantage to several Dawley families which have been bereaved.

Several branches of the local War-Savings Association appear to be doing fairly well — Dawley Church branch, for instance, has banked £25.

One day last week two strangers were gazing admiringly at the little Chapel (Mount Gilead) at Lawley Bank (now used by us as an Infant School). They had travelled 50 miles, they said, to have another look at the old place where they first learned the Better Life.

Last night, the Rock Primitives had a concert for the purpose of providing comforts for soldiers from the Rock — several of their men are on our list.

Our own Chapel, Lawley Bank Wesleyan, Dawley Wesleyan and Malinslee Church held a special service on Sunday at 3.15 — abandoning the evening service. All other Churches and Chapels in the district appear to be going on as usual.

"Some Dawley tradesmen and some Chapels do complain but I'm making a pot of money"

4ᵈ A PINT

LONG PULL ABOLISHED BY ORDER

The local publicans at a recent meeting decided to charge 4ᵈ a pint and to abolish the "long pull". You know what our views are about public-houses in war-time, don't you?

Thank You!

We are deeply obliged to the following friends for their kind gifts to our Postage Fund:—

"Ineligible" - £1
Sgt W.L. Thomason - 5/-
"Porch" - 2/6
"B.A. Dunn" - 2/6
"M.E.B's Class - 1/-

Also, for the upkeep of this little paper (which is being sent to upwards of 200 soldiers every week) from "Ineligible". £1.

L/Cpl Frank Buttery writing from France on Oct: 6th says:- "Thank you for your valuable paper.... We are out of the trenches now for a few days' rest and we have earned it, for we went "over the top" twice in 8 days and I am glad to say the good old Shropshires were successful on each occasion. We took over a mile of ground, two villages and a nice lot of prisoners.

We had very few casualties but I am sorry to say two from Dawley were killed - William Dunning from Chapel Street on the 18th September and Ernest Candlin from Horsehay on the 25th. I am very sorry these men have gone.

I myself got a good shaking-up as they blew our trench in and buried me and two more. It only made us stiff and sore for a few days. One could not help but laugh when we went "over the top" to see the Germans come running towards us, giving themselves up. A few kept on working their machine-guns but their time was short .... We are expecting to have another go at them soon, with I hope the same luck. Let us now get it over for this is my third winter out here.... I had the pleasure of seeing the "Tanks" three days before they went into action."

"We took a nice lot of prisoners."

EXTRA QUALITY

Petty Officer G. S. Picken of the R. N. Air Station, Vendôme, France writes:- "Thank you for the "Dawley News" - you will see I am at a Flying School where they are training some more "Zepp-Strafers." A very pleasant part of the country it is, reminding one of Shropshire, nearly all agriculture with Vendôme a good example of a French country town. We are about four and a half miles out and when we go on leave they take us on motor-lorries. I will send you a few views of this district later on, which I hope may interest you."

To-night we are distributing collecting-books in connection with our Soldiers' Comforts Fund. Last year we collected by means of little envelopes but this was not quite satisfactory. Mr. F. J. Wooding will issue the books and Miss Breeze and Miss Walker will co-operate with him as the treasurers of this special fund.

Among wounded soldiers we regret to report the following:—
Pte. S. Davies wounded on Sept. 30th by gun-shot — he is going on nicely in Aux: M. Hospital W. 3. Ward, 10, Worcester, Belmont Rd. Liverpool.
Sgt. J. W. Vaughan — who is going on well at No 3. Wilson's War Hospital, No 9. Ward, Wilsons Rd. Reading.
Pte. H. Evans writes from No 3 Ward, S. G. Hospital. Stourbridge, that he has been wounded in the left arm — where he has still a piece of metal. This is the third time he has been sent to England having been at the Marne, on the Aisne, and at Ypres.
Pte. J. Machin writes from Ancoats Convalescent Home, Great Warford, Alderley Edge that he is nearly well and now hopes to get a few days at home, after 16 months of knocking about in the Grenadiers. "I think Dawley has suffered more since the Somme affair than ever before. I have met Charlie Marsh and I have also been with Tom Archer and Jim Roberts."

"I had been driven many times to my knees by the overwhelming conviction that I had nowhere else to go. My own wisdom. and that of all about me, seemed insufficient for that day." — Abraham Lincoln —

"And we know that all things work together for good to them that love God. I am persuaded that neither death nor life shall be able to separate us from the love of God which is in Christ Jesus our Lord" — St. Paul —

"Hast thee got anythin' hextra, Sarah?"

The Dawley and Dawley Bank Post Offices were very lively last week, the Old Age Pensioners were quite excited at the prospect of extra allowances.

Dawley News: October 1916

Cpl. E. Shepherd says he was very surprised to see the D.N. last week – the first he has received during his 19 months at the Front.

Pte. W. Woodvine of the Cheshires writes:– "Send me the 'D.N' regularly as I like to know how the boys are getting on. I have just had a talk with W. Dunning from the Finger."

Pte. E. Lane (New Town) writes from France:– "When the 'D.N' comes the boys are all round me like a lot of bees. When our platoon has done with it I give it to a Corporal from —— who used to attend your Chapel on Sunday nights where he wanted to make a love affair and he seems more anxious to see it than I am. When I lend it to the boys from round Madeley they say– "Good old Dawley again". Thank you for the fags which I shared – some of them were cut in two so that the boys could say they had had a pull off a fag that had come from Dawley."

Thank you for the letters we have received this week – please keep on writing!

Jobs for Germans in Dawley.

The glass globes have been taken off – no street lamps are lighted in Dawley now.

He might have been set to catch that Squirrel!
(It may be remembered we brought a German prisoner (in imagination) from —— to Dawley for work of public importance).

A few days ago a very lively little squirrel was caught in a back-garden at Lawley Bank. After several exciting adventures it was captured and caged in a house in Sling Street. By some means it escaped. It was last seen on the Capt: Webb monument, where a boy attempting to capture it, was bitten!

209

"I shall run to Wellington."

Bombardier C. Woolger writes from France:— "We are still rubbing it into the Huns and I can tell you they don't like it now they have not got deep trenches and dug-outs to get into. I guess it must be cheering you all up to read of our great victory— we shall keep at them now until we have finished them off once and for all!!! I see they are still getting a few more men to come and do their bit out here from Dawley— I know of a nice few yet who ought to be out here. I heard one man say while I was on leave "Let them come to Dawley, then I shall run to Wellington" — not so bad, but we are not all like that. As regards the 'Tanks', well, we cannot speak too highly of them for they are "all there"— I tell you nothing will stop them. Thank you for the "Dawley News", hurry up and send the next number for me and my pals are waiting for it."

We had a fine attendance at our Meeting last Tuesday. Selections on violin and piano were given by Messrs P. Jones and E. Watkiss. Miss Blocksidge gave an effective address on "Keep the Home-Fires Burning". Not only a fire in the grate, she said, but a warm place in the heart, a happy home-life which should have in it the invisible altar of religion, the fire of which should never be allowed to go out. At the close everyone sang the well-worn song— copies of the words being distributed to all.

Pte. S. W. Archer writes from France on Oct. 6th:— "We have been having it rather rough lately but not so rough as Mr. Hun has had it, now we have got him on the run. We had the 'Tanks' up with us and they did good work, I can tell you.... Jim Roberts is quite well. My officer got wounded but not seriously, I expect he will soon be back again. I met the K.S.L.I. going up to the trenches as we were coming out and they were cheerful.... Thank you for the "D.N." I hope to hear again from one of you next week."

We have secured through our Enquiry Department (Mr. W. Preece) the following among other information which has been sent privately to soldiers friends. There is no trace of Pte. O. Bryce having passed through the Field Ambulance — the hope of this life therefore is slender. In respect to Pte Dunning, the Sergeant. Major of his Company says—"None of the men who returned can give any information regarding him after the attack commenced. If he were killed we should have found him as we advanced, yet it is unlikely that he is a prisoner since none of our men were taken. He is one of three unaccounted for."

The O/c A Coy - 1/8 West Yorks reports they cannot trace Rfn. E. Davies for whom we are searching. This soldier took part in an attack on Sept: 3rd and many of his Company managed to reach the German front lines — which were later recovered by them — he may therefore be taken prisoner. The area between the trenches has been searched but no trace of him can be found. We have been able to secure additional details as to Pte. R. Hetley who was killed on July 1st and now believe he was buried in what the soldiers call "Sausage Valley" near the remains of the village of La Boiselle. (We are now calling the attention of the Graves Registration Authorities to this case).

Note. When casualties affecting Dawley soldiers happen, we shall be greatly obliged if soldiers will kindly send a private note to Mr. Lester at once, particularly when it is known, for certain, that a man is killed. Needless to say, the information so sent must be in all cases quite reliable and not based upon mere hearsay.

We regret to say that L/Cpl. F. Buttery's letter (see page 3) received last Wednesday morning brought the bad news of the death of L/Cpl. Ernest. S. Candlin. Official intimation was received from the War Office the same morning that he was "wounded" (another proof that we are able to hear from soldiers often more quickly and accurately than from official sources). L/Cpl. Candlin was an old soldier of the K.S.L.I. At the outbreak of war he went to Tipperary and thence to France, where he saw a good deal of fighting. He used to be a moulder at Days Pipe Works. His age was 29 — his brother Arthur is a soldier in the Salonica region.

The house in Station Road, Horsehay, where L/Cpl. Candlin was born.

FOULE

L/Cpl. L. Tart writes from Singapore:- "I am very pleased to sit down and write a short letter to you thanking you for the "Weekly Report", for all the boys out here are delighted with it – we all laugh when we look at it.

I am sorry to hear of so many Dawley boys who have gone under in this great crisis but there is one thing we can all say, and that is they died brave heroes fighting for their King and Country.

I also see in four "W.R." that you are trying to get some information

"we boys out here are delighted with it."

"Can't we send some sketches?"

of my dear brother, L/Cpl. W. Tart who has been reported "missing" since Easter. I hope you will succeed for it will relieve many broken hearts. I wish this war was all over so that we could come back to the Homeland once again for it seems such a long time since we came out here. I must admit we were lucky to come out here instead of going to France but of course we are all willing to go in the firing line any time if they would let us. The weather here is a treat at present."

Sergeant. W. L. Thomason of the Australian Auxiliary Forces now in France, had been home on short leave. He apologises for not coming to see us but sends 5/- for our Postage Fund – a fine tribute to the worth of our little paper from the soldier's point of view.

Price One Penny.

Only sold at the Brotherhood and Sisterhood Meeting at Dawley Baptist Chapel on condition it is sent (preferably in our Envelope) when read to a soldier.

Dawley News

Tuesday, October 24th 1916.

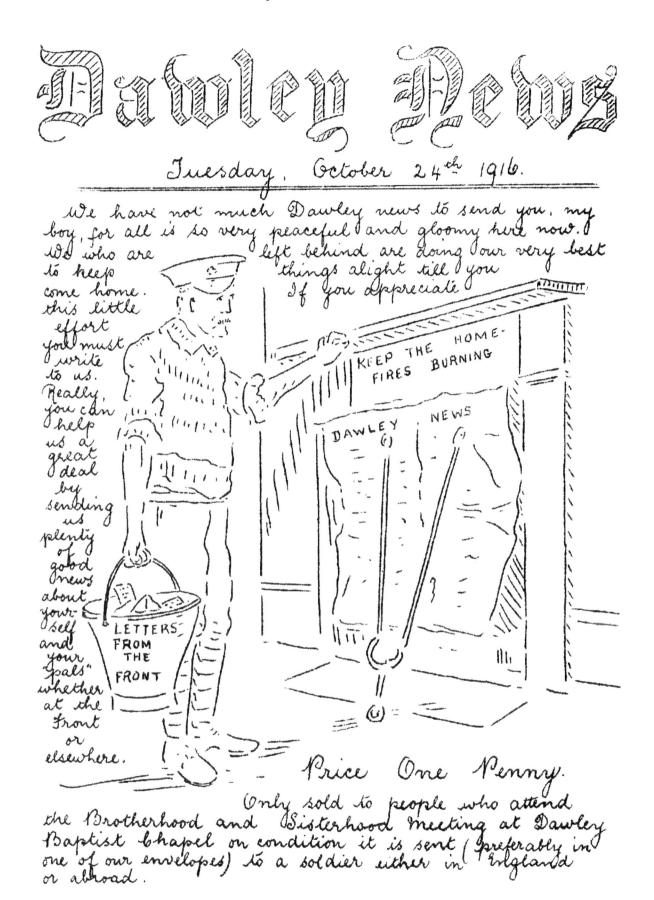

We have not much Dawley news to send you, my boy, for all is so very peaceful and gloomy here now. We who are left behind are doing our very best to keep things alight till you come home. If you appreciate this little effort you must write to us. Really, you can help us a great deal by sending us plenty of good news about yourself and your "pals" whether at the Front or elsewhere.

KEEP THE HOME-FIRES BURNING

DAWLEY (?) NEWS

LETTERS FROM THE FRONT

Price One Penny.

Only sold to people who attend the Brotherhood and Sisterhood meeting at Dawley Baptist Chapel on condition it is sent (preferably in one of our envelopes) to a soldier either in England or abroad.

Pte. Enoch Chilton writes from a camp in the South of England :- "I write to congratulate you on the splendid work of the B and S and your Church Members who are taking so much trouble for the sake of the boys who are in this great War. For months I have been trying to find out who the boys are who are serving their King and Country and your little paper puts me on their track.... Before leaving home for Canada I used to live at 40 Chapel St and Horsehay Common. I joined the Canadian Army last February and landed in Liverpool on Aug: 23rd After being in camp a week I got six days' leave which I spent at Horsehay. I was delighted to see the old town after an absence of three years. When on leave I heard that Pte. Crocker was killed (I was pleased to see in the D.N. that he isn't) Here we are learning how to shoot, we have to put on gas-masks, run 100 yards and fire - what a sensation!.... I would like you to sing my favourite hymn at one of your meetings - "Blest be the tie that binds."

"They teach us to make Xmas plum puddings there now"

At Pool Hill School a very useful Cooking and Domestic Teaching Centre is now being carried on under the supervision of local ladies.

Pte. W. H. Peake writes from France :- "Having now received two copies of the "Dawley News" from some member of your society I feel I must acknowledge them. It is indeed a very interesting paper. It is cheering to think someone remembers me though I have spent very little time in the old district for the past 18 years. I was especially interested in your note about Pte. Harry Bryce - he was in the same class at Dawley School - I hope you will be able to give us better news of him this week. No doubt there are many of my old school-chums out here but I have not come across any of them."

One of our men (so a C.O tells us) has been wounded by a regrettable accident. He was undergoing a course of instruction in a Bombing School and while at his work a box of bombs exploded, the cause not being known. He was wounded in several places; head, arms, hips and legs but his wounds, we are glad to say are not of a serious nature and the latest report is that he is going on very favourably (for private reasons we withhold this man's name)

Postage Fund. We have received nothing for this during the past week.
(1/- has been received from Mr. Round for Bible)

We are glad to say we are now able to send a parcel of magazines etc., each week to the old soldiers stationed at ——, for which they are grateful. We acknowledge with thanks parcels from the following friends:- Mr H. Simpson (2), Mrs Rowe (2), Mr J. R. Smith (2), Mr F. T. Wooding, Mr R. Bemrose, Mr Bailey (The Grange), Mr J. H. Jones, Mr S. T. Jones, Mr J. Jones, Mr Phillips (Glenmore), Mr A. Rowe and Dr Woodhouse. A few useful books have also been brought to the Meeting. May we beg our friends to bring more!

Our plan is to make a selection each week from our store, hoping in this way to keep up a fresh and interesting supply for these soldiers all through the winter.

Please send all communications on this matter to Mr Hubert Bailey, High Street or at the Tuesday Meeting.

Pte H. Darrall writes from France on Oct: 14th :- "I received your most welcome news on the 11th - it is very good of you to send it. as we all wonder how things are going on round the old district.

There are a few Dawley lads in this Battalion - some of whom you would know I Ernest Hyde, H. Edwards and Jones from the Rock, we are all together and quite well.

It is rough out here now, especially now the winter is coming on, but things are looking a bit better."

As the "Parish Lantern" is out this week we might use one to light us home after to-night's Meeting.

(It will be remembered we recently brought a German prisoner (in imagination) into the town to do odd jobs of local importance.)

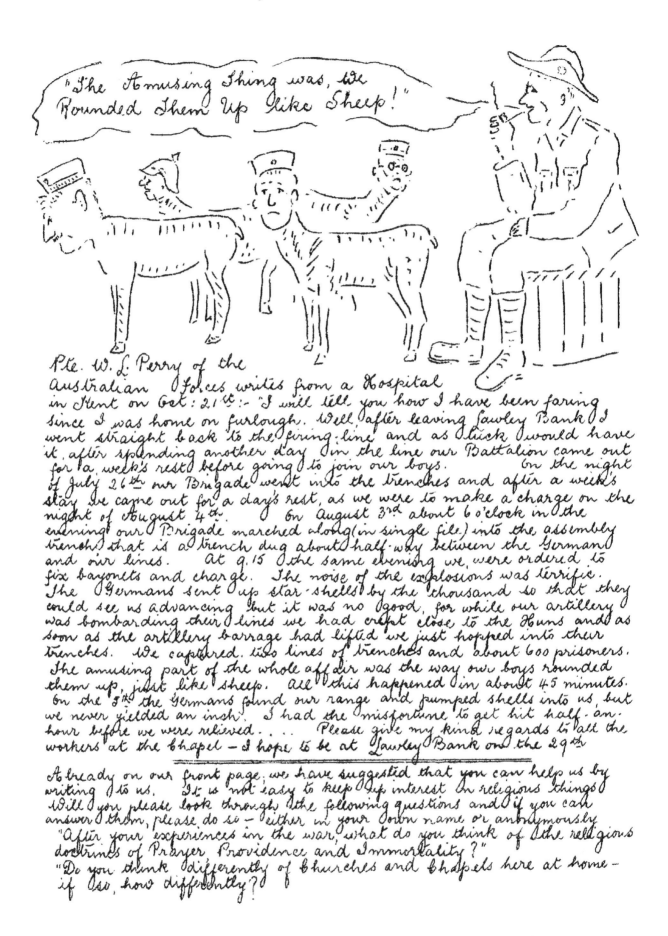

"The Amusing Thing was, We Rounded Them Up like Sheep!"

Pte. W. L. Perry of the Australian Forces writes from a Hospital in Kent on Oct: 21st:- "I will tell you how I have been faring since I was home on furlough. Well, after leaving Sawley Bank I went straight back to the firing-line and as luck would have it, after spending another day in the line our Battalion came out for a week's rest before going to join our boys. On the night of July 26th our Brigade went into the trenches and after a week's stay we came out for a day's rest, as we were to make a charge on the night of August 4th. On August 3rd about 6 o'clock in the evening our Brigade marched along (in single file) into the assembly trench that is a trench dug about half-way between the German and our lines. At 9.15 the same evening we were ordered to fix bayonets and charge. The noise of the explosions was terrific. The Germans sent up star-shells by the thousand so that they could see us advancing but it was no good, for while our artillery was bombarding their lines we had crept close to the Huns and as soon as the artillery barrage had lifted we just hopped into their trenches. We captured two lines of trenches and about 600 prisoners. The amusing part of the whole affair was the way our boys rounded them up, just like sheep. All this happened in about 45 minutes. On the 5th the Germans found our range and pumped shells into us, but we never yielded an inch. I had the misfortune to get hit half-an-hour before we were relieved.... Please give my kind regards to all the workers at the Chapel — I hope to be at Sawley Bank on the 29th

Already on our front page, we have suggested that you can help us by writing to us. It is not easy to keep up interest in religious things Will you please look through the following questions and if you can answer them, please do so — either in your own name or anonymously "After your experiences in the war, what do you think of the religious doctrines of Prayer Providence and Immortality?" "Do you think differently of Churches and Chapels here at home — if so, how differently?"

"Our Day" was not celebrated in Dawley last Saturday simply by youngsters at play — the town was canvassed by the members of the Dawley Nursing Division in aid of the Red Cross and a fair sum was realised.

Under the new regulations it is illegal for persons to collect for war charities without authority. We are applying for the necessary papers in order to collect from the public for our Dawley Soldiers' Comforts Fund.

In a picture paper of Saturday last there were illustrations of the work being carried on in a convalescent Home in Shropshire in making splints for wounded soldiers — One of the portraits has been recognised by Dawley people.

On Sunday evening about 7 o'clock in spite of the darkness and the rain there were about 100 young people parading the High Street, flashing electric lamps in each other's faces and otherwise "carrying on" — you see how lively we are!

General Sir. W. P. Campbell, K.C.B. the Military Chief of the Western Command is visiting Shrewsbury to-morrow and several Dawley gentlemen — representing the local Recruiting Authorities and the Tribunal are attending.

By arrangement with the Ministry of Munitions a certain number of soldiers are working side by side with some Dawley men, just outside the parish. Some of these soldiers, neglecting their work, have been fined. as they do not pay the fine they have been sent to gaol and on release will be handed over to the military Authorities.

A brother of the famous Captain Webb (who swam the Channel and to whose honour the monument above was erected) died last week at Birkenhead. Mr. W. H. Webb was connected with the Institute of Naval Architects and the Institute of Marine Engineers. He was born, we think, in a house which stood somewhere near Mrs H. S. Jones' china-shop.

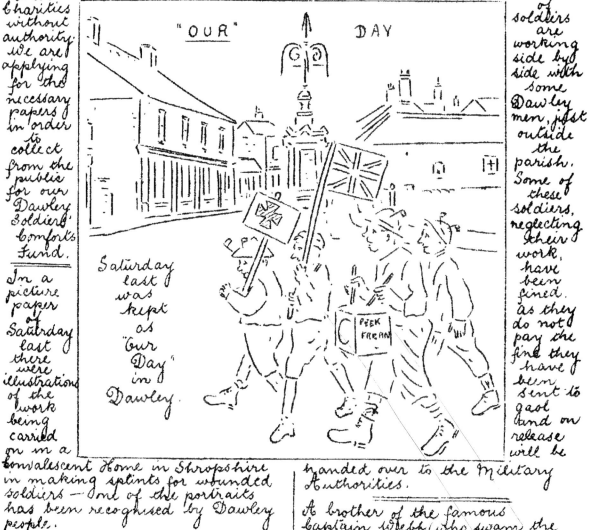

"OUR" DAY

Saturday last was kept as "Our Day" in Dawley.

Stoker George Rowe writes from Groningen, Holland on October 8th:- "Thank you for sending me the "W.R" again - I was beginning to think I had done with it for good. It is very nice to read of what is going on in my native place, of which I so long to hear, and also about the men who are fighting for their hearth and homes and how they appreciate your work. I hope it will be the means of drawing a closer fellowship and unity for our common cause. We lost one of our fellows by death last week and was buried last Tuesday with military honours. This makes four deaths since our entry into Holland, which is just two years to-day."

Pte S. Davies (Worcester Regt.) writes:- "I see you say in last week's "D.N" that I was wounded by gun-shot on Sept. 30th." No, I was wounded by shrapnel on July 30th but I am going on well and shall soon be alright again. It is nice to read the little paper and see how the lads are going on, I often think of them, though I am in old England."

The following is an exact transcript of part of a letter Mr. Lister has received from the lad, Albert Mortier (Belgian Refugee) whose family has now left Lawley Bank for Birmingham.

My Mother's sending you the note from the Railway (we promised to pay the cost of the carriage of the furniture we gave them) Please will you send the note back to us when you have done whigh it Me Mother & father thank you very much for what you have done for us (we are appealing for the money at our collection to-night) your cinsierly Albert

Further information has been received respecting Pte Harry Bryce, which we regret to say is not very re-assuring.

2nd Lieut: G.P. Bulmer writes:-

"I am afraid all the news I can give is that Pte Bryce was wounded on August 24th and the stretcher-bearer who dressed him said he walked down from him quite alright but he can't remember the nature of the wound as he had so many to dress on that day. But I think that the fact of his walking-down to the casualty clearing-station means that he could not have been wounded very seriously. I knew him very well as he was in my platoon and also orderly for some time - he was one of the very best." (We have made enquiries in many directions but Harry seems to have gone altogether)

The first local sharp frost was visible on Saturday morning last - the ground being quite white.

Many women were to be seen last week working in the potato-fields of the district.

"Lord give me faith - to live
from day to day,
With tranquil heart to do my
simple part,
And with my hand in Thine,
just go Thy way"
— John Oxenham —

A Dawley soldier translates the "Dawley News" for the benefit of his landlady in a French billet.

Sergeant S.G. Pitchford writes from Salonica Headquarters on Oct: 5th:- "Many thanks for the "D.N" - the new name is very appropriate, I think. I was pleased to have the last issue of the paper before your holidays - I was able to write to many of my chums who are doing their little bit in another theatre of war.

Since last I wrote things have changed in our favour though I am sorry so many Dawley boys have been called to make the supreme sacrifice. Dawley has already given some of her best - "Greater love hath no man than this." You will see that things have started to move now in the Balkans and as you know, many boys are out here." (Sergeant Pitchford sends us a copy of "The Balkan News" for which we thank him)

"Build a little fence of trust
around to-day.
Fill the space with loving work,
and therein stay.
Look not through the sheltering
bars
Upon to-morrow.
God will help thee bear what
comes
Of joy or sorrow."
— Mary. F. Butt —

Sergeant. F. Langford writes from France:— "It is a long time ago since I first received your very interesting paper — There must be quite a lot to do in its production and it is very good of you to send it out to the fellows.

I rather missed it during the time you suspended publication and when it started again it came as a pleasant surprise. I like the new name better than the old one, though we all speak of it as the "Weekly Report."

We are still trying to summon up a cheerful old grin but it is a bit difficult sometimes. I expect you would like to hear of our part in the "B.P." Well it is over 2 months now since our Battalion was sent to play its part, though for 18 months we have been in a hot part of the line. On Aug: 24th we shifted the Boches from a particularly strongly-fortified position in a wood, which we held for 48 hours. It rained in torrents — the trenches were flooded in no time and we were continually bombarded with heavy artillery but I am thankful to say we came through that little lot alright.

We were in the battle on Sept: 15th which the papers speak of as the greatest victory since the Marne. It was the occasion upon which the "Tank". "Land-Shark" etc. made its first public appearance and we had them to support us. Through a storm of machine-gun fire we strained our eyes to catch a first glimpse of them and at last we saw them. Over ground honey-combed with shell-holes they waddled along like an old tramp-steamer in a heavy sea. But forward they went as inexorable as Fate.

On other occasions since then we have been "over the top" but on that day our fellows were really magnificent and when the enemy counter-attacked they were driven off quite easily. Taking into consideration all we have been through, our casualties have been slight and I thank God I am through all without a scratch."

(We are glad to know that Sergeant Langford has been awarded the Military Medal — we congratulate him)

___

To A Soldier. When next you write home tell your people you receive this from us and ask them to come to our Meeting — it will help them.

"I should soon be in the Pantry

Pte. Edward Archer (who is ill at Malta) writes on October 18th. "I am still keeping my bed and am as weak as a cat.... If I were at home I should soon be in the pantry, I can't tell you. Send me a packet or two of "fags" out here as I cannot get any. This is a very nice place but I would rather be at home" (Will his old "pals" write to him? – 15444, Pte. E. Archer, A Block, No 3 Ward Sigue Military Hospital, Malta.)

Also at Malta is Pte. Solomon Shepherd who was wounded at Salonica first on Sept: 5th and then more seriously on the 24th being shot in the thigh and spine.

Rev. W. H. Compton (late Baptist Minister of Shrewsbury and who it will be remembered gave us at our Meeting since the outbreak of war, an excellent Dickens Recital) has gone with an Ambulance Unit to Mesopotamia.

Driver Harold Rowe is home from the Front for 10 days – he had a great welcome at the Chapel on Sunday. Pte. T. Bailey, wounded in a recent engagement and invalided to a hospital in Norfolk is now home on short leave, also Pte. W. L. Perry of the Australians, who was wounded and has been in hospital in Kent.

"German Measles!"

Sergeant W. Hughes writes on Oct: 23rd. "I am sorry to say I cannot send any more picture-postcards as they have stopped all photographic matter going through the post from France.... I am at a Hospital now and the other day I had a pleasant surprise: I met with two Dawley boys – the first I have seen since landing in France – Pte. Bishop of Bank Road and Pte. Adlington of Horsehay, both of whom belong to the Gloucesters, having been transferred from the Shropshires. They are suffering from German measles – the only thing of hospital fame they don't get from the Germans, though it bears their name. They had not seen the "D.N." for some weeks and were delighted to see the three or four copies I had kept. I am sorry I cannot give you any interesting news that sort is generally of a military character and therefore not allowed."

Message for the Week.

"He never turned his back, but marched breast forward.
Never doubted clouds would break,
Never dreamed, though right were worsted, wrong would triumph
Held, we fall to rise, are baffled to fight better
Sleep to wake"

Sergeant Sidney Rowe writes from a camp in Yorkshire on Wednesday last:- "I am out of hospital again and back at work. We are busy here getting the new Army into working order and some of them require a lot of getting ready - still we are making soldiers of them.... I expect I shall be going out to the front again before long, but that doesn't trouble me - for it will be over "the top" and good luck. I shall go with the best of spirits when the time comes."

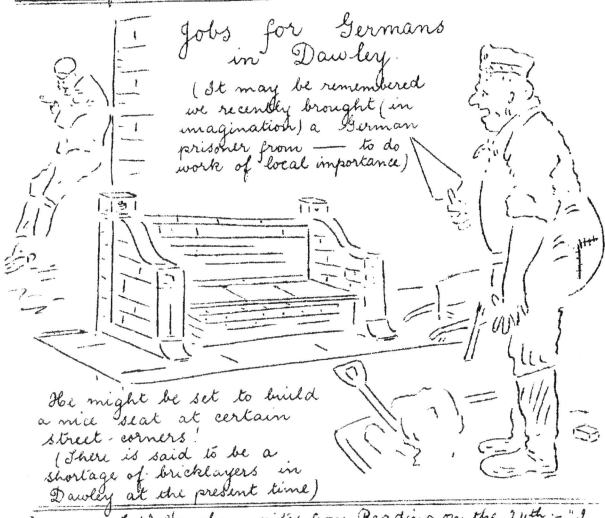

Jobs for Germans in Dawley.

(It may be remembered we recently brought (in imagination) a German prisoner from ⸺ to do work of local importance)

He might be set to build a nice seat at certain street - corners!
(There is said to be a shortage of bricklayers in Dawley at the present time)

Sergeant S. W. Vaughan writes from Reading on the 24th:- "I am going on well considering how badly I got 'blowed". The worst wounds are in my thigh and groin.... You must excuse my bad writing as I have got a wound over my eye and I can't see very well. Thank you for the "Dawley News" - I am sorry to see what you say about Harry Bryce, he was in my Battalion and he went "over the top" with me - he was a good soldier.... I have got about 8 wounds altogether, so I am not at all selfish."

"Turn the dark cloud inside out..."

This old chap with a wheezy melodion went singing(?) through Dawley Lane on Friday morning. The funny thing was he wore khaki puttees (properly fastened) and good boots – it almost looked as if some soldier had had mercy on him!

A "Bit of Sport"

Pte. Geo. Growcott writes from France on October 21st. Nothing pleases me better than the 'D.N.' which brings back to my mind the happy times I used to spend at the Brotherhood which was the best thing ever started in Dawley. But duty has called nearly all of us away.... I am at present out of the trenches but when we are in we have a bit of sport with the Germans until at last he gets his temper up and sends us iron rations.. Then our machine-guns and "Jack-Johnson" guns begin, followed by our infantry and then he starts and sings at the top of his voice "Mercy comrade". You can hear them a long way off.... I hope you will write to me again soon."

A "Top-Hole" Dinner.

Pte. G. V. Lovatt also writes from France:– I have just enjoyed a top-hole dinner so you can imagine how I feel at the present moment. No doubt you will say we are lucky in getting warm meals but Fritz is very quiet in this part of the line and we are able to do lots of things which add to our comfort.... Jack Butler had a letter from Jim Alford the other day but as I am not near him I cannot tell you about it..... The Boche is just giving us his mid-day 'strafe" with trench mortars, but it sounds as if he is getting the worst end of the bargain for there's about five of ours gone back in place of his one.'

Water Water Everywhere, and not a Drop to Drink."

Sapper J. Parton, in a letter received on October 27th, says:– "The D.N. is an excellent little paper and I should have written in reply to it before but we have really very little time. The weather now is wet and cold, we have had a continuous downpour of rain for two or three days making the trenches knee-deep in water.... I am very sorry to hear of the casualties among our boys but they suffer in a good cause. I shall be glad to see some of the old faces at Dawley, it will be a good thing when we are able to congregate in the Brotherhood again."

We are much obliged to friends who are helping us with our Soldiers' Comforts Fund by money or goods. During the week we have received a useful parcel of cigarettes, lighters, etc, from Mrs H. C. Woodhouse – part of which has already been despatched. We shall be very pleased to send socks or cigarettes to any soldier, who cares to ask for them. We shall send some without asking!

There was a Whist-Drive in Malinslee National Schools on Saturday afternoon in aid of the Red Cross Funds.

As nearly all the members have gone from the Liberal Club, it is being asked by some of the leaders whether the building might not be used for some other useful purpose to help the war.

The Dawley Sewing Guild — which knits socks, etc, for soldiers and provides other useful articles for needs arising out of the war — is now busy at work — doubtless for some of you who read this!

Mr. J. E. Gough has retired from the post of District Secretary of the Foresters' Friendly Society — a position he has held for 19 years! His father, the late Mr. Edwin Gough, held the same post for 31 years.

The Daily Mail on Friday last declared the Dawley Military Tribunal to be "under the thumb of the farmers." There isn't a single farmer on it!

In Malinslee parish, Churchpeople are interesting themselves in the National Mission. In the little leaflet personally handed by Rev. E. Parry to many of his parishioners the Bishop of Lichfield says:- "Of course I claim no sort of authority over those who do not worship with the Church of England but I wish to be considered their friend and I ask for their sympathy and prayers." Good!

Each evening last week special Mission Services were held in Dawley Church. As it must be inconvenient to walk so far in the dark, we have transplanted the church to High Street. We hope our church friends won't object!

Some of us here have been very desirous of helping wounded soldiers but it seems impossible for us to receive any in Dawley. But there is no reason why we should not share responsibility with others in the district. Mr Lester, mentioning the matter to the Secretary of the Wellington V.A.D Hospital the other day, received the following letter:-

"St John V.A.D. Wellington College, Salop, Auxiliary Hospital Western 27. Dear Mr Lester, we have accommodation for 34 men here and are quite full up. The men are being well cared for by a band of enthusiastic voluntary workers.

The capitation grant is quite inadequate to meet the outgoings and we are, therefore, dependent upon help from outside sources. We have a number of generous friends who assist by gifts in money and kind, but we are still needing further assistance. You have a number of people round you at Dawley who have not been slow to show their appreciation of the doings of our brave men at the front. Do you think you could influence them on behalf of a number of those who have returned from the fray? Gifts of vegetables, fruit, eggs and cigarettes are very acceptable. Last week, and again this week we received several couples of Rabbits. These eased the butchers bill somewhat. A little help week by week is highly appreciated.

Probably you know that Mr John Bayley has placed the free use of two houses – Newlands and College House – for the purposes of the Hospital, and has given generous gifts in other ways. In fact, he is the responsible man in this local effort. Help us a little, please! Visitors from Dawley would be welcomed.

Yours truly
J. F. Robinson
(Hon Sec)"

(We are hoping to bring this matter before our meeting to-night and may be able to organise some help)

Sergeant G. Collis writes from France:- I have been interested in "Old Remembrances" in the "D.N" but I have not been able so far to trace any of them. I have had the pleasure of meeting a few Dawley lads lately. We are having very changeable weather here now and rather sharp frosts but we are well off in the way of shelter and the health of our Regiment is good."

To Our Boys.

Here – or hereafter, you shall see it ended –
This mighty work to which your souls are set.
If from beyond – then, with the vision splendid,
You shall smile back and never know regret.

Or soon or late, for each – the life immortal!
And not for us to choose the How or When
Or late or soon – what matter? – since the Portal
Leads but to glories passing mortal ken.

O Lads! Dear Lads! Our men of God's anointing!
Press on in hope! Your faith and courage prove!
Pass – by these Highways of the Lord's appointing!
You cannot pass beyond our boundless love.

– John Oxenham –

There is apparently no uniform rule as to the degree of restriction of lighting of places of worship used on Sunday evenings. Some congregations meet in their Schoolroom, where the windows are closely curtained, in other places the main buildings are used and no particular care is taken. In one case no blinds are used - the inside lights are just shaded, and the building can be seen on Sunday nights for miles.

In looking through a list of old members of Dawley Bank Institute the other day it was discovered that no less than 40 of its old members are at the war. It may interest these to know that at the wish of a group of younger lads - all under military age - the place is being re-opened on Friday nights - with football on Saturdays much as in the old days.

Morning and afternoon services only were held at our Chapel last Sunday when collections were taken for Hospitals - two-thirds to be sent to the Royal Salop Infirmary and one-third to Wellington Cottage Hospital. The collection amounted to £7. 2. 9.

The three Nonconformist ministers are talking of establishing an after-church and chapel Lantern Evangelistic Service on Sunday nights probably in the Town Hall.

Our Postage Fund.
With grateful thanks we acknowledge the following amounts:-
"A Member of the Sisterhood - 2/6., Mrs Pugh (School House) 1/-. "C.H." 6d.
This Fund is used for the purchase of penny postage stamps for the despatch of this little paper to soldiers. Do please send us more money for this.

"We've got two pigs and a sheep for our Red Cross Sale in the Market Hall. Can you tell us where we can get more!"

He's Still at Sea.

Cook's Mate W. Hitchman of H.M.S. King George V writes on Oct: 18th:– "When a chap was home for good in days of peace he took his native place and everything connected with it as a matter of course, but how different the place seems now! How eagerly we await our mails to see if there is a line from the folks at home and that is why I for one so much appreciate the "Dawley News."

I am sure — deserves great praise for it."

Pte. Noah Vaughan writes from a Hospital in Sunderland:– "I lend the "Dawley News" to one of the nurses here to read who says it is very good indeed." (We do not apologise for these remarks – they alone keep us going)

A Quantity of Coal fell on E. Williams (Southall) on Tuesday last at Kemberton Colliery. He died on the way to Wenlock Hospital.

We are Going Ahead!

We had a crowded meeting last Tuesday and encouraging progress is being made. New helpers are rallying and we hope we shall shortly be able to introduce new work specially for soldiers wives and mothers, in addition to our usual Tuesday work. At our meeting Messrs J. W. Roberts and A. O. Callear sang splendidly and an earnest evangelistic address was given by Mr. R. A. Rhodes. Mr. F. J. Wooding read a number of letters sent by soldiers and Mr. W. Preece reported the results of his enquiries respecting "missing" men. Mr. E. Brookes and Mr. A. Bryce also took part. Several friends paid in money collected for the Soldiers' Comforts Fund and the collection was devoted to the payment of the cost of removal of Belgian Refugees' furniture.

If you have never written us a letter please send us a few lines at your first opportunity.

Price One Penny.

Only sold to people who attend the Brotherhood and Sisterhood Meeting at Dawley Baptist Chapel on condition it is sent in one of our envelopes to a soldier abroad or privately to a soldier in England (name to be furnished to Mr. Lester)

Dawley News

Tuesday. November 14th 1916.

We are now hoping to have a Monthly Monday-afternoon Meeting for the Wives and Mothers of all Dawley soldiers - whether in or out of this country. You will all agree with this project, we are quite sure. It is very lonely now for some of your women at home. Their allowances are alright - happily few of them have anxieties on that account. But the fact that you are away, exposed to the dangers and risks that you are is a constant worry to them. We are trying to help you a bit; we want to help them also.

Will you please write home, directly you receive this, and ask your wife or your mother to accept the invitation we are sending to her?

Next Monday afternoon at 2.30 is the first gathering we expect a big crowd and a grand time. Meeting in the Chapel a cup of tea etc. will be served in the Schoolroom.

"It's no use looking out for Daddy to-night. Granny dear. he wont come home yet."

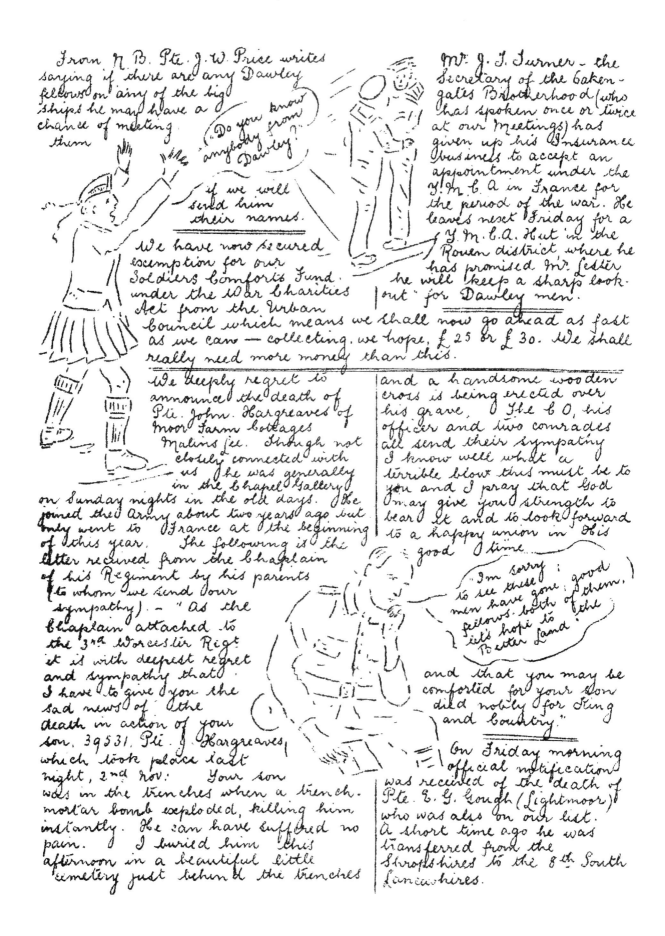

From H.B. Pte. J.W. Price writes saying if there are any Dawley fellows on any of the big ships he may have a chance of meeting them "Do you know anybody from Dawley?" if we will send him their names.

We have now secured exemption for our Soldiers Comforts Fund under the War Charities Act from the Urban Council which means we shall now go ahead as fast as we can — collecting, we hope, £25 or £30. We shall really need more money than this.

Mr. J.S. Turner - the Secretary of the Oakengates Brotherhood (who has spoken once or twice at our meetings) has given up his Insurance business to accept an appointment under the Y.M.C.A. in France for the period of the war. He leaves next Friday for a Y.M.C.A. Hut in the Rouen district where he has promised Mr. Lester he will keep a sharp look-out for Dawley men.

We deeply regret to announce the death of Pte. John Hargreaves of Moor Farm Cottages Malins Lee. Though not closely connected with us he was generally in the Chapel Gallery on Sunday nights in the old days. He joined the Army about two years ago but only went to France at the beginning of this year. The following is the letter received from the Chaplain of his Regiment by his parents (to whom we send our sympathy). – "As the Chaplain attached to the 3rd Worcester Regt it is with deepest regret and sympathy that I have to give you the sad news of the death in action of your son, 39531, Pte. J. Hargreaves, which took place last night, 2nd Nov. Your son was in the trenches when a trench mortar bomb exploded, killing him instantly. He can have suffered no pain. I buried him this afternoon in a beautiful little cemetery just behind the trenches

and a handsome wooden cross is being erected over his grave. The C.O, his officer and two comrades all send their sympathy I know well what a terrible blow this must be to you and I pray that God may give you strength to bear it and to look forward to a happy union in His good time. I'm sorry to see these good men have gone; good fellows both of them, let's hope to the Better Land and that you may be comforted for your son died nobly for King and country."

On Friday morning official notification was received of the death of Pte. E.G. Gough (Lightmoor) who was also on our list. A short time ago he was transferred from the Shropshires to the 8th South Lancashires.

Can You Send Us A Washerwoman?

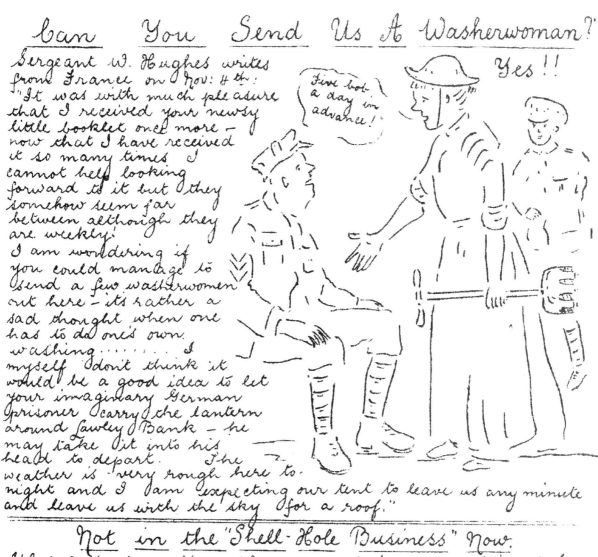

Yes!!

Five bob a day in advance!

Sergeant W. Hughes writes from France on Nov: 4th: "It was with much pleasure that I received your newsy little booklet once more – now that I have received it so many times I cannot help looking forward to it but they somehow seem far between although they are weekly. I am wondering if you could manage to send a few washerwomen out here – its rather a sad thought when one has to do one's own washing......... I myself don't think it would be a good idea to let your imaginary German prisoner carry the lantern around Lawley Bank – he may take it into his head to depart. The weather is very rough here to-night and I am expecting our tent to leave us any minute and leave us with the sky for a roof."

Not in the "Shell-Hole Business" Now.

L/Cpl. J. Davies writes:- "I am sorry to keep you waiting so long for a few lines but times, places and circumstances make all the difference, but now we are at rest for awhile - well away from the sound of the guns. It is a pleasure to feel good solid roads under our feet again after so much of the shell-hole business. Have you found out any more about Harry Bryce? I am very interested in his case for we were close friends." (No, we are sorry to say we haven't).

Are your letters lost? The G.P.O announces that the Arabia (torpedoed in the Mediterranean) had on board letter mails which have been lost. Will Dawley men note that we are not likely to receive letters posted at Singapore Oct: 7-13; Egypt, Oct: 27, Nov: 3, or papers (not letters) Hong Kong. Sept: 24 Oct: 6th. Will soldiers in these places please write again.

At our Meeting last Tuesday the address was given by Miss Dorothy Staunton (Birkenhead), solos being rendered by Miss Nellie Clay (Oakengates)

Bombardier C. Woolger writes from France on Nov: 8th :- "When I receive the D.N. I have to take it to pieces to give my pals a bit apiece for they all want it at the same time. The weather is very bad out here now but we are doing well under the circumstances as you can see in the papers.... I am glad you are going to introduce a new work for soldiers wives and mothers for it must be very

hard for those who have lost their loved ones... I trust it will not be long before I shall be able to see old faces again - in about another 12 months I think we shall all have our reward."

Pte. John Bishop writes from Malta :- "I am in a Hospital at Malta as I expect you have heard there have been a lot of boys bad in this place. We have had malaria fever and we have had enough of it. In many ways this place is like

JEALOUSY!

"Why should we Dawley women have to go down to Wellington?"

"Are you going to do yourself out of an out on Market Day?"

£10

DAWLEY

DAWLEY URBAN COUNCIL

WELLINGTON INFANT WELFARE CENTRE

The Dawley Urban Council voted £10 last Tuesday to the Wellington Infant Welfare and Maternity Centre, which is attended by a number of Dawley mothers. The Chairman suggested there ought to be a centre in Dawley. Why not?

England in money etc. but for all that give me England.

Soldiers' Comforts Fund.

The following amounts have been paid in. Oct: 19th Miss Tranter 5/-; Oct: 22nd Mrs M. H. Bailey £1-0-0; Oct: 26th Miss S. Ball (collected) £1-5-0. Oct: 26th Mrs Collis (collected) 16-2; Oct: 26th Mrs C. Tranter (collected) 3/-; Nov: 7th Mrs Boycott (collected) 10/10; Nov: 7th Mrs J. S. Smith. 10/-. making a total to date of £4-10-0 received by the Treasurers.

Last Sunday three public services were held at our Chapel,— morning, afternoon and evening. Being Temperance Sunday, Mr Lester preached on this subject in the afternoon — it was very appropriate as there had been a drunken fight in Lawley Bank

an hour or two previously. The Choir sang the Anthem — "I will lift up mine eyes unto the hills." A soldier in khaki was present at the evening mission service in the school-room, where Mr. C. H. Taylor read the lesson and Mr. C. Brookes rendered a Sacred Song "Into Thy Hands."

During this week we have received for our Postage Fund the following, for which we express thanks. Miss Simpson 10/-: Mr. J. Buttery 2/6. "A member of the Sisterhood" 2/-

Jobs for Germans in Dawley.
(We have brought (in imagination) a German prisoner from his work at — to do things of local importance.)

HADLEY GLEE SINGERS — SILVER COLLECT...

"ask for a crown from you she says!"

PAY - BOX

He might be set to forcibly demand adequate amounts from people who attend the next Red Cross Concert in the Town Hall!

The Hall was crowded last Tuesday and we understand from a disappointed Red Cross official the "silver" collection at the doors amounted to only £3-14-0. another collection was made on retiring which made a total of £5, out of which £2 expenses have to be paid!!!

The Urban Council at its meeting last week elected a new member in place of the late Mr. J. Payne. Three names were submitted — Messrs A. Phillips, W. Kerr and J. G. Watkiss — the first-named being the winner after a close contest

Will soldiers please send us a few lines for our next week's issue.

Dawley News: November 1916

"The Mountainous Scenery is Grand."

Corporal Nelson Rhodes writes from Salonica:— "I am very much surprised to see by the "Dawley News" that so many local fellows are out here — it seems a pity that situated as we are so far away from home, we cannot see each other in order to pass away the time more pleasantly. As regards this country, I haven't much to say in its favour. The mountainous scenery of course is grand but when one sees nothing else from morning till night it gets somewhat monotonous. Up to the present we have been favoured with ideal weather and a Balkan winter, which one never looks forward to, has yet to tell its tale.... It is a pleasing and interesting sight to see Russian, French, Italian, Serbian and British soldiers encamped side by side and to think they are all fighting for one cause... I should like to tell you more interesting news but, alas, I cannot."

"As A Scientific Instrument Maker."

I Like my Work Very Much."

Pte. W. G. Roberts who is attached to the A.O.C. writes from the Base Work-shops, Salonica:— "as you will see by the address I am attached to the Army Ordnance Corps as a watchmaker and scientific instrument maker and I like my work very much. But we fellows in the workshops don't feel half so jolly as the boys in the fighting-line — they put more heart into singing to a mouth organ than they do to a piano in a wood hut at the base. I have been in hospital for a month with fever but I am going on very well now."

"My Old Shop-Mate."

Pte. S. Bird, 5586, 69 M. G. Coy, 69 Brigade, B.E.F. writes:— "I am writing to thank you all for the very valuable help we receive in the shape of the "D.N.; In one of the recent ones I recognised one of my old shop-mates, W. L. Perry of the Australian Forces. As he nicely puts it we have done quite a lot of rounding-up. We are now in a quieter part of the line for a much-needed rest."

Pte. S. Davies (Sky Light Row) and Pte. G. Jackson (Church Rd West) have been discharged from the army through ill-health and have returned to civil employment.

We understand that Pte. Philip Powell and several other Dawley lads have removed from Singapore. After a few days in India it is thought they have gone to Mesopotamia.

234

One Day At A Time.

Life is lived only a day at a time, and the very darkest to day will be gone to-morrow. The consequences of its sorrow or its sin may throw a long shadow ahead, but we at least shall have passed through it and shall have reached the farther side. It is the massing of days and their troubles that throws the soul into panic. "Take my hand, and don't try to see any farther than the next step" said the reassuring voice of one who was guiding a friend over a broken and perilous bridge. And when we come to life's hardest places, our Heavenly Friend offers the same counsel and help. It is the only safe way through hours of bewilderment, bereavement and pain. The long look ahead brings despair; one step at-a-time, guided by the Master's hand, will lead us through.

The Dawley British Women's Temperance Association held its Annual Meeting at its Rooms in the High Street last Monday week. All the women of Dawley are not teetotallers yet! (A Stirchley woman-publican said at Wellington last week that she has permission to brew 200 extra bushels of beer if she can get a man to do it!)

Ptes. Jack Butler and A. Morton write a joint letter from France on Nov: 7th: "We are both in the best of health and spirits, though it has been very trying these last few weeks — raining nearly all the time. I used to think Dawley was about the wettest place in the world but I have changed my opinion now... We were very sorry to hear of so many of our old Dawley pals being so unfortunate. We had a fine view of a fight in the air a few days ago. Four of our aeroplanes and three Germans. It was the finest exhibition of flying I have ever seen and it resulted in one of ours coming down and one of the Germans — it was "a sight for sore eyes" as they say in Dawley."

Pte. S. Machin writes from Ancoats Con: Home, Alderley Edge, Great Warford, Cheshire:- "My injury was not so serious, only two shrapnel bullets in the right arm... Yes the "Tanks" are great, they paved the way for us on Sept: 15th and also when our boys took Lesboeufs."

Several small gifts were brought in for wounded soldiers at Wellington on Tuesday last – we hope to secure a really good weekly collection as time goes on.

The Somme Battle Pictures were exhibited at Wellington on the first three days of last week and at Oakengates on the last three days. Some people who have seen them seem somewhat disappointed! We only hope everyone who has seen them will be inspired to do more for you men who have actually taken part in the fray – you have found the real thing sufficiently sensational, we are sure!

We are sending a parcel of reading matter to the old soldiers at —— each week. We shall be glad of magazines for this purpose, if any of your people at home can send us any

Bombardier J. Parkes writes from France :- 'I should have acknowledged the "D.N." sooner but we have been in action for a considerable time which means work and plenty of it. I am at this moment waiting to send Fritz his night-cap before turning in. I rarely meet any of the boys from Dawley. The weather has been dead against us these last few days and has made us unearth our paddling-kit, but we do not mind as we are seasoned mud-larks and more or less enjoy it. I am sorry to read of so many casualties from Dawley – some of my old chums were among them but it cannot be helped. I have been very lucky myself, having been in and out of the firing-line since August 14th and I hope to carry my bat through. Things are now going greatly in our favour which we have been waiting a long while for. My present back-rest is a picture to glory in, piles of food for the breech, which makes every gunner feel happy."

Price One Penny.

Only sold at the Brotherhood and Sisterhood meeting at Dawley Baptist Chapel on condition it is sent in one of our addressed envelopes to a soldier abroad or privately to a soldier at home (name to be given to us to avoid duplication of copies)

Dawley News

Tuesday. Nov: 21st 1916.

We can imagine what it is like at the Front, this weather!

Price One Penny.

This little paper is sent to over 200 Dawley soldiers out of England every week. It is only sold at the Brotherhood and Sisterhood meeting at Dawley Baptist Chapel on condition it is posted in one of our addressed envelopes Every Dawley soldier is supposed to have a copy regularly — if any man is not getting it, please write to Mr Lester or Mr Wooding. giving the exact address.

As the result of the recent local efforts for the funds of the Red Cross the sum of £55 has been forwarded by Miss Briscoe treasurer of the St. John Ambulance Brigade of which Miss Edith Rowe is the secretary. (We may say that your envelope is addressed each week by Miss May Rowe)

Nurse Everest, who came to Dawley about 10 months ago as District Nurse has been appointed nurse at Madeley Union. A collection for Dawley Nursing Association is to be held shortly

"Old Remembrances are Thronging Through My Memory" alright! The first Dawley soldier who sends us a post card identifying this shall receive a book prize.

Pte. Albert Bishop writes from France:—
"I have been in the trenches 3 times now, it is very hot there on both sides."
(Commenting on the report that the German Government is confiscating pewter vessels of every kind he sends the following lines):—
"Pewter pots and pewter pans
Jugs and mugs of pewter
Yield up all your vessels Fritz
Female, male and neuter
Well we understand the strain
On your pride and little
How can men their pluck retain
Unless they keep their metal?"
(Mr. Wooding says the above goes very well to tune of "Little Drop of Water" — he has tried it)

We are deeply grateful to friends who have kindly subscribed to our new Fund "Soldiers' Wives and Mothers Monthly Socials" — Mr. J. A. Jones £1, Mr. C. Beddard £1. "Weekly Donor" 2/6 We hope these amounts will about cover the cost of yesterday's meeting reported elsewhere in this paper.

Again we thank our friends for the following gifts to our Postage Fund:— "Anon" (by post) 2/6; "A member of the Sisterhood" 2/-; Miss Vaughan, 1/6; Miss P.B. 1/-; Mr. Francis 1/- Mrs. B. 6d; Mrs. Morton 6d. Miss Jonks 2½. From this Fund we meet the expenses of posting this paper to soldiers week by week

In The Lull

A Soldier's Prayer.

Ere the blood-red dawn has broken,
Ere the clash of steel begins,
Ere the dread command is spoken,
Lord absolve us from our sins:
Ere we war with men, may we
Humbly make our peace with Thee.

When the darts of death are flying
Shrieking through the startled air,
When, with demon powers vying
Men lay all their passions bare,
Lord in that tremendous day,
While we fight we cannot pray

Hear us, therefore, for Thy mercies'
And Thy loving kindness' sake,
And to-morrow hide the curses
Which upon our lips we take,
Heedless in our time of stress,
In Thy deep forgetfulness.

Turn Thine ear then to the others,
Praying in a peaceful land,
Brethren, sisters, fathers, mothers
That for us their words may stand,
Hear their prayers, the warrior pleads
Now by nothing else but deeds.

A. W. B.

Sir Charles Henry M. P.
asked two questions in
Parliament last week – one
in respect to the number
of men under 30 engaged
in anti-aircraft service
and the other respecting
men of military age
engaged in canteens.
The official reply to both
questions was that steps
are being taken to provide
substitutes for these men

Jobs for Germans in Dawley.

(We recently brought (in
imagination) a German
prisoner from —— to do things
of local importance)

He might be
set to draw a few
portraits of local
celebrities for this paper!
(If he cannot do better than
this he is as bad a
draughtsman as our own artist!)

Last week a letter to Stoker George Rowe (interned in Holland) was written on notepaper embellished with the Union Jack — it has been returned to us by the censor on account of this!

We acknowledge with thanks gifts of books from the following friends for the old soldiers at ___ Mr. W. G. Bailey, Mr. Lavender, Mr. Wooding, Mr. John Bishop and Mr. Harry Bailey.

A few days ago, Pte. Albert Jovatt (who is just finishing his training) was married to Miss Elsie Bryce at Malins Lee Church.

As a result of the donation of £10 by the Dawley Urban Council to the Wellington Child Welfare Association four representatives are to be asked to serve on the committee.

"The Artillery Bombarded Us With Heavy Stuff."

Pte. A. Percy Jones writes from France on Nov. 13th :- I appreciate the "D.N" very much... The winter is now coming on adding to the general hardship of everything, changing many a whistle into a groan and many a groan into what the Baroness Orczy calls "a good old English ___ Our friends over the way do not seem to have so much ammunition to spare as was the case 12 months ago, still we won't grumble about that ___ but perhaps the Somme is taking most of their attention at the present time. I have now got my second wind and am not bothering much about leave (which seems farther off than it did 9 months ago). I am hardly getting fonder of this country and I would willingly change it for the old one at any time to suit the convenience of the military authorities... If anyone asks you you can tell them from me that I really think the war will end ___ sometime. Of course, I cannot be too certain about that but I think it will. I have recently taken part in a football match against some Artillery boys, I was not on the winning-side but better luck next time. They are a heavy set of fellows and they bombarded us with heavy stuff — they whacked us 4-1, the last two goals being scored in the last 10 minutes.... I see some of the Dawley boys have been having a taste of the "B.P" and find it not all honey — my Battalion has not escaped."

Dawley Military Tribunal sat for three hours at the Town Hall on Friday last, when forty or fifty appeals were dealt with. Thirteen exemptions granted to Horsehay workmen at the last meeting were returned by the military authorities for revision. The Tribunal refused to review them, simply confirming their previous decisions. The new military Representative, Mr. C. Clarke-Bruff gave notice that he would send the whole of these cases to the Central appeal Tribunal. The engine-driver at the Council's pumping station was granted six months exemption - a member remarking it would not do to stop the Water-Supply. The new regulations regarding medical examination proved advantageous to applicants - several men in low health categories being granted temporary exemption on these grounds. Several appeals by men employed at the Coalbrookdale Works were adjourned in order to see the result of the Company's appeal for 150 of their men. A man who asked for exemption on the ground that he was paying 13/-

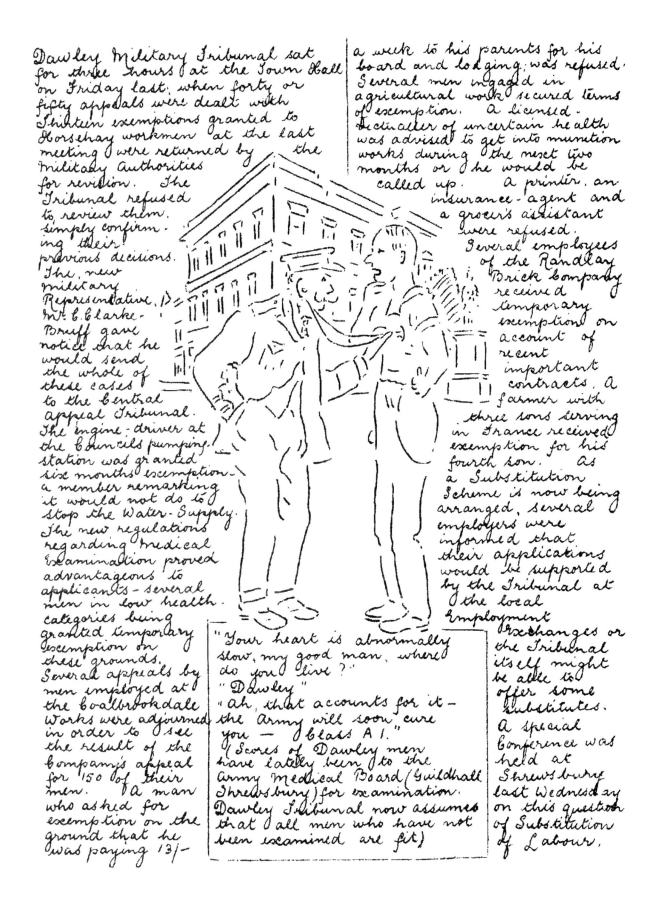

"Your heart is abnormally slow, my good man, where do you live?"
"Dawley"
"Ah, that accounts for it - the Army will soon cure you — Class A1."
(Scores of Dawley men have lately been to the Army Medical Board (Guildhall Shrewsbury) for examination. Dawley Tribunal now assumes that all men who have not been examined are fit)

a week to his parents for his board and lodging was refused. Several men engaged in agricultural work secured terms of exemption. A licensed-Victualler of uncertain health was advised to get into munition works during the next two months or he would be called up. A printer, an insurance-agent and a grocer's assistant were refused. Several employees of the Randlay Brick Company received temporary exemption on account of recent important contracts. A farmer with three sons serving in France received exemption for his fourth son. As a Substitution Scheme is now being arranged, several employers were informed that their applications would be supported by the Tribunal at the local Employment Exchanges or the Tribunal itself might be able to offer some Substitutes. A special Conference was held at Shrewsbury last Wednesday on this question of Substitution of Labour.

Driver. J. W. Rowlands writes from France :- "I have not come across any Dawley lads out here as I am the only one from the old town in our corps. But I have got some chums who come from adjoining districts and they look forward to the "D. N" as much as I do".

At our meeting last week Mr Alfred Hoggins (Chairman of Oakengates Military Tribunal) was the speaker and Mr F. Forgham sang. Time only allowed for one song from Miss. G. Waterton but she has promised to come and sing again soon. There was a fine crowd present, despite the darkness and the fog.

Signaller G. Lloyd Roberts writes from a Hospital at Salonica :- I can assure you the "D. N" is very much appreciated. I am sorry so many of our lads are getting put out in the "B. P" for we cannot spare them very well... I have not been enjoying very good health and am at present in hospital. I got better once but I had a relapse and

"You cannot tell the joy a chap feels when he is reading a letter in the "D. N" which actually comes from an old pal."

had to return to bed but I am pleased to say I am progressing nicely now. I cannot write more as it is difficult to write in bed."

A Trench Poet

Pte. George Growcott writes from France :- "I am keeping my spirits up and my head down. We are enjoying ourselves singing the good old songs but our latest song has been composed by the lads in our Machine Gun corps and it runs like this :-

"Away down Communication Trench.
Away down Whiz-bang Lane;
I've got a cosy little dug out.
Where the great Jack Johnsons rain.

Very close to the sniper's post,
Where the aerial torpedoes visit us most,
You can get some machine-gun toast,
Away down Whiz-bang Lane."

(Will Pte. Growcott please send us the music of the above so that the choir can sing it ?)

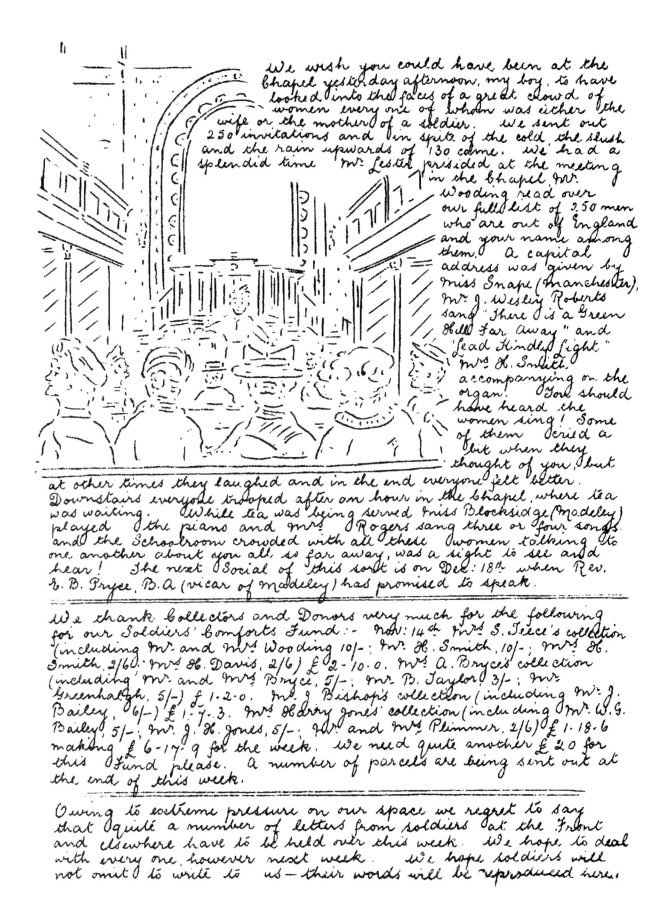

We wish you could have been at the Chapel yesterday afternoon, my boy, to have looked into the faces of a great crowd of women every one of whom was either the wife or the mother of a soldier. We sent out 250 invitations and in spite of the cold, the slush and the rain upwards of 130 came. We had a splendid time. Mr Lester presided at the meeting in the Chapel. Mr Wooding read over our full list of 250 men who are out of England and your name among them. A capital address was given by Miss Snape (Manchester). Mr J. Wesley Roberts sang "There is a Green Hill Far Away" and "Lead Kindly Light", Mrs H. Smith accompanying on the organ. You should have heard the women sing! Some of them cried a bit when they thought of you, but at other times they laughed and in the end everyone felt better. Downstairs everyone trooped after an hour in the Chapel, where tea was waiting. While tea was being served Miss Blocksidge (Madeley) played the piano and Mrs Rogers sang three or four songs and the Schoolroom crowded with all these women talking to one another about you all so far away, was a sight to see and hear! The next Social of this sort is on Dec: 18th when Rev. E. B. Pryce, B.A (vicar of Madeley) has promised to speak.

We thank Collectors and Donors very much for the following for our Soldiers' Comforts Fund:- Nov: 14th Mrs S. Teece's collection (including Mr. and Mrs Wooding 10/-; Mr. H. Smith, 10/-; Mrs H. Smith, 2/6; Mrs H. Davis, 2/6) £2-10-0. Mrs A. Bryce's collection (including Mr. and Mrs Bryce, 5/-; Mr. B. Taylor 3/-; Mr Greenhalgh, 5/-) £1-2-0. Mr J Bishop's collection (including Mr J. Bailey, 6/-) £1-7-3. Mrs Harry Jones' collection (including Mr. W.G. Bailey, 5/-; Mr. J. H. Jones, 5/-; Mr. and Mrs Plimmer, 2/6) £1-18-6 making £6-17-9 for the week. We need quite another £20 for this Fund please. A number of parcels are being sent out at the end of this week.

Owing to extreme pressure on our space we regret to say that quite a number of letters from soldiers at the Front and elsewhere have to be held over this week. We hope to deal with every one however next week. We hope soldiers will not omit to write to us — their words will be reproduced here.

Sapper. A. Upton writes from France :- "I show the D. N to my pals and they are delighted .... I wish someone would send me a small prayer-book as I have lost the one the Vicar of Doseley sent me last year... I only hope the weather clears up and then we shall be able to show the Germans what the British soldier is made of, for we shall come out top and keep the old flag flying."

"If people only knew how much your paper is appreciated, you would get your money immediately!"

We have to pay nearly £ 5 this week for a fresh supply of paper - we shall be glad of extra help for the upkeep of this little weekly.

Pte. H. Darrall writing from France, says :- "J. Hyde Edwards and myself are all in the same billet and you bet we were soon having a look at "Dawley News" when it came. We hope you will continue to send it... We are sorry to hear of Pte. H. Bryce." (At our meeting last Tuesday Mr. Lester reported that a Swiss Agency which undertakes to search the lists of British prisoners in Germany, is unable to find this man's name. We are compelled to draw our own sorrowful conclusions from this. Alas! he is not the only Dawley man who is "missing" - in one or two cases we have been making enquiries for months)

Dawley News

Tuesday, November 28th 1916.

Here We Are!

"I wish I could bring one of our camels to Dawley — it would be a novelty!"

Sapper Thompson writes as follows:— "It is a real treat to get a paper from the dear old place and I cannot tell you how much the boys out here enjoy reading it.

The sketch of the camel has been sent by Sapper. A. Thompson from Egypt — we have just put him on the point of leaving the old circus at Field, at the bottom of Meadow Road!

I am sending you a sketch but there is not much to sketch about here as we are far out in the desert, right away from any town... I am sorry to hear of so many boys going under but I suppose it is the fortunes of war."

Price One Penny.

This little paper is only sold at the Brotherhood and Sisterhood meeting at Dawley Baptist Chapel on condition it is sent in one of our addressed envelopes to a Dawley soldier, of whom we have about 250 on our list — every one out of England.

Pte A. Barker writes from France saying he is sorry to hear of so many Dawley boys being lost but they have died heroes' deaths. He says all the boys flock round him once a week when he receives the "D.N" and they all had a laugh when they read about Billy Lloyd and more so when I explained to them who he was. In the trenches where he is now it is fairly quiet but they had some severe fighting a short time ago — he himself is wounded but he is now almost alright again.

Last week we sent out 33 parcels to soldiers each containing a shirt, socks, cigarettes peppermints stationery, shoe-laces, etc. The average value of each parcel is about 6/- plus carriage. In selecting names we have endeavoured to choose the men who belong to apparently the poorest families. We hope to send a small Xmas parcel to each soldier on our list at Hong Kong and Singapore — 30 in all — to-day. We beg our friends to send us much more money for our Comforts Fund — we need at least another £20 at once.

Our Last Week's Post-Bag

DAWLEY POST OFFICE

33 PARCELS. 200 LETTERS

When we have persuaded all the people we can at our Tuesday meeting to take envelopes we generally have 120 or so left on our hands, which are dealt with at the close of the meeting and posted at once.

That means we have to find on an average 10/- a week for postage stamps. We shall be grateful for help towards this. The following amounts have been received during the week:- Sir C. S. Henry Bart. M.P. - £1. A member of the Sisterhood 2/-. Mrs H - 6d.

About a score of soldiers on foreign service write to us every week saying how much they appreciate the "D.N." a copy having reached Sir Charles Henry our M.P. writes a few words of kindly cheer, enclosing £2 towards our expenses. We are very grateful for this donation and have assigned £1 to the Paper Fund and £1 to the Postage Fund.

We have now a direct representative of the "D.N." "on the spot" in France. Look out for him a tall chap in a fur coat somewhere in the neighbourhood of a gigantic blue-black gun which needs a couple of traction-engines to move it. See him if you can (Cyril F. Jester) and tell him some of your experiences.

If any soldier desires any particular pal's address, please ask us. If you change for it — we cannot put addresses in here. yours kindly let us know.

"Tank" Secrets Out At Last!

"Thank you Dawley for doing your bit."

At last, pictures of the famous "Tanks" are published. We are bringing one (in imagination) through Dawley, where it is an open secret – we are specially interested in them!

Pte. A. E. Corbett writes sadly from Hong Kong on Oct: 22nd in reply to the news of the death of his mother. He says that when coming back from Australia where he took German prisoners he slipped and caused a dislocation for which an operation has become necessary at once. (We deeply sympathise with this man in his troubles)

Cook's Mate W. Hitchman writes from H.M.S. King George V.:-

"I think all the members of the B and S have done yeoman work all through the war. For not only the "D.N" and your parcels of books but the personal letters from different friends connected with the movement have helped to brighten my own life and the lives of many others.... I am in the best of health and although I expect to spend another Xmas at sea it is all for a good cause and when the struggle is over we shall be able to say we have done our bit."

Pte. E. Brown writes from Great Yarmouth:- "I have been away on farm-work since August 26th but have now returned to settle down once more to Army life. There are not many Dawley boys with us now as most of them went to France while I was away, ie I found myself among new faces when I came back Joe Dunning is still here, though."

A few days ago a wounded soldier, tired of being in another part of the country wrote to Mr. Lester, asking if he could not secure for him a transfer. Last Saturday the man had the joy of arriving at one of the V.A.D Hospitals in Wellington. Please do not expect this to be repeated, boys!!

The members of the Dawley Nursing Division have offered to share the nursing of wounded soldiers located in one of the Wellington V.A.D. Hospitals. They are also collecting food-stuffs for these Hospitals — just as we are attempting to do at our Tuesday meeting.

Lieutenant. H.A.L. Bayley second son of Mr. H.R.G. Bayley, Horsehay. has been promoted Captain in the R.E.
Lance-Corporal H.C. Reade, who was formerly employed at Horsehay Works, has received a Second-Lieutenancy and is now with the Royal Flying Corps.

Pte. R. Nickless writes from France:- "We have been out of action for a fortnight now and some of us are farming - getting up mangolds and potatoes. They always keep us busy. Some people seem to think that the R.A.M.C have a soft time of it and don't go near the trenches but they would think different if they could see us. We go where the infantry go and we are not able to take cover like the other lads for

Let me first of all ascertain how many you have punched!

Les pommes de terre françaises évacuées par les soldats anglais.

(The rule laid down by certain potato-growers to their women-potato-pickers who were working in the fields last week was "no pinch-ing!")

we have to go up and down with cases. The lights are awful but we must not grumble. I have met ever so many Shropshire lads out here and they are always smiling. I had the pleasure of meeting my own brother at the Base... We shall all welcome the end of the war — I think it is in sight now. I see by the D.N we have lost some of our gallant boys but we feel sure they are in Heaven above — where all is Peace.."

Church-people are taking steps to erect Shrines containing the names of soldiers who have gone from the several ecclesiastical parishes of Dawley. We are asked to supply some names to the clergy. We hope this will not prevent the erection of a permanent memorial later on, to bear the names of all Dawley men without religious or parochial distinctions.

A few days ago, an aeroplane passed over Lawley Bank. Several people did not see it, thinking the sound was that of a passing motor-car.

In spite of the dearness of eggs (they are now sold at 4d each) about 350 have been collected by Mrs Greenhalgh and her friends in the district for wounded soldiers during the past fortnight.

At Wellington Police Court last week a Stirchley school-girl was

Jobs for Germans in Dawley.

(Some time ago we brought (in imagination) a German prisoner into the town to do work of great importance).

He might be set to keep children out of the way of motor-cars at a certain corner!

Two children have recently had narrow escapes from heavy motor-lorries rushing round a certain corner. (Rev. C.W. Hickman at our meeting last Tuesday said it was very important that we do everything we can to protect child-life at the present time)

A soldier in his letter this week suggests we might set our German prisoner to work with pick, shovel and wheelbarrow to level Dun Cow Bank! (If so, these wild motors would tear round the corner faster than ever!)

charged with stopping a little boy of seven years who was sent on an errand and stealing 2/6 from the purse.

A Dawley soldier (who has lately joined up) was recently fined for keeping a lurcher dog without a license. The defence was he had given the dog away several times but it always came back home!

Pte. J. Frost writes from Egypt:- "I was quite surprised to receive such nice letters from you - I thought I had lost all touch of Dawley people but I see now that there is someone who has not forgotten us. When I am on duty I often pull the letters out of my pocket and read them again - it makes me think of the old town where I have spent the best part of my days.... I have been a few miles in different countries but this land is the limit. We have nowhere to go at night, except the Y.M.C.A, and if we are a bit lively at times it soon goes dead and makes us wish we were back in old Blighty again."

"If William Lloyd Came Over the Top" —

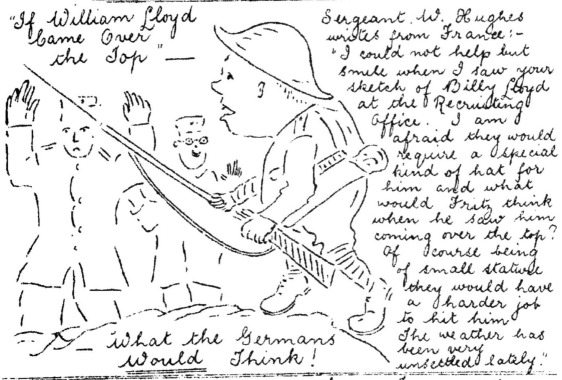

What the Germans Would Think!

Sergeant W. Hughes writes from France:- "I could not help but smile when I saw your sketch of Billy Lloyd at the Recruiting Office. I am afraid they would require a special kind of hat for him and what would Fritz think when he saw him coming over the top? Of course being of small stature they would have a harder job to hit him. The weather has been very unsettled lately."

Corporal J. Smith writes on Nov: 15th from France:- "You will know by the time you receive this that a terrible battle has been raging incessantly now for three days in this part and we have captured thousands of Germans. I have seen the Red Cross cars bringing down wounded by the score but mostly Germans and to see our slightly wounded men helping the slightly wounded Germans out of our Red Cross cars is a sight worth seeing. It reminds me of some lines I used to know when I was in Dawley years ago —
"Lions they were in battle my lords.
But lambs when the battle was o'er."
I am exceedingly grateful for your valuable little paper which I receive every week and I must say that I have obtained more local information from it than from any other source whatever. I am proud to think that our little town has done so well in the struggle for freedom and right."

For our Comforts Fund we are deeply grateful to the following friends. "Ineligible" £1. Bootlaces (value 17/6) Mr. Preece; Cigarettes (value 5/-) Mr. Greenhalgh; Peppermints (value 7/6). Mr. Tranter (St. Georges)

Pte. A. Morton writes from France - "We are in the trenches up to our knees in water in places. When we have finished our shift in the sap we go into cellars behind the firing-line where we can almost put out our hands when in bed and touch grave-stones in a cemetery"

Pte. Maurice Cadman writes from Egypt that he is very busy though he cannot say what he is busy at – but he will tell us when the war is over. He says it is more than two years since he received the first letters from us

Letters have been received from Pte. H. Hoof and Driver Fred Vaughan also from L/Cpl. Noah Jones who is at Singapore

L/Cpl W. H. Oliver writes from Malta saying the same shell wounded both himself and Solomon Shepherd. Pte. Shepherd seems to have got the worst of it and is now on his way home to England. L/Cpl. Oliver has been in hospital since September 18th.

A Bit of "Spurgeon."

Our Lord meant by saying men ought always to pray, that they ought to be always in the spirit of prayer always ready to pray. Like the old knights, always in warfare not always on their steeds dashing forward with their lances to unhorse an adversary, but always wearing their weapons where they could readily reach them and always ready to encounter wounds or death for the sake of the cause which they championed. Those grim warriors often slept in their armour, so even when we sleep, we are still to be in the spirit of prayer so that if perchance we wake in the night we may be with God. Our heart is to be like those beacons and watch-towers which were prepared along the coast of England when the invasion of the Armada was hourly expected, not always blazing but with the wood always dry and the match always there the whole pile being ready to blaze up at the appointed moment. Our souls should be in such a condition that ejaculatory prayer should be very frequent with us – silent, short, swift petitions to the throne of grace.

"We have to keep them from rising against one another,"

says Pte Albert Powell writing from Singapore on Oct: 20th. "We are with some funny people Chinese. Malays. Indians. and people called Klinks – you would be surprised to see so many on so small an island. We are alright out here – we can go for a ride in a rickshaw and the coolie will take you for miles for about 2/- I am a bit down-hearted, because my brother Phil has gone to Mesopotamia to fight. I only with I was going too, so that we could both have a go at them but I am afraid they will keep us here till after the war is over.

I don't expect there are many elder boys left in the Sunday School now well, no one can say but what our school has done its share for the war. The Brotherhood has not written to me lately. Tell them it cheers us up when we can get a letter from dear old England. We look forward to the mail coming in once a week and you should see us all running about after our letters and papers then and I tell you we look very downhearted if there are none for us. It is very hot out here and we cannot work long together because the sun plays on your back so much."

Bombardier. G. Duckett of the R.F.A writes from France :– Before the war I was employed by Mr. W. G. Bailey in High Street ... I have not met a Dawley lad out here for a long time so I am glad to read about them all in the "D.N." We get a church service every Sunday night but not so warm and comfortable as your service for by the time we have sung a hymn we are about frost-bitten."

Pioneer. I. Swift also writes from France :– "I have received a copy of the "D.N" – I had never heard of the paper. I should be pleased if you will send it every week... We are enjoying ourselves out here the best way we can."

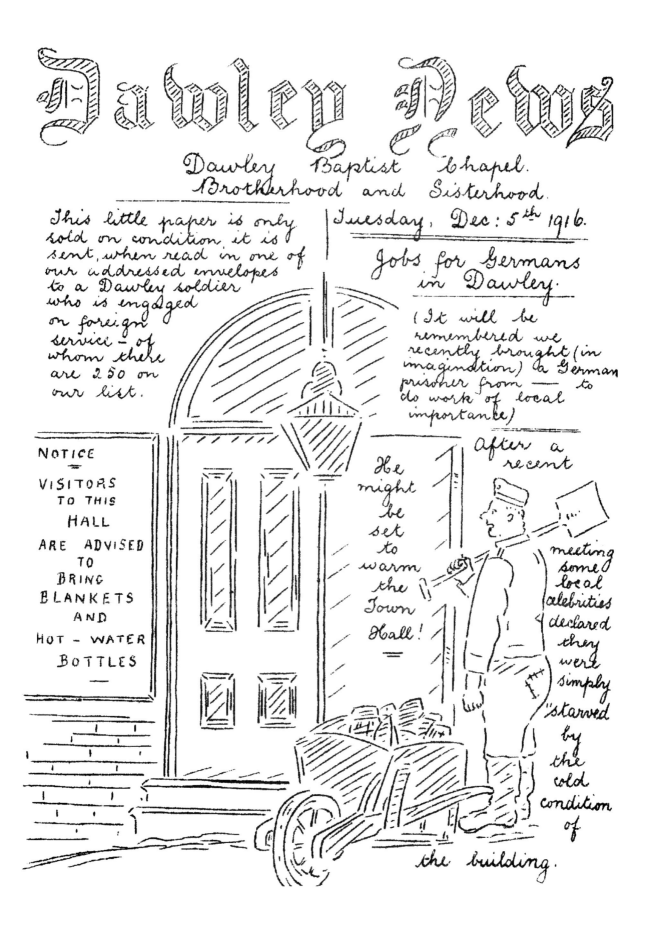

Dawley News

Dawley Baptist Chapel.
Brotherhood and Sisterhood.

This little paper is only sold on condition it is sent, when read in one of our addressed envelopes to a Dawley soldier who is engaged on foreign service — of whom there are 250 on our list.

Tuesday, Dec: 5th 1916.

Jobs for Germans in Dawley.

(It will be remembered we recently brought (in imagination) a German prisoner from —— to do work of local importance)

NOTICE
=
VISITORS
TO THIS
HALL
ARE ADVISED
TO
BRING
BLANKETS
AND
HOT - WATER
BOTTLES

He might be set to warm the Town Hall!
=

after a recent

meeting some local celebrities declared they were simply "starved by the cold condition of the building.

Bombardier. A. Round of the R.I.A writes from France, saying:- "The "D.N" keeps us in touch with the old place – I have received many copies of the "W.R" and D.N and I am sure it is very good of you to send them. I have only seen the Shropshires at one place and then I met two Dawley boys, Archer and Frost."

Pte. Seth Baugh writes from France that he never felt better in his life and that he is working on roads just behind the firing-line at present.

We have pleasure in acknowledging the following amounts received during the week for our Comforts Fund. Mr. H. C. Simpson £2; Mr. H. R. G. Bayley, 5/-; Mr. J. Simpson, 5/-; Mr. Herbert Simpson, £1; Mr. J. S. Smith, 2/6; Mr. J. P. Bayley, 2/6; Horsehay Drawing Office, 7/-; Mr. J. Barker, 10/6; "Porch" 7/6 (2/6) = 10/-; Mrs. Woodhouse, 10/-; Mr. and Mrs. J. W. Roberts, 2/6 (also 3 prs mittens); Mr. J. Wood, 10/-.

We remind our friends we sent off last week 30 parcels value about £10. This week-end we have despatched almost a similar number to Hong Kong and Singapore. In a few days we hope to make up the number of parcels to 100. We shall be very glad of much more money for this Fund.

We thank the following friends for their kind contributions to the Postage Fund:- "In Memory" 10/-, "Porch" 2/6, Mr. W. J. Shepherd 2/6, Mrs. Lovatt, 2/- "A. B." 10d

"Won't You Buy My Pretty Flowers?" ("Didst thee say 'arf-a-crown or 'arf-a-quid?")

Mr. Harry Smith kindly gave us the whole of his fine show of beautiful Chrysanthemums. The blossoms were sold by several of our friends this week-end and the sum of nearly £3 has been realised for our Comforts Fund.

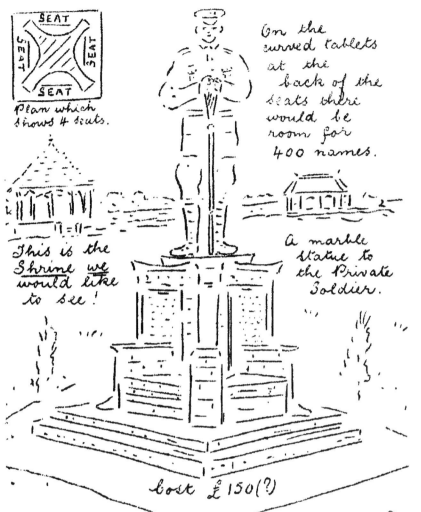

SEAT | SEAT | SEAT | SEAT

Plan which shows 4 seats.

On the curved tablets at the back of the seats there would be room for 400 names.

This is the Shrine we would like to see!

A marble statue to the Private Soldier.

Cost £150(?)

Set up at the entrance to Dawley Park

Pte. W. A. Brooks writes from France:- my best thanks for the "D. N." Sander Edwards is in my company. he wishes to be remembered to all friends... We are having a rest at present and we have earned it for we have seen something since we have been out here and we shall be glad to see what peace is like once again. Remember me to all the friends at the Brotherhood and tell them it is grand to have some news from the old place and to know they are still having a decent time."

Sapper: A. Upton again writes from France saying he hopes every available man will come forward to keep the name of the Dawley district in good reputation. After an engagement he says, it is really a sight to see the Germans coming into the British lines in streams.

Pte. R. Deakin (Old Park) is at Pembroke Dock awaiting his discharge - or substitution in one or other of the local pits. He was wounded at Loos and has been in the doctor's hands practically ever since. We regret to say he has lost the sight of his left eye.

We are in communication with the General Post Office authorities in London with respect to this little paper. The official Censor in Whitehall has, as you know, passed it for publication now we think the P.O ought to let it go for 1½ instead of 1s. Mr. Thomason, on behalf of the P.O visited us the other day to see how it is produced. There are no patents in our processes — other people please copy!

A meeting of the Dawley Military Tribunal takes place to-night. when 34 appeals have to be heard.

Pte. Ned Archer writes from a Hospital in Malta on Nov 20th. I thank you for the parcel you so kindly sent to me - I am sure the B and S is doing its best for the men who are doing their duty... Before I was taken ill we were preparing the theatre of war on the ——— front and since then the curtain has risen and the enemy has been defeated more than once. Some of our men have had to make the Great Sacrifice but then a Greater One made a Sacrifice for us. We are pleased with the "D.N." which some of the boy's call the "Balkan news." (Ned also sends us the following which he says "me and my bed-mate have made up since we have been in hospital")

"Cheery Words from "Neddock"" (of which verses 7.9 and 10 run):-

"We are lads from good old Dawley
And places round about
You bet we try between us
To clear the Bulgars out

Now you at home who cannot help
To close this cruel war;
Just think a bit about the lads
Across the sea so far.

Two years we done and still the war
Continues in full swing:
We wont come home to Dawley Bank
Till victory we bring"

Pte. E. Shepherd writes from a Field Bakery in France saying he has reverted to the ranks at his own request. He will explain the reason at another opportunity.

Bloodshed in Lawley Bank!

Last Friday night

A Fox visited a Hen Roost and destroyed several chick-a-biddies!

L/Cpl Brumaley in a letter received on Dec: 2nd says he has had a stripe since he received the last copy of the "D.N." He seems to think the Army will want a lot more boys from Dawley. They have had it a bit rough at times, but they laugh at things when they have quietened down again.

Rfn. J. H. Collier writes from France:- "Thanks for the "D.N." I met in the trenches the other day another Dawley boy (Rfn. A. Johnson) who had never seen the little paper. We had a good smile over it and hope you will forward it every week.... We often wish the Germans would come out and have a final set-to so that we could finish it showing what the British are made of, with an extra one for Dawley."

Apparently Dawley has several men who know the weight of a pig or a sheep when they see it. At a Block-Test competition at Wellington last week (in connection with the Red Cross effort) the winners in regard to the weight of a sheep (56 lbs) were H. Gaundrell (Burton St) 56½ lbs and C. Morris (Station Road). In regard to the weight of a pig (14 score, 8 lbs) R. Williams (High Street) won a prize by his estimate of 14 score, 4 lbs.

Cooks Mate W. Hitchman writes from "Somewhere at Sea" on Nov: 29th :- "Thank you for the useful parcel just received — I am more than grateful for your kindness. This is my second Yule-tide at sea, still I am not grumbling. There are times when you almost forget that war is on or that Germany exists... I have no doubt that Xmas will find many empty chairs and lonely firesides in Dawley. Though some will never again return it is not for us to complain, we can rest assured that they who trust in God and do the right will have their reward in Heaven... It is very cold now at sea, with choppy winds and heavy frosts and the sky looks to me as if we shall have some snow. I wish all the friends who work with you a merry Xmas and a better new Year than the last.

Two of our local special constables recently spent a whole night on the summit of certain pit-mounds they were watching over us all while we peacefully slept. It has been suggested that we send you a sketch of these "Guardian Angels" - fitted with wings — but we daren't! We get into quite sufficient trouble with our sketches-as it is!

Owing to the displacement of a flaming gas-burner on Sunday night a beam in the Baptist Schoolroom became ignited. As the people began to arrive for the evening mission service the place was found to be full of smoke. It is generally agreed that the effects might have been serious if it had not been discovered for, say, an hour.

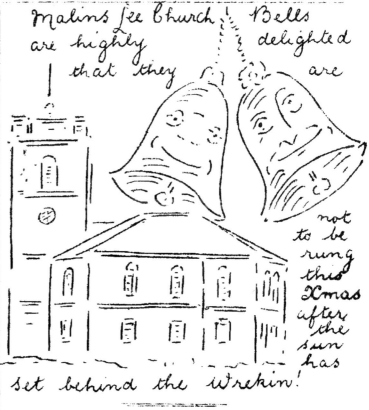

Malins Lee Church Bells are highly delighted that they are not to be rung this Xmas after the sun has set behind the Wrekin!

Some of the parishioners are equally delighted to escape the evening "practices" which usually begin this week.

To-night we are expecting at our meeting Rev. G. W. Rhodes the Dawley Wesleyan Minister, who came here last September from Cornwall. Certain structural repairs have lately been done at the chapel in the High Street and it may therefore be of interest to give you a sketch of the old chapel which once occupied that site and which was pulled down about 50 years ago to make room for the present edifice. It was a curious little place and as may be seen the main entrance was in Chapel Street, the School, vestries etc. facing High Street. It only seated about 200 persons and there was a big window between the School and the chapel which was opened on anniversaries and revivals to increase the accommodation. The School was not only used on Sundays but on week-days as an elementary school and for some years a Miss Trigger was the mistress of whom little is known except that she did her duty. The sketch is rough as all our sketches produced on a Cyclostyle have necessarily to be but if your friends at home are interested in Wesleyan Methodism we advise you to send it to them. We do not think there is any other sketch of this building anywhere in Dawley!

A Bit of the Old ✠ Dawley.

Mr. H. Smitlis

Chapel Street

Pte. Jim Alford (Prisoner of War formerly in Germany now transferred to Switzerland) writes:- I have not gone into hospital here yet; I told the doctor I was alright but he says I shall have to go in and under the X Rays to see if there is anything in that has to come out.... I saw the last lot of English prisoners wives who came out to Switzerland to see their husbands they said they had had so much travelling that they were fairly done up. Much as I should like to see some of my relatives, it is a long way to come and they would only have a short time here and its across the Channel is the worst — at least that is what some of the women told me. We are not allowed many free letters now and we have to pay for stamps and they cost 2½ each, so I'm thinking someone will have to go short. I heard from Mr. S. T. Jones the other day and also from Jack Butler from the Front, he's still going strong. He's had a good turn out there and I can't make out how he still goes on without getting wounded, but I suppose its his luck. I hope he'll go on without getting one."

A Soldier's Wisdom.

Here are some extracts from the writings of "A Student-in-Arms" a brilliant young soldier writer in the Spectator:—

"The true wisdom is that it is not what a man does, or has, or says that matters; but what he is."

"The world judges a man by his station, inherited or acquired. God judges by his character. To be our best we must share God's view-point."

"To the world death is always a tragedy; to the Christian it is never a tragedy, unless a man has been a contemptible character."

"Religion is the widening of a man's horizon so as to include God."

"The recognition of God's presence upsets the balance of a man's environment, and means a new birth into a new life."

"To be the centre of one's universe is misery. To have one's universe centred in God is the peace that passeth understanding."

"Greatness is founded on inward peace. Energy is only effective when it springs from deep calm."

A sketch sent from France by a Dawley soldier for this paper.

Mr. William Lloyd is easily the most popular of all our local celebrities!

A.P.O. S.13.

Billy — "Bit too big, aint they Sargunt?"
Serg. — "That's alright — you'll have all the more room for boarders!"

Malins Lee National Schools were closed all last week owing to some slight infection among a few of the children.

A Dawley miner was fined £1-11-0 at Shifnal last week for neglecting his work.

We hope to send out Invitations next week to all wives and mothers of Dawley soldiers for our second "Monday Social." In your next letter home please ask your people to make a point of coming, especially if they did not happen to be at the first.

It has been very dark at night lately and old people have found great difficulty in getting about after sunset. The corner of the malt-house opposite the Chapel has been artistically plastered with whitewash, also the posts in the short-cut between the Chapel into the Old Park.

If you are the soldier who never writes to us, please mend your ways at once and let us have a letter!

At our Tuesday meeting we are now compelled to adhere rigorously to our new rule — that this little paper is not sold unless an envelope addressed to a Dawley soldier is taken with it. Naturally a few of our friends find a little difficulty in falling in with this arrangement, but we hope all will loyally co-operate. Last week, every soldier on foreign service on our list was supplied with a copy of the "D.N"!

We have been able to make a start in collecting for wounded soldiers at Wellington

removed and others have taken their place. We are sending them a good parcel of reading matter each week. We hope to be able to invite these men to a Christmas Party — half one week, the other half the next.

All the Churches and Chapels have now gone back to a Sunday evening service — except Malins Lee Church. At our own Chapel, three services are now being conducted each Sunday. At the mission service in the Schoolroom on Sunday evenings we are glad to see new

DAWLEY SEWING GUILD

The Dawley Sewing Guild has generously sent us for distribution among Dawley soldiers 77 pairs of socks, 2 mufflers and 6 shirts. We appreciate most warmly this kind and magnificent gift. Each article is marked "From Dawley Sewing Guild" — if you receive any of these you will know to whom thanks are due.

About 12/- or 15/- worth of eatables were brought to our meeting last Tuesday we shall be glad of more helpers for this good work.

All the old soldiers who were at —— have recently been

faces and it is hoped in time to see quite a fresh congregation there. Invitations from other churches to inaugurate an after-service Evangelistic meeting in the Town Hall are impossible for us to accept at present.

Dawley News

Dec: 12th 1916.

Sapper. A. V. J. Poole writes from France:-
"I have some very good news for you. I was lying on my bed two nights ago when a pal who sleeps close to me was reading a small book and I thought I had seen one like it before so I enquired what it was and he told me it was the "Dawley News". His name is Pte. Morton from Dawley. I have known him about two months now and if it wasn't for that little book we shouldn't have had some good times. He has lent me some copies of the "D.N." to read and they are jolly interesting although I don't know anybody but my relations. but it shows what your little book will do."

A Soldier writing from the Front on Dec. 2nd asks:- "Is there to be a Christmas Double Number of the "D.N."?"

Our Artist arrives on the scene to make a few sketches for our Christmas Number which will be posted to you next Tuesday night.

IF YOU HEAR OF A DAWLEY MAN WHO DOES NOT GET A XMAS PARCEL FROM ANYONE PLEASE LET US KNOW

DAWLEY NEWS XMAS NUMBER

NEXT WEEK 1D

Price One Penny.

This little paper is only sold at the Brotherhood and Sisterhood meeting at Dawley Baptist Chapel on condition it is sent when read. to a soldier on foreign service in one of our addressed envelopes of which we issue over 200 every week.

Because you are a soldier my boy that is no reason why you should not be a devout Christian. General Gordon was a fine soldier — you can see his memorial in St. Pauls, the next time you go through London and he was one of the greatest Christians of his day. Read the inscription on the memorial "At all times he gave his strength to the weak his substance to the poor his sympathy to the suffering and his heart to God." During his Egyptian campaign, he could be seen going into the desert all alone and there perched high on the back of a camel, he would pore over the pages of his little pocket Bible. In another campaign, he used a bell-tent and in the early morning, for a few minutes, would be seen a white handkerchief over the entrance which signified to his fellow-soldiers that he must not be disturbed - he was at prayer. Here are two of his sayings :- "No comfort is equal to that which he has who has God for his stay". "There will be times when a severe strain will come on you but it is only for a time and if you look to God, as the strain is, so will your strength be."

We regret to announce that Pte. W. J. Morrall (Old Park) has been missing since Nov: 13th. He was not a Dawley man and was employed at the Rudge-Whitworth works in Birmingham. He joined up on June 10th was placed in the 3rd Royal Berks at first but later transferred to the 2nd Oxford and Bucks. His wife who has relatives in the locality came here with her three children in August last.

Official intimation has been received that Pte. Thos. H. Phillips (Station Road, Lawley Bank) was wounded in the Salonica region on Nov: 27th.

By the death of Mrs. Matthew Henry Bailey, the Baptist Chapel and the Tuesday B and S meeting have lost a very good friend, whose passing many Dawley soldiers, if they knew the facts, would deplore.

Sapper Hill of the R.E writes:- "A dear friend of mine at Dawley sends me the "D.N" — I hope it will meet with the success it deserves. I do not think there is a Shropshire man in my company, if I did find one I should pass the little paper on to him... I am sorry to tell you there is a sad little tale attached to a recent number. After reading it I passed it on to six or seven of our fellows and lost sight of it for a week or two until one morning about 2.30 one poor fellow named Morris — I think he came from London — was hit by shrapnel and died almost immediately... Among his belongings I found my copy of the "Dawley News" which I have kept and will send to you if you desire it." (We have asked this soldier to return this copy to us)

We are to-day sending out Invitations to about 250 Wives and mothers of Dawley soldiers for our second Social which takes place next Monday afternoon.

A Christmas Day local Collection for the Relief of Children in Belguim is to be arranged, as last year, here in Dawley.

The Urban Council has decided to purchase five additional 50 feet lengths of fire hose – this is good news. When you boys come home we must have a fire brigade!

Sergeant J. E. Davies writes from Netley Hospital Hants that he is going on well and much appreciates the D.N. because it tells him about his pals (We ask our friends to write to this crippled hero)

Pte. A. Bishop writes from France thanking us for a parcel and especially the bootlaces which he says cannot be procured in France. "We are standing all night in mud and water – I wish you could come to France and see us coming out of the trenches with mud on our clothes and a smile on our faces. The war will not last long after Xmas, I think so you can look out for the lucky month."

P. B. ROOM 11
No. 83440
5 DEC 1916
Recd
Despd 12
.M.
M.

We have received permission from the Censor to publish this little paper, as you know. We have been anxious to tell you

are so interested in the exploits of the "Tanks".

We therefore submitted a Sketch and a Paragraph to London. This is the result!

PRESS BUREAU,
Passed as censored
12

Some of the Dawley boys in France have told us of the wonderful exploits of the "Tanks," – You will be glad to know that some of your old pals though still at home are doing their bit to win the war. We wish the same could be said of everybody.

Pte. J. W. Price of the Cameron Highlanders who is again at the Front, writes:- Thanks for the parcel – my old shirt was alive so the new one will come in very handy. I had been looking for the "D. N." every post and not having met any Dawley boys no one could help me in my search for it. We have a picture-house out here and the other night I tried to fancy I was at "Bannister's Pictures" in Dawley Town Hall again. Last week it was the National Mission of Repentance and Hope all through the camp."

"my old Shirt was alive!"

Sergeant W. Hughes writes on Dec 2nd - "Behold, our tent has departed; as I thought it would, at about 3 a.m." The first inkling I had of the matter was a wild yell and on completing the difficult task of opening my eyes I wondered who had thrown me outside. ... I tell you the air was quite ruddy and warm for a few minutes although the frost was on the ground."

Pte. R. E. Breeze writes from France – We have had another scrap with the Boche and I am pleased to say I have come out safe and sound but we have had a rough time, I can tell you... I think the drawing is that of Dawley Bank Day School." (Quite right a book prize is being sent to you.)

Pte. G. Round says:- All my comrades ask me for the little paper... I am glad to see so many Dawley chaps are doing their best for their King and Country."

Pte. A. Lloyd writes – I did not think we should have another winter out here but it looks like it now, but never mind so long as we beat the Germans. The war out here has taught us many lessons which I hope we shall not forget when we come home."

During the week letters have been received from Gunner A. Round (who is now at Weymouth Hospital) and Pte. Percy Jonks, who acknowledges the receipt of a parcel.

Pte. A. E. Collier writing from France, says his birthday is on Dec. 7th and he is spending his birthday for a second time in the firing line. He hopes his next will be in "dear old Dawley."

During the week-end we have had a visit from Pte. Jonathan Jones R.A.M.C. who is leaving Southampton, where he has been since the outbreak of war for the Macedonia Region.

Dawley News: December 1916

Pte. A. Jones of the 1st North Staffs. Regt writes:- I don't agree with the artists imagination of what it is like at the Front,- according to that we are having a very good time (I don't think!) I used to work with Mr G. Morgan when I was at home. I joined up in December last in the K.S.L.I but have been transferred to the N.S.R.

Pte. George Growcott writes from France on Nov: 26th:- I am out of the trenches again for a rest after another shot at Johnny. I don't know whether I hit him or not but I know he has got the wind up for he expected our brave lads over the top... You asked me for the music of that song— I am composing it now and will send it along.

Jobs for Germans in Dawley.

(We brought it will be remembered a German prisoner from — to do work of local importance)

Sergeant S. Brey Morgan writes from Salonica. The labour and patience which the D.N. entails must be enormous... most of the Dawley boys in this Battalion are keeping fairly well. We have had a spell of wet weather which has made the trenches in rather a bad state but we keep trying to remember 'There's a Silver Lining. etc.' I have met quite a lot of Dawley boys who have just come out here.

Pte. A.F. Morton writes from France:- I can assure you every Dawley soldier appreciates the D.N.... I am keeping my head despite all the dangers and hardships one has to endure. Accept my best wishes for your organisation.

He might be set to carry home the —— extra Xmas allotment.

265

There were 33 appeals dealt with at the local Tribunal on Tuesday last and if the exact number of claims allowed were given, you would probably say "why should all these men be exempted?" But if you knew all the facts you would see that the majority of them are men of good age. Indeed several are nearly 40. They are in business for themselves and according to the Medical Board at Shrewsbury are not fit for general service. Nearly a dozen are in business in the High Street and if the food supply of the place is to be carried on, these men must be kept at home. The new rule that all applicants must produce the Army medical certificate is being kept and in four cases where the necessary certificate was not forthcoming consideration was adjourned. The Tribunal always refuses to consider claims by miners and refers them to the colliery court.

Where young men say under 30 are de-badged by the Ministry of Munitions in any of the local Government Controlled Works there is difficulty now in gaining exemption and several of these were refused. The case of inn-keepers is a difficult one but now in every instance the Tribunal is insisting that licensees put part of their time in local munition works or some other work of direct national importance. The Military Representative appeals against decisions he does not agree with and these are, as a rule, heard at the County Appeal Court at Wellington.

At this Court last Friday the Military Authorities appealed against a number of decisions made by the Dawley Tribunal in favour of Hordehay workmen. In about half the cases the decisions of the Tribunal were upheld, while half have to be substituted.

WEIGHING THEM UP!

NO SUGAR

TRIBUNAL

To decide whether a man will best serve the country in civil life or in the army is not as easy as it looks!

It is very amusing to watch the endeavours of soldiers to send their letters to the people responsible for the publication of this little paper. Last week we received letters addressed as follows:- The Vicar, "Dawley News" etc; "Dawley News c/o Miss Rowe" and a third – "Dawley News Mr. Goodyear"! Happily the post woman knows where the publishing-house is! Can't you recognise the features of our artist on the front page?

Pte. J. Forgham writes from Ashford:- I appreciate the "D.N" very much... I am now out of hospital and my wound has healed nicely, though I still have some of Fritz's dirty metal in my back. I am now attached to the Royal West Kents for home-service."

A successful Red Cross Sale was conducted in the Market Hall on Saturday. Among the gifts were loads of coal, swedes and firewood. Also two pigs, a calf and a sheep (which got out and ran amok among the people)

We are glad to say we have received for our Comforts Fund up to last Saturday night the sum of £30-1-10. We have now despatched 106 different parcels of comforts to Dawley men on foreign service and as they cost us 5/- or 6/- each on an average — plus 1/- each parcel for carriage — you will see we have not very much money left. We are therefore making an effort to make £30-1-10 into £50 — indeed, we have ordered shirts, etc., in the hope and expectation of getting this amount. We gratefully acknowledge the following contributions received during the week (included in the above total):- Mr. F. Taylor (Langley Farm) £1., Mr. and Mrs. J. G. Lavender, 10/6; Miss Elsie Smith's S. S. class, 7/6; Mrs. Greenhalgh, 5/-.

Mr. J. Jones, 5/-. Mr. T. Ellis' Collection (including Mr. Ellis, 5/-) 14/-; Mrs. Boycott's Collection, 2/8; Mrs. A. Evans' Collection (including Mr. A. Evans, 2/- and Mr. E. Evans, 2/-) 9/2; Miss A. M. Thomas' Collection (including Mr. Thomas, 2/6, Mr. B. Rogers, 2/6, Mr. F. Blocksidge 2/-, Mr. S. Bird 2/-, Mr. F. Rogers, 2/6) £1.6.3; Mr. Joe. Williams 2/6; "Letter-Box (per A.L) 2/-.

We thank the following friends for their kind donations to our Postage Fund:- Mr. H. C. Simpson, 10/-; "An Old R.E" (per F. T. W) 2/6, Rev. C. W. Rhodes, 2/-; "A. B" 9d.

For the upkeep of this little paper we acknowledge with thanks 10/- from Mr. H. C. Simpson.

"any advance beyond eighteen pence?"

We had a capital meeting last Tuesday when the address was given by Rev. C. W. Rhodes, the Wesleyan Minister, Miss V. Swift being the soloist. At the close one of the Chrysanthemum Blooms (of which upwards of £3 worth have already been sold) was put up for sale and in the course of an amusing contest 14/- or so was realised for our Comforts Fund. Not only the auctioneer but his clerk had quite a busy time putting down the bids. The flower was ultimately sold for 1/6.

Dawley News: December 1916

Pte. W. A. Brooks writes from France on Nov. 30th. The parcel came in very handy I can tell you. I also thank you for the little paper I am receiving every week. I am sorry I cannot give you any information about Pte. H. Bryce — he was in my Battalion and I was with him the day before he was missing. It is grand to think that while we are out here fighting for right you are fighting for us at home.

Lieutenant J. E. Smith (eldest son of the late Mr J. S. Smith, High St.) of the British East African Forces writes:— I have to work very hard and long to keep things going (as Accountant for the B.E.A. Military Govt) but that does not hurt me. I expect to leave here very soon and to have an exciting journey in this country which is like a huge zoo. My journey will include four days across the lake. The war here is taking place in a very difficult district — all swamps and fever stricken so that sickness is one of our enemies now. It often plays havoc with some of our splendid men — I am thankful I am not subject to it.

I have an invitation to a levee at Government House to-morrow and expect to have a good time. A man eating lion is invading this district and has already had two men (Blacks) so I hope he will keep to that idea and miss out the Whites. The other morning I woke up early and found several wild pigs in our mess-tent eating our rations so I lit the lamps and got out and scared them off. We also killed a cobra a few days ago. The papers reach me occasionally and I was sorry to read of the death of many boys I used to know.

"I woke up early ..... we killed a cobra"

Pte. E. Lane writes:— I must thank you very much for your parcel which came safely. It is most useful and compact and all the things are such as a soldier needs. When I look at the sketches in the D.N. I think of the happy times I have spent in Dawley. We have now plenty of rain and there is any amount of mud and water but nothing daunts us — we are just as cheerful as if we were going to the Dawley Demonstration.

We have received letters of appreciation from Mr John Bayley C.B. the Commandant and from the Secretary and Quartermaster of the V.A.D Hospital in Wellington for the boxes of eatables sent for the wounded soldiers there. We are collecting now each Tuesday night — under the general management of Mr A. Bryce, who will be glad of extra helpers for new districts.

268

Dawley News

Dawley Baptist Chapel.
Brotherhood & Sisterhood

Tuesday, Dec: 19th 1916.

The Xmas number of the little paper which is sent to upwards of 200 Dawley soldiers weekly.

God give you a good Xmas my boy. This comes to you with the fervent good wishes of a great host of Dawley folk who do not fail to think of you. We send you a sprig of mistletoe to put in your hat. May God bless you!

We are trying to send out about 150 parcels before Xmas, but it may happen you may not get one. Other people, we hope, will remember you. If they don't, please give us a chance to send you some little token of our good-will by writing to us.

You will be glad to know we had another delightful time yesterday when 150 of your mothers and wives came to our Second Monthly Social. Soon after 2.30 they came streaming into the Chapel till the middle was full. There were not many left on the premises at 4.30 but in the meanwhile a very pleasant time had been spent. A splendid address was given by Rev. E. Bulstrode Pryce, B.A. the vicar of Madeley. It was a homely, forceful talk of a "Christmassy" sort, full of heartening cheer for the women you have left behind. He dwelt on the loneliness of the birth of Christ, the loneliness of his life and death — a loneliness which has the most amazing results that no one really need be lonely. The solitary, anxious woman at home, equally with her soldier on the battlefield or her sailor at sea may have the constant sympathy and the abiding presence of the living Christ. After the service was over Mr. Pryce produced a stained copy of the "D.N." for which he announced he would not take £5. A Madeley soldier had sent it to him after having been through a fearful engagement, and there were little marks about that paper which made it for ever to the Vicar of Madeley a sacred treasure.

"I hold in my hand a little paper for which I would not take £5"

Mrs March of Wellington during the service sang two wonderfully telling solos to her zither accompaniment and while the 150 women were having tea Mrs March was again responsible for a musical programme, Mrs Watkiss rendering various songs. There is no doubt your friends all enjoyed themselves and those of us who are responsible for this monthly effort are glad to do it in order to show our admiration of you. Towards the cost of this Second Social, Mrs J. Bailey acknowledges the following gifts:— Mrs Bemrose, 2/6; Mr H. Smith, 10/6; Mr J. O. Steventon, 10/-; "Weekly Donor" 10/-; Mrs J. R. Smith, £1.

"No trumpet-blast profaned the hour in which the Prince of Peace was born.

No bloody streamlet stained earth's silver rivers on that sacred morn."

If you change your address, please let Mr. Wooding know at once.

Jobs for Germans in Dawley this Xmas.

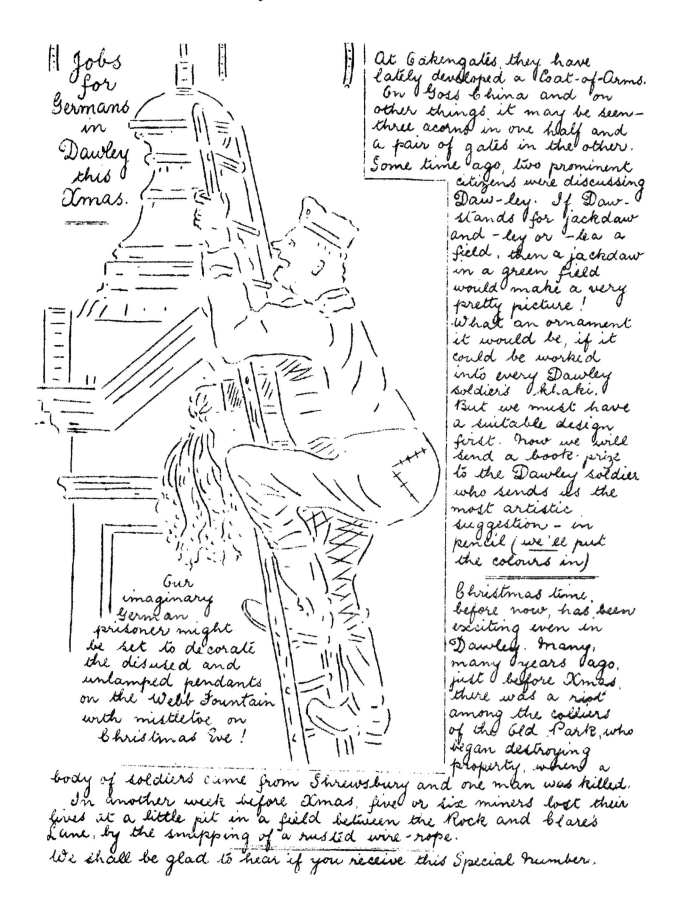

Our imaginary German prisoner might be set to decorate the disused and unlamped pendants on the Webb Fountain with mistletoe on Christmas Eve!

At Oakengates they have lately developed a Coat-of-Arms. On Goss China and on other things it may be seen — three acorns in one half and a pair of gates in the other. Some time ago, two prominent citizens were discussing Daw-ley. If Daw- stands for jackdaw and -ley or -lea a field, then a jackdaw in a green field would make a very pretty picture! What an ornament it would be, if it could be worked into every Dawley soldier's khaki. But we must have a suitable design first. Now we will send a book-prize to the Dawley soldier who sends us the most artistic suggestion — in pencil (we'll put the colours in)

Christmas time, before now, has been exciting even in Dawley. Many, many years ago, just before Xmas, there was a riot among the soldiers of the Old Park, who began destroying property, when a body of soldiers came from Shrewsbury and one man was killed.

In another week before Xmas, five or six miners lost their lives at a little pit in a field between the Rock and Clare's Lane, by the snapping of a rusted wire-rope.

We shall be glad to hear if you receive this Special Number.

Dawley News: December 1916

We have bought ourselves this Plough

for a Christmas Box!

D.U.D.C. SNOW-PLOUGH

Pte. G. Phillips writes from France:– "I hope it wont be long before I am able to come and see you all again ... When I was coming back last time I said I didn't want to come to Dawley again until the war was over but I have altered my mind since then. The weather is awfully wet and I have such a cold I can hardly speak."

We may have our new Snow-Plough out on Boxing-Day!

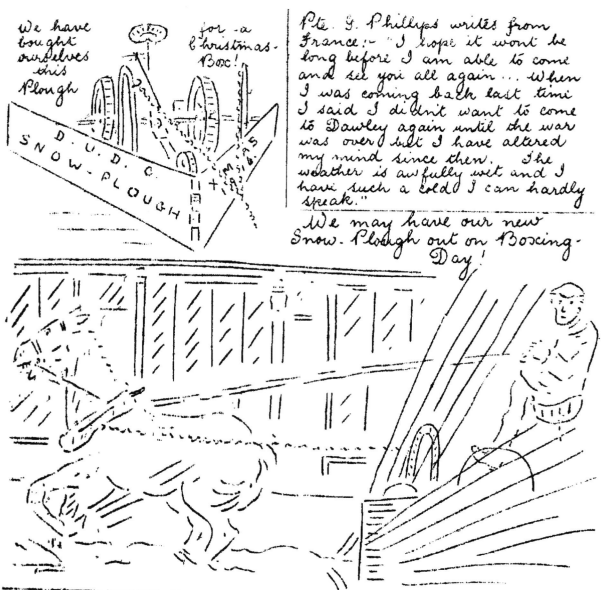

Sergeant. G. Collis from "Somewhere in France" writes:– "I must say it is some consolation to us to know that while we are out here you are doing your best to look after our wives and mothers at home, helping to brighten, if ever so little, the dark hours which must come to them... I shall keep a strict look-out for the representative of the "D.N" — I rather fancy he is in this neighbourhood, as we have some decent-sized material."

Corporal. R. M. Stanley says:– "I have always a warm place in my heart for the little town of Dawley, my parents are there and I have a dear friend there. I feel quite ashamed to say it but I have learnt more about Dawley from your little paper than from any other source."

Sergeant. Percy Morgan writes from the Salonica Region:- "Your constant work for us proves that distance does not sever friendships... L/Cpl. Collier (Horsehay) is now with us, also Pte. H. Mawdsley of Dawley F. C. is in my Platoon. Pte. L. Roberts of Burton Street wishes to be remembered to you all."

Pte. W. H. Parton writes from St. Patrick's Hospital, Malta:- "The copies of the "D.N" you sent to Salonica have followed me here. When I get it, all the men in the ward want it first but I tell them I read it first and they must draw lots and so have it in turn."

Pte. G. Jones says:- "It is very cold and wet out here and the guns are roaring like lions, we bombard them very heavy, they don't get much rest, I can tell you."

Pte. A. Jones writes from France:- I think your sketches of the Webb monument are very good and they remind me of the old times when I used to play round it."

Pte Jack Rogers of the Canadians writes:- I have not seen any Shropshires in this part of the line, we are mainly colonial troops here.... Wouldn't it be a fine Xmas. box if Peace were declared! We shall have as bright and as merry a time as circumstances will allow."

"Imitation is the Sincerest Form of Flattery"

For the new use of the gas-pendants see elsewhere.

For Captain Webb's smile — see elsewhere.

Children will march about the High Street in Toy-Costumes.

The Shropshire Society in London awards every year a Captain Webb Memorial Medal for feats of life-saving — the medal was last week awarded to Mr. H. Jenks of Shrewsbury for heroism in saving a boy's life from drowning in the Severn.

Dawley is not dead yet, when at a Saturday afternoon sale the sum of £90 can be realised for the Red Cross and that is what happened last Saturday week.

Referring to our remark in last week's "D. N" that we need a Fire Brigade there is, it appears, an understanding among the councils employees and others as to what is to be done in case of an outbreak at night. The water-pressure seems to be alright for the bulk of the district, but some time ago when it was tried, it is not sufficient to throw water on to the roof of the Baptist Chapel, though it will over Mr. E. H. Plimmer's near by.

The Bronze Medallion of Captain Webb (on the Memorial Fountain) has a good laugh to itself, not at the mistletoe over its head but at the gratifying number of Dawley lads who have crossed the Channel to serve their Country.

Rolls of Honour of Members who have volunteered their services for King and Country were unveiled by the Captain Webb Rechabite Tent, in the Dawley Wesleyan School-room last Saturday afternoon.

Several soldiers have lately enquired why Dawley — a town of 7,000 people — is not on the map? The answer is - Because it is left to you to put it on the map! When you are asked where you come from, don't say "Lawley Bank, Old Park, Finger or Horsehay" but — Dawley. If we are going to perpetuate our smaller place-names for ever, then we'll have more of them — "Ragged - End" "Dog-in-the-Lane" "Brick-Kill-Hole" "Ganderfield". "Dawley" ought to be good enough for anyone! Good old Dawley!

"It is the Christmas time:
And up and down 'twixt
Heaven and earth.
In glorious grief and solemn mirth
The shining angels climb."

274

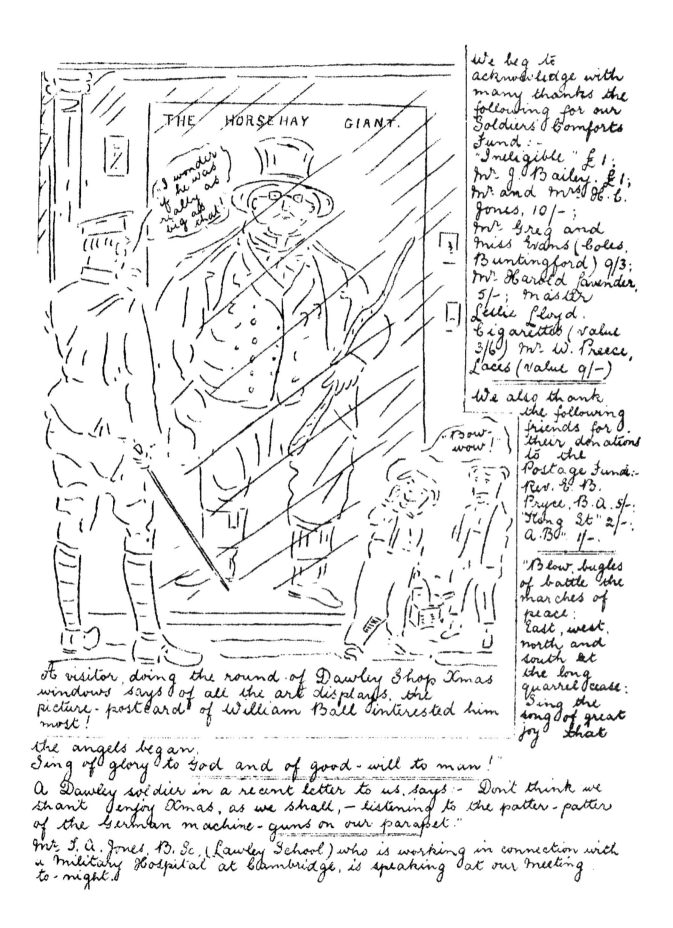

THE HORSEHAY GIANT.

We beg to acknowledge with many thanks the following for our Soldiers' Comforts Fund:—
"Ineligible" £1.
Mr. J. Bailey. £1;
Mr. and Mrs H. C. Jones, 10/-;
Mr. Greg and Miss Evans (Coles, Buntingford) 9/3;
Mr. Harold Lavender. 5/-; Master Leslie Lloyd.
Cigarettes (value 3/6) Mr. W. Preece,
Laces (value 9/-)

We also thank the following friends for their donations to the Postage Fund:-
Rev. E. B. Pryce. B.A. 5/-;
"Hong St" 2/-;
A. B." 1/-.

"Blow bugles of battle the marches of peace:
East, west, north and south let the long quarrel cease:
Sing the song of great joy that the angels began,
Sing of glory to God and of good-will to man!"

A visitor, doing the round of Dawley Shop Xmas windows says of all the art displays, the picture-postcard of William Ball interested him most!

A Dawley soldier in a recent letter to us, says:- Don't think we shan't enjoy Xmas, as we shall, — listening to the patter-patter of the German machine-guns on our parapet."

Mr. J. A. Jones, B.Sc. (Lawley School) who is working in connection with a military Hospital at Cambridge, is speaking at our meeting to-night.

Some of us who are left at home do not expect a very lively Christmas this year, because so many of you are away. We have very little heart to be merry and if the truth be told, I expect you will be having a really more lively time than we shall. The Church bells will ring — do you recollect the sound of them — can you tell the difference between the bells of Dawley Church and Malinslee, could you say off hand the difference between the bell at Doseley and Lawley Churches? We shall have the youngsters round with their "While Shepherds Watched", the Dawley Band on Boxing Day and the

young ragamuffins, with their black faces, their sticks and their "Somebodys in the house I know," but for all that, our hearts will be with you. scattered in various places as you are, far away. On Xmas Sunday Mr Lester

with our Best wishes for a merry Xmas.

says he is going to preach once again on the "Angel Song of Peace on earth. good-will among men." It is not easy to preach on such a subject he says. but he believes that the war is not Christ's fault. While he believes it is necessary to fight on and to win this war his idea is that there will be no real guarantee of brotherhood among the different nations till the Prince of Peace is given full control of the life of each one of us and of the policies of all the nations.

OBITUARIES 1915-1916

(These are of people mentioned in these surviving copies of Dawley News. The details here are extracted from the Dawley News; the local newspaper, the Wellington Journal and Shrewsbury News; and the Commonwealth War Graves Commission website)

Private G. Kearsley: Lived at Bank Road, Dawley, and disappeared on November 11, 1914, during an attack by the 2nd West Riding Battalion on German trenches in which the attackers suffered heavy losses and were forced to retire. The name G. Kearsley-Clarke is recorded on the Dawley War Memorial panels.

Sergeant A. Eric Bailey: Died "somewhere in France" on March 29, 1916, at the age of 23. He served with the 1st/6th Battalion of the South Staffordshire Regiment. A soldier from Coalmoor who was with him at the time of his death, Private Boycott, reported on a visit to Dawley a few weeks later that they were among five soldiers together on a firing platform in the trenches when a German shell buried all five of them. When Sergeant Bailey was extricated he was lifeless. A former pupil of Lawley School, he won a county council scholarship which secured him a place in Newport Grammar School. He became an elementary school teacher, first at Pool Hill School, Dawley, and then at Malinslee School. Later he went to Goldsmith's Training College, London, to train to enter the teaching profession. Sergeant Bailey was a member of Dawley Baptist Chapel, and was also a Sunday School teacher. His parents lived at 16 High Street, Dawley.

Lieutenant Cyril Charles Henry: He was the only son of Dawley's local MP, Sir Charles Henry. Educated at Harrow, he served in the 2nd Worcestershire Regiment. At the outbreak of war he was in the 4th Hussars, but requested a transfer to the Worcestershire Regiment in May 1915. He was reported missing in action at Loos on September 26, 1915. He was seen to fall by his platoon sergeant, Sergeant Birch, while leading his platoon in an attack. A search later failed to find him.  It was confirmed in April 1916 that he had been killed by machinegun fire on the night of that date. He was 22.

Private Henry Howells: Harry Howells was killed in action in France on April 25, 1916, while serving in the 7th Battalion King's Shropshire Light Infantry. A comrade reported that he and a sergeant were both killed on the same day by a shell. He was 34 and had formerly been a miner working at the Stafford pits. He enlisted on November 10, 1914, and had been in France about five months. His wife and five children lived at 29 Old Park, although the *Wellington*

Journal and Shrewsbury News gave his address as 34 Park Lane, Old Park.

Lance Corporal William Tart: Reported missing on April 23, 1916, and his parents received official notification of his death on February 3, 1917.

He lived at The Finger, Dawley. The CWGC website gives his unit as the 1st Battalion KSLI, although a report in the *Wellington Journal and Shrewsbury News* says he joined the "2nd Shropshires" five years previously and was drafted out to India. At the start of the war he went to France, was wounded, and invalided home. Recovering, he went to the Front once more and again returned home wounded. He went out a third time, but it was third time unlucky. He was 25 and the eldest son of Mr W. Tart, of Hinkshay Road, Dawley.

"Locke from Newport": The death of this soldier was mentioned by Gunner Garnet Tart in a letter written to the *Dawley News* on May 22, 1916. Locke received a wound from which he died shortly afterwards. This soldier could be Gunner F Locke of 112th Battery, 24th Brigade Royal Field Artillery, who is recorded on the CWGC website as dying on May 9, 1916, at the age of 19. His parents were from Raven Cottage, 54 High Street, Newport.

William Taylor: A lay official at Dawley Church. Lived at Chapel Street, Dawley. His death is mentioned in the *Dawley News* of May 30, 1916.

Boy Telegraphist Noah Round: Killed at the Battle of Jutland on May 31, 1916. He was a 17-year-old boy telegraphist on the battlecruiser HMS Invincible, which was hit and blew up. There were only a handful of survivors. He left a stepmother and a sister aged 13. His father Alfred had been killed in a pit accident in about 1913. He lived at 3 Ball's Hill, Dawley, and had been in the Royal Navy for two years, serving on HMS Impregnable, Vernon, and Invincible.

Private Enoch Round: Brother of Noah, killed at Gallipoli. The CWGC website records a soldier of this name serving in the 5th Battalion Connaught Rangers being killed at Gallipoli on August 21, 1915.

Corporal Norman Jones: Reported missing July 1916, the younger son of the late Mr Thomas Jones, of Prospect House, Lawley Bank. Before enlisting he was in Lloyds Bank. He served in the Berkshire Regiment.

Private Harry Ashley: Son of Mr A. Teece, of 18 Church Road, Dawley, reported killed in action in about July 1916, having been previously reported as missing. He was 27. A death notice in the *Wellington Journal and Shrewsbury News* says he died of wounds on July 26, 1916, in France. He was in the 1st Battalion KSLI. He was son of Susannah Teece (formerly Ashley), and stepfather Alfred Teece.

Sergeant Richard Everard B.H. Soame: Elder son of Sir Charles Buckworth-Herne-Soame and Lady Soame of Horsehay, died in hospital as a result of wounds received in action. He was taken to Kempston Hospital,

Eastbourne, in a critical condition. He was apparently making a little progress when he had a relapse and died at midnight on July 29, 1916. He was 24 and in the 7th Battalion KSLI.

Private Raymond Ketley: Of the 10th Battalion, Lincolnshire Regiment. Killed in action July 2, 1916, at the age of 23 or 21 (reports vary). He was the son of Mr and Mrs Ketley of the Queen's Arms, Finger Road, Dawley. Private Ketley completed his education at Newport Grammar School and after serving his apprenticeship as a draper's assistant with Messrs J.L. and E.T. Morgan, Wellington, he worked for Messrs Yarnold and Yarnold drapers, West Bromwich, before enlisting on September 17, 1914.

Gunner William Baugh: From Horsehay, served in a machinegun section. Killed in action July 1916, according to the *Dawley News*. He was 20 and the son of Mr and Mrs William Baugh, of Bridge Road, Horsehay. He had enlisted in the KSLI in November 1914 and later transferred to the Machine Gun Company (sic), according to the *Wellington Journal and Shrewsbury News*. Before joining up he worked at the Horsehay Company. He was a scholar of Horsehay Methodist Sunday School and a prominent member of a local football team. The CWGC records a William Baugh of the 69th Battalion Machine Gun Corps being killed on August 7, 1916.

Private Alfred Bowers: Killed at Albert, France, on August 18, 1916, while carrying in a wounded man. He had only enlisted on March 24 and was in training at Pembroke Dock for 15 weeks. He was in the 7th Battalion KSLI. A.J. Bowers was the son of William Bowers, of King Street, Dawley, and before joining up worked for Messrs J. Sankey and Sons, Hadley, and was also for many years in the service of Mr J. Clayton. He was a member of Wellington St John Ambulance Corps, and an ex-scholar of Lawley Bank Wesleyan Sunday School.

Private Frederick William Bowers: Served in the 1st Battalion KSLI, an elder brother of Private A. Bowers. Died of wounds received in action on August 24, 1916. Survived by a wife and five children at The Finger, Dawley. He was 35, the son of William and Esther Bowers, of Dawley.

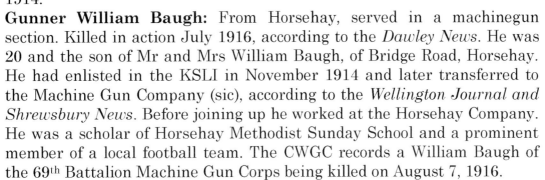

Private George Baugh: Of 65 Aqueduct. Served in the 5th Battalion KSLI. Had worked for the Madeley Wood Colliery Company before the war and had enlisted 16 months before his death in action, at the age of 31. He was a keen footballer who had played for Aqueduct before he enlisted. He was killed on August 28, 1916.

Private Samuel Small: Died on July 24, 1916, at about 11am. He attended the ambulance classes in Dawley, and at the outbreak of war volunteered first for Netley, and later on for the Front, serving in the 142nd Field Ambulance, Royal Army Medical Corps. He is thought to have been killed by a bursting shell while attending to a wounded comrade. He left a wife Bertha, nee Corbett, and three little boys. Before joining up he had worked at Randlay Brickworks.

Private Albert Ball: Of Church Road. He enlisted the day after his mother's funeral, having been employed at the Castle Car Works at

Christian Albert Ball, KSLI, killed in action September 4, 1916.

Hadley, and had been out at the front less than three months when he was killed on September 4, 1916. He was killed by a German shell while carrying wiring material to put up entanglements in front of a newly captured position. He was buried, with three others killed by the same shell, near the spot where he fell, this being done spontaneously by comrades at risk of their own lives. Among those with him when he was killed was Private H. Hollis, and Private J. Davies had helped to bury him. Christian Albert Ball had been selected and trained as a reserve stretcher bearer. The circumstances of his death caused some confusion back in Dawley, where no-one knew him as a stretcher bearer, and the authorities were asked to double check. Replying, one Captain Latham said there was no doubt of the identity of the man killed about 200 yards beyond Trones Wood. Although no identity disc was found on him when his pockets were searched, a paybook and a packet of letters addressed to Private A. Ball were. Private Ball, he added, had been through a recent 10 day course of stretcher-bearing and had only just taken on these duties to fill a vacancy.

Christian Albert Ball was 20 – he would have been 21 on Christmas Day - and served with the 6th Battalion KSLI. He was son of John Henry and Helen Ball, of 25 Church Road. A keen footballer, he had played football for various local clubs. He was a bellringer at St Leonard's Church, Malinslee.

As a matter of interest, his nephew Albert Rogers was killed in an accident while a prisoner of war in 1944.

Mr Thomas Payne: Of Dark Lane. Was for years a member of the Dawley Urban Council and Madeley Board of Guardians, and one of the chief supporters of the Dark Lane Primitive Methodist Chapel. His death is mentioned in the Dawley News of October 3, 1916.

Private William Joseph Harrison: Received severe gunshot wounds to his back in action during the Battle of the Somme on September 16, 1916, and died at a hospital at Rouen, France, on September 26. He was 22 or 23 and had worked at the Kemberton pit. A member of the Royal Army Medical Corps, he was attached to the 6th Battalion KSLI and had been recommended for the Distinguished Conduct Medal. He had gone out into No Man's Land and brought in a wounded Sergeant Major on his back. His father, Sergeant William Harrison, had won the DCM in the Boer War. Private Harrison's parents lived at 3 Hodgkiss Fold, Old Park.

Private Len Bailey: Was shot in the head on September 17, 1916, and died of his wound. He was 25 and his mother and brothers lived at Stony Fold, Lawley Bank. He had worked at the Stafford pits. Private Bailey was holding a bombing-post in the most advanced position in newly-won trenches which came under attack by the Germans. He was in the 6th Battalion KSLI. He had a brother serving at the Front in the 1st Battalion KSLI.

Private Len Taylor: Killed by a shell on September 18, 1916. He was badly wounded and the ambulance men went out under heavy fire to do what they could for him in dressing his wounds, but to no avail. He had only reached his 18th birthday in August. He had three brothers in the Army – Ted, Will, and George. His parents lived at Powis Fold, Lawley Bank. Private Taylor was in the 6th Battalion KSLI.

Private Harry Bryce: Officially posted as missing in about October 1916. He had been wounded on August 24 and the stretcher-bearer who dressed him said he walked down from him towards the Casualty Clearing Station "quite all right", but he could not remember the nature of the wound because he had so many to dress on that day. What happened to him thereafter seems to be a mystery, and all inquiries drew a blank. There turned out to have been no trace of him having passed through the Field Ambulance. He was in the 5th Battalion KSLI and was 39  years old. He was the husband of Mrs Hancock Bryce, of 11 Alice Street, Dane Road, Bolton, who made unsuccessful attempts to find out what had happened to him. Harry Bryce was a former pupil of Lawley School.

Private William Dunning: Killed September 18, 1916. Lived in Chapel Street, Dawley. None of his colleagues could give any information regarding him after the attack commenced. He was in the 1st Battalion KSLI.

Lance Corporal Ernest Samuel Candlin: Of Horsehay, killed September 25, 1916, at the age of 29 (although the CWGC says he was 32). Was born in Station Road, Horsehay, and was a moulder at Day's Pipe Works in civilian life. He served in the 1st Battalion KSLI. Incidentally the *Dawley News* learned of his death in a letter from a soldier at the Front, which arrived on the same day as the War Office said that he was "wounded". It was one of a number of occasions in which the *Dawley News* received the bad news first.

Rifleman Edward Davies: Took part in an attack on September 3, 1916. Many of his Company managed to reach the German front lines, which were later recovered in a German counter attack, leading to the belief that he may have been taken prisoner. The area between the trenches was searched but no trace was found of him. The magazine implies that he was in A Company, the 1st/8th West Yorks, although the CWGC gives his unit as the 1st/5th West Yorks. He was 36 and was the son of Mrs Mary Ann Davies, of 18 Horsehay Potteries.

Mr W.H. Webb: A brother of the famous Captain Matthew Webb, the first person to swim the English Channel, who was born in Dawley. He died in Birkenhead (the death was reported by the *Dawley News* on October 24, 1916) and was connected with the Institute of Naval Architects and the Institute of Marine Engineers.

E. Williams: Coal fell on him at Kemberton Colliery and he died on the way to Wenlock Hospital. He lived in Southall. His death was reported in the *Dawley News* on October 31, 1916.

Private John Hargreaves: Of Moor Farm Cottages, Malinslee. Killed on the night of November 2, 1916, while serving in the 3rd Worcester Regiment. He was in the trenches when a trench mortar bomb exploded, killing him. He had been in France since the beginning of the year. He had originally enlisted in the 4th Battalion KSLI in 1914 before transferring to the Worcesters.

Private Ernest Gilbert Gough: Gilbert Gough transferred from the KSLI to the 8th South Lancashires a short time before his death in action on October 21, 1916, at the age of 18. He lived at 4 Lightmoor. The son of Mr and Mrs Thomas Gough, he had enlisted in the KSLI in June 1915. Before enlistment he had worked at the Sinclair Iron Company, Ketley. He was a regular worshipper at the Lightmoor New Connexion Chapel.

Private William John Morrall: Missing since November 13, 1916. Although not a Dawley man, his wife, who had relatives in the locality, came to the area with her three children in August 1916. They lived in Old Park.

"Mrs Matthew Henry Bailey": Said to have been a very good friend of the Dawley Baptist Chapel and the Tuesday Brotherhood and Sisterhood meeting "whose passing many Dawley soldiers, if they knew the facts, would deplore" the magazine said, rather mysteriously, in its December 12, 1916, edition.

DAWLEY SOLDIERS LIST

(As compiled by the Dawley News of August 1, 1916)

Here are the names and addresses of Dawley men who are prisoners of war in Germany and Holland: Pte J. Alford, 5th KSLI; Lazaret M.P.K. Baraque A, Giessen, Germany. Bugler E. Round, 9th R.W.F., Zeneig, Gefangenenlager, Meyenburger Moor, Krieg Blumanthial, Hanover, Germany. Stoker G. Rowe, R.N.R., 25 Mess, Hawke Batt., Intermeering Depot, Groningen, Holland.

Remember, lots of you who are interested in our work have been content to let <u>us</u> write for you for a year. Now it's your turn – will you fail the brave men abroad?

Pte Bert Archer, 6th KSLI, 20th Div I.B.D., A.P.O., S/17, B.E.F. Pte J. Bailey, E. Coy, 4th KSLI, Singapore. Cyclist A. Barker, 22nd Div Cyclist Corps, Salonica Forces, Greece. Pte E. Baxter, C. Coy, 8th KSLI, B.E.F. Pte S. Bird, no. 2 section, 69 M.G. Coy, M.G. Corps, B.E.F. Pte J. Bishop, 8th KSLI, B.E.F. Sgt Frank Bott, 2nd Cavalry Division, Aux Horse Transport Coy, B.E.F. Pte W.A. Brooks, B. Coy, 5th KSLI, B.E.F. Cpl J. Bullock, 4th KSLI, Hong Kong. Pte T. Butler, D. Coy, Sappers Platoon, 2nd South Staffs, B.E.F. Pte M. Cadman, B. Coy, 2nd Garr Batt, R.W. Fusiliers, Egyptian Forces.
Pte E. Archer, 8th KSLI, B.E.F. Sgt J. Arden, Headquarters Co, 12 Div Train A.S.C., B.E.F. Pte Chas Ayres, A. Coy, 3 Platoon, 1st King's Liverpool Regt, B.E.F. Pte Seth Baugh, A. Coy, 6th KSLI, B.E.F.
Gunner Bodkin, C. Coy, 1st Canadian Contingent Divisional Artillery, 1st Heavy Battery, 1st Group, B.E.F. Sapper H.L. Brown, 3rd Sig Squadron, 3rd Cavalry Div, B.E.F. Pte Jack Butler, 14 Div Mining Co, New Zealand T.C., B.E.F. Pte F. Buttery, B Coy, 5 Platoon, 1st KSLI, B.E.F. Pte A.E. Corbett, A. Coy, 4th KSLI, Hong Kong.
Pte H. Corbett, 69 Machine Gun Co, 69 Brigade, M.G. Corps, B.E.F. Driver E. Edwards, No 1 Sec, P.A.C., 12 F.A., 9th Division, B.E.F.
Pte W. Ewings, B. Coy, 6 Platoon, 8th KSLI, B.E.F. Sgt J. Farr, No 1 Canadian Vet Hospital, Le Havre, France. Bombadier R. Harley, 1st Siege Battery, R.G.A., B.E.F. Sapper R. James, 82 Field Coy, R.E., B.E.F. L/Cpl G. Frost, E. Coy, 4th KSLI, Singapore.
Pte Herbert Bailey, A. Coy, 6th KSLI, B.E.F. Pte L. Bailey, A. Coy, 6th KSLI, B.E.F. Pte T. Bailey, 1st KSLI, 6th Inf. Base Depot, B.E.F. Pte C.A. Ball, 6th KSLI, 20th Div S/14, Inf. Base Depot, A.P.O., B.E.F. Sgt C.P. Ball, A. Coy, 4th KSLI, Hong Kong. Cpl T. Brickley, C. Coy, 1st KSLI, B.E.F. Pte E.P. Brown, C. Coy, 4th KSLI, Hong Kong. Cpl E. Candlin, A. Coy, 3 Platoon, 1st KSLI, B.E.F. Pte W. Crocker, D. Coy, 3rd KSLI, B.E.F.

Pte C.T. Collier, D. Coy, 14 Platoon, 8th KSLI, B.E.F. Pte E. Deakin, A. Coy, 1st KSLI, 6th Inf. Div., B.E.F. L/Cpl H. Dacre, C. Coy., 12 Platoon, 2nd South Staffords, B.E.F. Pte L. Halford, 2 Platoon, 8th KSLI, B.E.F.

Pte A. Harriman, B. Coy, 6th KSLI, B.E.F. Pte Percy Howells, Machine Gunner, 2nd Northumberland Fusiliers, B.E.F. Pte John Holmes, A. Coy, 8th KSLI, B.E.F. Pte A. Holbrook, I. Coy, 3rd KSLI, B.E.F.

Sgt W. Hughes, 4th Garr. Batt., R.W.F., A.P.O., S/8, B.E.F. Pte J. Kelsey, 4th KSLI, Hong Kong. Sgt F. Langford, D. Coy, 5th KSLI, B.E.F. Pte Alf Lloyd, A. Coy, 7th KSLI, B.E.F. Pte H. Mason, 2nd KSLI, 27th Inf. Base Depot, Rouen, France. Pte A. Kelsey, Z. Coy, 2nd KSLI, B.E.F.

Staff Sgt H. Morris, A.S.C., S2/016339, 9 Field Bakery, B.E.F. Ptes G&W Oakley, 4th KSLI, Hong Kong. Pte Phillips, B. Coy, 8th KSLI, B.E.F. Driver A. Round, 459 Battery, R.F.A., 1 Canadian Div, B.E.F. Sgt Skelton, B. Coy, 4th KSLI, Singapore. Pte T.E. Tart, A. Coy, 4th KSLI, Hong Kong. Pte Jack Williams, 177 Coy, R.E., B.E.F. Pte W. Williams, A. Coy, 4 Platoon, 2nd South Staffs, B.E.F.

Pte A. Morton, 14 Div. Mining Co., New Zealand Tunnelling Co., B.E.F. L/Cpl W. Oliver, Y. Coy, 2nd KSLI, Salonica Forces. Pte H. Purcell, E. Coy, 4th KSLI, Singapore. Pte G. Roberts, C. Coy, 4th KSLI, Hong Kong. Pte Jos Shepherd, R.A.M.C., HMS Letitia.

Pte James Sherwood, 4th KSLI, Hong Kong. Pte H. Skelton, A. Coy, 4th KSLI, Hong Kong. L/Cpl L. Tart, B. Coy, 4th KSLI, Singapore. Driver C. Woolger, 147 M.M.L., Section 3, 46 Divisional Ammunition Column, B.E.F.

L/Cpl J. Davies, 84 Field Coy, R.E., B.E.F. Pte Stephen Davies, 8th KSLI, B.E.F. Sgt T.E. Davies, 46 Coy, Machine Gun Corps, B.E.F. Rifleman J.A. Davies, B. Coy, 8 Platoon, 1st King's Royal Rifles, B.E.F. Pte J. Evans, 2nd KSLI, B.E.F. Pte A.P. Jones, D. Group, Observation Section, 2nd Field Survey Coy, Anzac H.A., B.E.F. Pte W. Jones, B. Coy, 5 Platoon, 8th KSLI, B.E.F. Sgt P. Morgan, D. Coy, 8th KSLI, B.E.F. L/Cpl Geo. Phillips, 42nd Brigade, Machine Gun Coy, 14th Light Division, B.E.F. Pte Philip Powell, E. Coy, 4th KSLI, Singapore.

Sgt J.H. Price, A. Coy, 5th KSLI, B.E.F. Pte H.R. Pugh, C. Coy, 15th Service Batt, Royal Warwick Regiment, B.E.F. Signaller E. Lloyd Roberts, B. Coy, 8th KSLI, Signalling Section, B.E.F.

Gunner E. Round, 21st Div, R.F.A., 94 Brigade, 6 Battery, Mediterranean Exped. Force. Pte G. Round, A. Coy, 1st KSLI, B.E.F. Driver H. Rowe, 63rd Field Ambulance, 21st Div. Train, R.A.M.C. Cpl J. Smith, No. 1 Siege Co, R.M.R.E. B.E.F. Pte G. Taylor, C. Coy, 10 Platoon, 8th KSLI, B.E.F.

Pte T. Tranter, C. Coy, 10 Platoon, 8th KSLI, B.E.F. Pte T. Tranter, A. Coy, 4th KSLI, Hong Kong.

Sgt L. Hardman, B. Battery, 61 (How) Brigade, R.F.A., Guards Div, B.E.F. Pte John Harley, A. Coy, 3 Platoon, 8th KSLI, B.E.F. W. Hitchman, Cook's Mate, 59 Mess, HMS King George V. Signaller Thos. Hobson, A. Coy, 6th

KSLI, B.E.F. Pte H. Hollis, A. Coy, 1 Platoon, 6th KSLI, B.E.F. Pte T.H. Jones, X. Coy, 2nd KSLI, B.E.F. Pte Noah Jones, E. Coy, 4th KSLI, Singapore. Pte T. Machin, No 2 Coy, 6 Platoon, 1st Grenadier Guards, B.E.F. Pte Merrington, Y Coy, 2nd KSLI, Salonica Forces. Pte W.H. Parton, R.A.M.C., 21st Stationary Hospital, Salonica Forces. Pte W.L. Perry, 27th Batt., 2nd A.D.B.D. c/o A.P.O., S/17, B.E.F.

Sgt T. Pitchford, A. Coy, 3 Platoon, 8th KSLI, B.E.F. Pte W.E. Powell, 1/1 Shropshire Yeomanry, British Mediterranean Forces. L/Cpl R.G. Richards, D. Coy, 7th KSLI, B.E.F. Pte L. Roberts, D. Coy, 8th KSLI, B.E.F. Gunner Tart, 112 Battery, R.F.A., B.E.F.

Pte S. Small, 142 F. Ambulance Corps, B.E.F. Pte L. Taylor, 6th KSLI, B.E.F. Pte P. Tonks, C. Coy, 6th KSLI, B.E.F.

GENERAL INDEX

INDEX OF SURNAMES

Acknowledgements: This book was produced with the kind help of the late Clive and Mary Westbrook, who loaned me the Dawley News magazines and gave this project their blessing. The photos are mainly from the collections of Bridgnorth postcard collector Ray Farlow and Mrs Freda Goucher, nee Bowyer, a niece of Dawley character Billy Lloyd. Cover design, logo, and Dawley map by Pete Doherty. Thanks too to Shropshire Regimental Museum and Shropshire Archives.